101 Ways to Boost Your Fortune on eBay

Get More Money for Everything You Sell

Dennis L. Prince
Bestselling Authority on eBay

McGraw-Hill

New York   Chicago   San Francisco   Lisbon
London   Madrid   Mexico City   Milan   New Delhi
San Juan   Seoul   Singapore   Sydney   Toronto

The McGraw·Hill Companies

DEDICATION

For my son, Eric. You clearly
show promise to take over the
family business. I'm proud of you.

1 2 3 4 5 6 7 8 9 0   DOC/DOC   0 9 8 7 6

ISBN 0-07-147012-3

101 Ways to Boost Your Fortune on eBay is in no way authorized by, endorsed, or affiliated with eBay or its subsidiaries. All references to eBay and other trademarked properties are used in accordance with the Fair Use Doctrine and are not meant to imply that this book is an eBay product for advertising or other commercial purposes.
Readers should know that online auctioning has risks. Readers who participate in online auctions do so at their own risk. The author and publisher of this book cannot guarantee financial success and therefore disclaim any liability, loss, or risk sustained, either directly or indirectly, as a result of using the information given in this book.

McGraw-Hill books are available at special quantity discounts to use as premiums and sales promotions, or for use in corporate training programs. For more information, please write to the Director of Special Sales, McGraw-Hill Professional, Two Penn Plaza, New York, NY 10121-2298. Or contact your local bookstore.

 This book is printed on recycled, acid-free paper containing a minimum of 50% recycled, de-inked fiber.

Library of Congress Cataloging-in-Publication Data

Prince, Dennis L.
    101 ways to boost your fortune on eBay / by Dennis Prince.
        p. cm.
    ISBN 0-07-147012-3 (alk. paper)
    1. eBay (Firm) 2. Internet auctions. 3. eBay (Firm) I. Title: One hundred
one ways to boost your fortune on eBay. II. Title: One hundred and one ways
to boost your fortune on eBay. III. Title.
    HF5478.P747 2006
    658.8'7—dc22   2006005488

Contents

Acknowledgments

A writer is only as successful as the team that surrounds, supports, and stabilizes him throughout a book project. It's been my unending pleasure to have worked, yet again, with an incredible group of folks on this book.

At McGraw-Hill, I must first recognize my project editor, Donya Dickerson. You've become my proverbial "right arm" in my work, and I can't imagine bringing a project to fruition without your incredible attitude, professionalism, and discipline to bring a book in on time. Also, I extend an equal gratitude to the rest of the terrific McGraw-Hill team with whom I've worked: Mary Glenn, Ruth Mannino, Bettina Faltermeier, Anthony Sarchiapone, Jeff Weeks, and all the fine folks who serve as the creative and inspirational heart of the McGraw-Hill Sales and Marketing teams. Thanks to each of you.

Next, my thanks to Wes Campbell Editorial Services for the excellent copy-edit. Thanks for your insightful observations and keen eye that resulted in such a fine interior layout. Your enthusiasm for this particular project was much appreciated.

Of course, I would be remiss if I didn't extend thanks to all the folks I've met at my seminars, conversed with via e-mail, or met whenever and wherever the subject of eBay arose. Many of you told me you wanted fast answers to specific questions and, thanks to your persistence in gaining that information from me, I've been able to assemble this book filled with your most-requested topics of interest. Thanks for your continual support, everyone, and I know we're still just on the tip of the iceberg in this exciting journey through our favored online realm.

Introduction

H ere's the good news of the day: No matter how well you may be doing with your online selling at eBay, you could still be doing better. That's not to say that your well-honed selling approach is deficient necessarily but, rather, there are always more ways to enhance your methodology, improve your online presence, and boost your fortune. That's what this book is all about—zeroing in on precise methods of working the eBay marketplace to increase your efficiency and profit while making the entire process more enjoyable and fulfilling. If you've been looking for more ways to better your eBay business approach, here are 101 tips just for you.

Don't expect just a prattling of 101 one-liners, though—some that might pithily suggest, "add better pictures to your auctions" or "list at lower opening bid amounts to reduce your fees." Those are good thoughts, but certainly not enough to actually implement any tangible improvements in your selling activities. Rather, in these pages you'll find 101 full-length discussions of very targeted topics, the sort that I'm continually asked to address discretely by readers and seminar attendees. Let's face it. Even if you've been selling at eBay for some time, there's usually a specific question you have where you want more elaboration—whether you need guidance to clear a particular selling hurdle or just affirmation that you've covered all the bases fully. In this book, then, you'll find discussions of specific selling methods that provide not only background to the situation but also actionable steps you can take to harness new approaches and techniques to improve the outcome of your efforts.

The better news, now, is that this collection of 101 profit-bearing and time-saving techniques is not intended solely for intermediate to advanced eBay users only. While those experienced sellers will certainly find value within these pages to help them push their success rates ever higher, newcomers can also benefit from the focused discussions, literally getting a leg up on other new eBay sellers who may elect to "find their way" by slowly going the route of learn-as-they-go. That's a fine enough approach, but if you're interested in getting better results from your auctions and fixed-price sales items, then this book has what you need to move ahead of your peers. This book won't cover the "getting started" aspects of using eBay (I suggest that you read my other book, *How to Sell Anything on eBay...and Make a Fortune!*) but, rather, will give you in-depth knowledge and awareness of specific ways to improve your tactics and bolster your bottom line. Really, it's a book for anyone who wants to propel their eBay results ever upward (and who doesn't?), and it's based on my decade of eBay analysis and activity, since the site's original inception in 1995.

I recognize that often answers can give rise to even more questions. While my approach here is to anticipate your specific queries and answer them within these pages, I realize that you may still wish to ask a follow-up question or gain one more point of clarification. As I've always maintained, I'm *your* advocate in gaining a better return for your efforts and deeper enjoyment of eBay, and I always welcome your questions, comments, and even experiences in the eBay realm. To that end, I invite you to drop me a line and let me know what's on your mind. You can reach me at dlprince@bigfoot.com.

But, for now, let's answer your burning questions. Just turn the page and we'll get started!

Choosing eBay—It's like
Finding Money Growing on Trees

FORTUNE BOOST #1
YES YOU *DO* HAVE TIME TO SELL AT EBAY

Perhaps the best "boost" you can get right away is the knowledge that selling at eBay doesn't require a full-time commitment or any major reshuffling of your current lifestyle. The beauty of eBay and its fortune-bearing prospects is that you control your level of involvement—and the height your of fortune.

It's actually much like that cluttered garage, basement, or attic you might have; so many items, so much to do, and so overwhelming to determine where to begin. Well, begin from the beginning by taking on the task in manageable "chunks," and when it comes to boosting (or perhaps *rebooting*) your eBay sales activities, the best way to begin is to recognize you *can* do it without turning your life and lifestyle inside out.

It's All about You

Yes, the eBay experience and your ultimate fortune does all revolve around you and your own world because eBay is made up of people like you who are using the site in a way that suits them best. Some are there to dabble, some are there build an entrepreneurial empire, and most others exist somewhere in between. The most important thing to recognize about the site is that it provides a steady and "always on" foundation upon which you can run your business. Whether you want to list and sell items daily, focus in on specific seasonal offerings only, or simply want to "do eBay" when you need cash or want to clean out your living space, you can manage precisely how much or how little you want to achieve based on your own ever-changing needs. So when compared to a more traditional "brick and mortar" storefront or even a constant presence at trade shows or various small-merchant booth venues, here's how eBay helps you save time whenever you're ready to sell:

- **Thousands of Sellers:** On eBay, your "competition" can actually help your efforts because they're keeping buyers busy when you're not actively selling. No need for you to spend time announcing you're "open for business" because the steady crowd of customers is constantly milling about.
- **24-x-7 Operation:** The site is always on and always available for your use whenever you want to list, day or night, unlike a store that keeps set hours.
- **A Managed Marketplace:** You needn't bother yourself with the mechanics of receiving bids or buys because eBay manages that for you. You're always able to focus squarely on your product presentation while leaving the overhead matters to eBay.

Just as the light in your refrigerator greets you each and every time you're ready for a bite to eat (even for your night owls), so, too, does eBay keep its light burning, always ready to serve you whenever you're ready to make a sale.

Stopwatch: Clocking the Common eBay Activities

"But it takes so long to list an item, from finding it to photographing, to putting it up for bid at eBay."

The above quote is a frequent complaint of newer eBay users who have found that selling at eBay does require effort. If you're going to be selling steadily, you do need to maintain a consistent time investment to keep the cash rolling in. Selling at eBay, however, is easy to streamline once you've developed a routine that you can repeat and reuse each and every time you sell. Consider the following *repeatable* tasks that can make your second, third, and all sales beyond extremely time-thrifty:

- Listing descriptions can be leveraged from item to item to reduce the amount of retyping necessary. Develop a template that will contain your static information such as sales policies, shipping details, and accepted payment methods. Narrow the unique information to just what is necessary to properly describe the product.
- A picture is still worth a thousand words, and a good digital picture (or two) can significantly reduce the amount of written description required.
- eBay's relist feature allows you to launch another auction for a same or similar item in mere seconds.

- Automated end-of-auction notifications relieve you of having to generate buyer notifications, and embedded payment instructions, managed through eBay, allow buyers to send online payments just minutes after the auction has ended.

While you're free to manage your auctions and fixed-price listings in whatever manner you choose, you'll find the most prolific sellers have learned to harness eBay's toolset in a time-efficient (and cost-efficient) manner such that they're happily working at "eBay speed" every step of the way.

How Did You Spend Your Time Today?

If you're still not convinced you have time to boost your own eBay fortune, consider these top "free time" consumers that eat up more of a person's day than they may care to admit:

1. **Television**—On average, citizens give up four hours every day to watching the boob tube.
2. **The Internet**—Yes, all surf and no work make Jack and Jane less profitable. One recent survey concluded that up to 25 percent of respondents' free time was devoted to 'Net surfing. It's up to you, of course, to ensure that time is spent in the pursuit of profits.
3. **E-Mail**—It's the close cousin to unchecked surfing and it's accounting for a tremendous amount of time spent. Constantly checking, reading, and responding to e-mail has become one of the world's newest time wasters, in some cases approaching addictive levels.
4. **Extended Phone Calls**—Yes, even those chats with your friends and family might be costing you a fortune if that time spent gets out of hand.

Of course, don't feel the need to go "cold turkey" on any of the above activities, as they do provide definite benefit to your value of life. Still, if you're wondering just where the day went, try tracking your hours each day for a week (or two) and see just how your time is really being spent. Try to reclaim at least 25 percent of that time to devote to your eBay sales, and you'll see your profits rise in a pleasant way.

You *do* have time sell on eBay, whenever you're ready to claim it. (See Figure 1-1.)

FORTUNE BOOST #2
WILL YOU TAKE $5,000 FOR THAT TRASH?

Isn't this what we'd all love to hear? Someone offers us big money for a box or bag of our worthless junk? It's not a fantasy, and it can happen to you today when you learn how to look at your castoffs in a different way.

Figure 1-1 Wouldn't it be nice to actually be able to get *more* time to sell at eBay? The folks at Golden Palace Casino shrewdly won this "time machine" at eBay in March 2005 for a time-thrifty price of just $647.59. Now *there's* an interesting new approach.

A True Story, Caught on Video

To share a personal anecdote, I recently cleaned out my old video collection, gathering VHS tapes and now-outdated laser discs since I had replaced the titles with spanking fresh DVD incarnations. It amounted to two grocery sacks of displaced entertainment "junk" that was about to see the inside of the trash can. On the way to the trash, though, I paused long enough to consider, just as an experiment, how much I might be able to earn if these items were listed on eBay. Taking the old "dollar days" approach, I listed each item for 99-cents each and let the bidders have their way. Many sold for less than a dollar while others stirred up some rather spirited bidding. At week's end, those two sacks of trash netted me a fast $500. My suspicions were confirmed and the old adage was once again propped up: one man's trash is another man's treasure.

And how.

Too often, everyday throwaways amount to easy fortunes lost. I've extrapolated that experience many times over and have come to the conclusion that each of us is enjoying close quarters with at least $5,000 worth of unwanted goods. Remember, the video collection was kept in one small converted coat closet; think about what treasures are tucked away in other closets, drawers, spare bedrooms, attics, basements, and garages.

A New Way to Look at Your Trash

Think about my previous anecdote, then take a second look at that box or bag of "trash" that you're about to toss in the back of the pickup or drag to the curb. Much of what you're throwing away can be easily converted into cash with little effort and potentially great reward. Here are the fortune-bearing finds that might await you in your load of castoffs:

- **Old Books:** Not all books you have stuffed away might be collectible, though some might be just the title a buyer is searching for. If the books are in reasonable condition, list them for auction. If you're not sure about listing them individually, list them in lots, maybe five or more. If you want to move the whole lot at once, list them as such and make sure your image features a few of the better titles.
- **Old Magazines and Magazine Pages:** Collect up those magazines and list them in lots of five or more (group them according to subject matter) and let the bidders take a look. If the magazines' spines have deteriorated but the pages themselves still look good, consider auctioning the various advertisements on their own. Vintage ads (from the 1970s and earlier) are regularly sold for $5, $10, and more for each page, sold to collectors who are eager to frame and display such great nostalgic pieces.
- **Old Products and Product Packaging:** Did you know that at eBay folks are actively bidding handsomely for things like empty milk cartons and TV dinner trays and boxes? Again, vintage products are a top draw and are bringing in big bids. If Mom or Grandma seemed to have a penchant for storing old Colonel Sanders buckets and so forth, you'll likely find they've left you quite an impressive inheritance. Don't throw it out!
- **Bottles and Glassware:** Aside from antique glassware (which is always in high demand) seemingly simple items like milk bottles, peanut-butter jars, and soda pop bottles are big treasures to collectors.
- **Vinyl Records:** You might be surprised to learn that you can't make a killing on selling LPs of days gone by; not like you'd hope, anyway. However, original vinyl records are big with DJs who are looking for vintage sampling and scratching material; they'll buy 'em by the box load, so don't toss that grooved licorice just because you don't have a turntable anymore.
- **Tools and Hardware:** Before you toss Grandpa's ancient monkey wrench and wood planes, think about letting the tool collectors at eBay

take a look first. The same goes for vintage hardware, especially if it's still in the original packaging. This, incidentally, is the sort of stuff that gets nabbed for mere pennies at neighborhood garage sales and turned into a fast fortune for the savvy shopper.

- **Vintage Technology:** One of the newest collectible categories to arise in our high-tech lifestyle is original technology goods like early video game consoles, LED wristwatches and calculators, and even cell phones.

These are just a few examples of the sorts of things many tend to think of as trash. The truth is, with just a bit of eBay effort, you'll be surprised to find out how much your junk is really worth. And, if what you offer doesn't sell, you can still throw out later. Don't be surprised, though, to find you've been kicking around $5,000 or more of junk.

FORTUNE BOOST #3
RESEARCH FOR REWARDING RESULTS

The old adage states, "good business is where you find it." The trick to that little phrase, though, is to actually *know* where to find such good business. While the implication seems that anyone can stumble into a business oasis, it makes better sense these days to leave nothing up to chance. So when it comes to knowing what to sell, how to sell, and where to sell, it becomes imperative that you actively drill deep into the online sales market and let the cyber-statistics guide you on your way to better results. See what others are doing and where they're doing it, then strive to emulate the best. Very soon, others will be emulating *you*.

Data at Your Fingertips

Perhaps one of the greatest contributions of the online marketplace (next to the ease with which we can all buy and sell goods) is its volume of real-time sales data, readily available $24 \times 7 \times 365$. This is the core of the online data mining potential, enabling sellers to seek out products similar to theirs and determine the mood of the marketplace for such items.

Easiest to mine are the online auction spaces where sellers can take a quick pulse of buying and selling trends. Yes, it starts with eBay itself, but don't forget to search other auction sites like Yahoo Auctions, Amazon Auction, ePier, and others. When mining, determine who's selling the sorts of items you'll offer. First, check their minimum bid prices as well as their "buy-it now" prices to see which sellers' strategies seem to be attracting the highest bids or fixed-price sales. Next, check the bidding activity to see which items are commanding the most active bidding. When you zero in on the listings that are generating the greatest "buzz," take note of the listing categories being used, an indication of where most buyers might be going to find this type of good. Beyond price and category, take a careful look at the listing title (watch for all-important key words), the listing description, the images presented, the seller's sales policies, and the seller's feedback. In short order, you'll be able to quickly ascertain which sellers are successful, which products are drawing activity and garnering the best prices, and what overall sales style seems to attract the most customers.

But what about other sales destinations on the Web? Now it's time to expand your data mining to the various "store" venues (such as at Yahoo, Froogle, Amazon, and others) and search those listings, too. Then perform a search engine query to comb the entire World Wide Web in order to locate merchant sites run by folks just like you. Standing in the customer's shoes, ask yourself how well each destination you encounter motivates you to inquire further and possibly compels you to buy. Check carefully to determine if the site is being regularly updated or if it appears to have been overrun by virtual cobwebs. Don't be bashful about contacting shop owners via e-mail to ask specific questions about their operations and their merchandise.

Don't Overlook the Past

The most telling statistics, naturally, are those found in history. Again, the online marketplace has plenty of information to offer here. Back at the auction spaces, take a careful look at completed listings, seeking out final selling prices as well as determining if prices are holding steady or are experiencing either upward or downward trends. Be particularly attentive to listings that seem to appear as "spikes" in the market (with a final price being either noticeably high or low); these are the listings to closely scrutinize as you seek to determine what contributed to the spike (was the item miscategorized, priced too high at the outset, poorly presented, or what?).

This sort of sales history data is often a bit more difficult to cull from fixed-price or merchant sites. Some sellers provide sales history (and you should too) whereby you can ascertain what goods they've dealt with in the past and how much activity they've seen over a period of time. Again, inquire (politely) about recently sold items if you have questions.

Counter Culture

Another way to gauge the appeal of products and sales strategies is to quantify the public response by way of a counter. Look for counters—either at auction sites or at fixed-price venues—to indicate the popularity or attractiveness of an item up for sale. Though these counters don't necessarily indicate unique page views or site visits, they are a good indicator of whether the seller's style and strategy seem to be successful with potential customers. If the counter numbers are low, then something in the seller's methodology could be amiss.

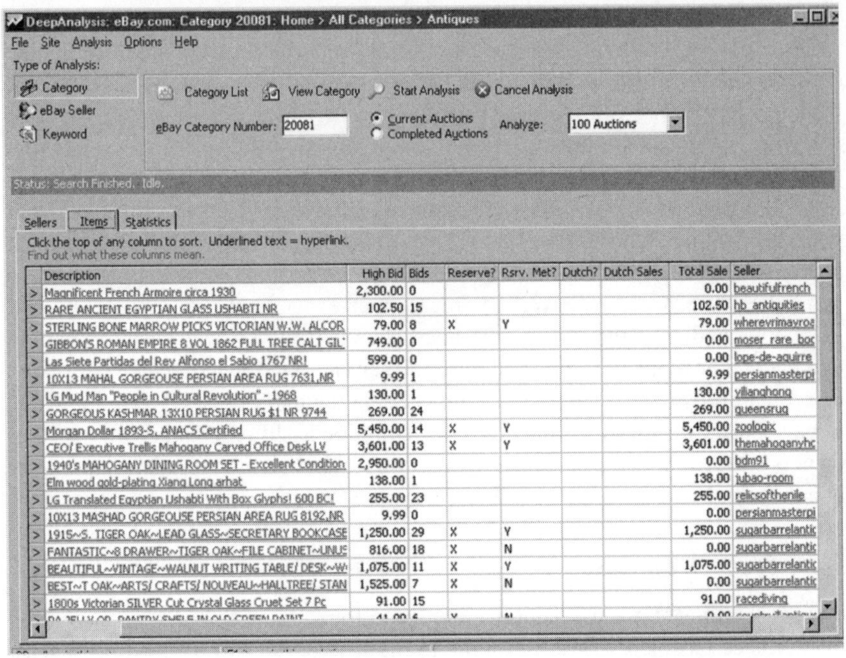

Figure 3-1 Look to HammerTap's Deep Analysis tool for detailed eBay sales statistics. Find it within the "Auction Tools" on. www.quotetracker.com.

Mine Your Own Business

While you're actively sifting through the items and actions of others around you, don't forget to carefully examine your own offerings as well. Keep close track of your eBay sales history, determining in which categories your items sell best, when they seem to be in greatest demand, and which transactions encouraged a customer to make a return visit. By regularly watching others while monitoring your own results, you'll have the conclusive data that will help you successfully navigate the ever-changing online marketplace.

FORTUNE BOOST #4
LISTING FOR LESS: SAVING A FORTUNE BY LOWERING FEES

Though many sellers feel they are at the mercy of eBay when it comes to the fees of doing business there, it might be comforting to know that many of the fees can be avoided (legally) with a bit of foresight and careful planning. If you feel you're losing too much profit at the hands of the eBay fee collectors, consider these tips about the fees you pay and how to keep them under control to the benefit of your business' bottom line.

The Fees That You Need

Be realistic—you *will* pay some sort of listing fee; that's just the reality of it all. Sure, you could elect to find some other free auction site (there's few to be found) but realize they don't receive the sort of bidder volume that will translate into the level of fortune you likely seek. Saving a few bucks in listing might cost you far more in lost opportunity and time wasted by listing at sites with little traffic and few bids.

And while many users argue that eBay is getting obscenely rich in their tariffs, those costs you pay provide the needed capital to fund useful features, infrastructure, and user services and tools. As eBay continues to grow, it needs to reinvest to ensure that it can satisfy the needs and wants of the more sophisticated online seller. The listing and usage fees wind up being a small price to pay for the ability to list, sell, and collect at this very active site while ensuring the availability of advanced methods that will save you time, effort, and, yes, money in the long run.

Little Pluses = Big Minuses

But there *is* a lot of fluff within eBay, and you *can* cut costs by carefully selecting which features and services you'll use in your listings. In fact, you'll find many "junk" adornments that add plenty of eye-candy to your listings but might offer little true return on the investment.

Cast a frugal eye on these questionable, and often costly, listing enhancements:

- **Title Enhancements:** Be it bold, highlighted, or whatever, few bidders really pay much attention to the visual style of your item's title. Save a buck and make conservative use of capital lettering (not exclusively, though) to highlight the key element of your title. Make sure you use plenty of good "hit words" because most items are found via keyword searches.
- **Special Icons:** Whether it's a birthday cake, a Christmas tree, or a firecracker, when it comes to added title icons—who cares? When did you last leap at an item because of the cutesy little gif that accompanied it? Again, save the buck.
- **Featured Placement:** This is one of the most expensive listing options out there and, unless you've got an item that will gain you thousands of dollars in high bids, leave this one out, plain and simple. Again, it's typically the keywords that get noticed, not the site real estate where your item's listed.
- **Cross-Category Listing:** Cross-category listing will cost you double your listing fees. Didn't you do just as well listing in the category where most similar items were to be found? If so, why change your strategy now and why pay twice the fees?

- Image Hosting: eBay provides many fancy photo features that will produce slide shows and all sorts of other whiz-bang photo effects—at a price. All you really need is a place to store and access your good digital images, so find a reliable yet inexpensive host site (you got free Web space when you signed up with an ISP) and forgo the cost of those high-end hosts.

Choosy Sellers Choose Fees Wisely

Of course, this isn't to say that *all* fees are inherently evil and detrimental to your eventual profit. Just as it makes perfect sense to pay reasonable fees for site and service usage, it's just as prudent to occasionally make use of features and enhancements when the situation calls for it. For example:

- **Reserve Prices:** You might hate to pay the reserve surcharge, but do the math between putting a $199 reserve price on your item versus listing it with an opening bid of $199. At eBay, you'll find listing the item with a $9.99 opening bid and a reserve of $199 costs $2.35 to list with the reserve fee of $2.00 being refunded if your item sells. If you opt for the opening bid of $199, sans reserve, the same listing will cost you $2.40 without the refund. If you need to protect the value of your investment, it makes more sense to use the reserve price feature than to risk taking a significant loss.
- **Opening Bids:** Of course, if current demand for your item will easily gain you your target price without the use of a reserve, then list in the lowest fee bracket and let the bidders work their magic.
- **Relisting:** Well, it's typically free (at eBay, you're refunded listing fees if you get a sale), and the benefit is you can make changes to the item title, description, and category to find your buyer on the site's dime. Take advantage of that.
- **Online Payment:** Sellers aren't universally happy that fees are being levied by online payment sites, but remember that buyers who can pay with credit cards (accepted at online payment sites) will invariably spend more than if they must surrender their limited cash on hand. If your items sell at good prices, make it easier for your buyers to pay by offering the online payment opportunity, then collect their higher bids at the relatively low cost to you.

No Sale and Additional Opportunities

Just when you thought sniping was the reigning hotbed of auction controversy, along comes "fee avoidance," the frowned-upon act of manipulating auctions and luring bidders off-venue to make a sale without paying site fees and commissions. But, just as the eBay is in the business of making money, well, so are you. Read the site policy carefully on this, but to date, there's still no infraction assessed if

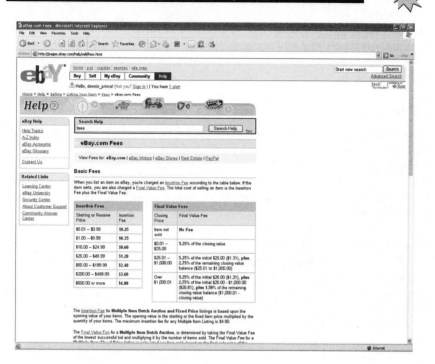

Figure 4-1 Visit http://pages.ebay.com/help/sell/fees.html to see the most up-to-date fee schedule in use at eBay.

you're contacted by a buyer who inquires about an item that fails to meet the reserve or possibly asks if you have more of the same to sell. It's a fine line, though: if the seller initiates such off-line transactions or additional sales, there could come a swift site warning and possible suspension, as those are considered acts of fee avoidance.

But, in the interest of your sales and over profit-to-cost ratio, be sure buyers can easily contact you (provide an e-mail or Web site link in your item description) to assist them with any inquiries they may have, informational or otherwise. If they initiate a potential transaction, then that's just simply good for business and may save you some operating costs in the process. And, if you're operating your business well, faithfully serving the customers you attract, they might elect to deal with you directly—and any savvy businessperson will assert it's much cheaper to keep the customers you already have, any day of the week.

FORTUNE BOOST #5
FROM KEYWORDS TO CASH

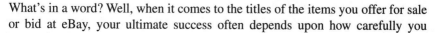

What's in a word? Well, when it comes to the titles of the items you offer for sale or bid at eBay, your ultimate success often depends upon how carefully you choose your words. If you wonder whether you're making optimum use of your item titles in a way that will boost your eBay fortune, consider these "keys" to keyword use, why they're so important to your sales success, and how to literally make every word count.

Hit Me

Your first order of duty is to ensure your items can be easily found. Keywords serve as the virtual searchlight that guides bidders to your goods. When you're listing in the vast sea of offerings eBay, your immediate challenge is to be seen among the millions of other items that vie for bidders' attention. Most bidders now make near-exclusive use of the site's search tools to locate those goods they seek (who has the time or patience to painstakingly scroll through pages upon pages of unfiltered listings?), and your effective use of keywords will better assure that your items are represented in keyword "hit lists."

So begin by including as many pertinent keywords that prospective bidders are likely to search for. Knowing what you are selling well will help you understand which words are typically searched for, in which combinations, and to what level of detail. As a rule, you'll want to include the following within the 55 characters that eBay offers:

- Brand name
- Item name
- Item origin
- Year (or period) of the item's origin
- Manufacturer

Depending on what you sell, color, size, and other such attributes might also be elemental information to include in your listing titles.

Check Your Spelling

Here, more than anywhere else, is where spelling counts. Buyers and sellers continually lament lost sales and missed purchasing opportunities due to misspelled keywords. Be sure to spell correctly, especially when items like yours feature intentional spelling variations or are identified by words that are commonly misspelled. Many sellers go so far as to include common misspellings in their item titles to better ensure that their listings will be included in a greater number of search results. Buyers, too, search for these commonly misspelled words to ensure that desirable—albeit misspelled—goods don't get away.

Perfunctory Punctuation

Believe it or not, punctuation marks such as hyphens, parentheses, and exclamation marks can actually sabotage your sales. Depending on the search tool being used, a keyword search for "Jadite" might actually ignore titles that include punctuated variations like "Jadite!" or "(Jadite)." Some search tools associate punctuation as part of a word and, in the literal sense, will not recognize the keyword match. While this isn't always the case—it varies among sites and search tools—it does pose the added risk of having your goods summarily passed over.

Don't Get Cute

Simply enough, don't waste valuable title space on words that do little to describe the item or properly identify it to the discriminating buyer. Words like "cute," "adorable," "desirable," and the like often do little to help attract let alone convince a buyer. Words like "rare," "hard to find," and so on are not only superfluous at times (especially when buyers are often already aware of the scarcity of an item) but they sometimes work to expose a seller's attempt to justify a higher price. Subjective words like "awesome," "unbelievable," "must see," could seem to be enticing but usually just succeed in wasting space. Finally, visual come-ons like "L@@K" and its ilk are nothing short of obnoxious and should be avoided.

Abbreviated Angst

Again, it goes back to search functions and the kinds of words your target buyers might be searching for. Abbreviations may make sense to you—may even be recognized among purveyors of certain products—but they may cost you a sale if they fail to show up on keyword search hit lists. Unless the abbreviations you employ are commonly used by your buyers (such as grading acronyms), it's best to avoid spontaneous contractions or concatenations whenever possible.

FORTUNE BOOST #6
CAN WE GET DESCRIPTIVE HERE?

You know how important good images are when buyers come to look at your eBay listings, but don't overlook the importance of terrific descriptions that spell out all the vital details—those of your item and those of your business policy. Though many buyers have bemoaned the bad habits of lazy sellers—exhibited through ambiguous facts or littered with horrendous spelling and grammatical errors—here are the keys to presenting professional item descriptions that you'll want to master to put your items in the best possible light.

Get the Facts

The first order of business is to offer a full disclosure of your item. Though images reveal much, supportive text can confirm visual details and illuminate unseen minutiae. Be sure your descriptions include the following:

- All distinguishing and authenticating details.
- Details of item completeness or lack thereof.
- Any and all imperfections.
- Provenance of the item (where you got it, how long you've owned it, and so on).

These facts, accompanied by high-quality images, will paint the full picture that helps potential buyers determine the complete nature of the item as well as your knowledge and integrity in presenting it.

School Daze

As trite as it may seem, spelling and grammar *do* still count and can quickly alienate buyers when they struggle through sloppily crafted descriptions from apparently unskilled sellers. Use a computer-based spelling and grammar checker, and dig out the dictionary when your electronic resources come up short. Though it can be a tough pill to swallow, your skills in the written language will have direct reflection on you and your business.

The Hook that Helps

Don't forget to add a certain amount of "sales appeal" to your descriptions. Though you'll want to get to the point when presenting the facts, there's still enough room for a bit of pitch that could entice a sale. A good sales "hook," then, might incorporate the following:

- A bit of nostalgic language or phraseology that's suited to the item's time period.
- A link to a current trend such as the revived interest in items like yours.
- A bit of humor that might invoke the sort of fun or whimsy your item represents.
- Historical events or styles that account for the manner in which your item was designed or manufactured.

Though you don't want to distract or annoy your buyers with the excessive promotion or hard-sell verbiage, recognize the persuasive power of a good sales hook that might be just the nudge to encourage a shopper to become convinced your item is the one they simply must have.

Make It Easy on the Eyes

The physical appearance of your description is of equal importance to its content. In other words, be sure that your text looks as good as it reads. Use paragraph breaks in your descriptions to make them more legible. A crowded block of text is more difficult to sift through than the same text with a well-placed break. And, if you plan to use HTML coding for your description, be sure to use a font style that's easy to read, a font color that doesn't clash with the background, and a font size such that isn't painfully tiny or overwhelmingly large. (See Fortune Boost #18 for more about HTML.)

Things to Avoid

As the previous paragraph noted proper visual technique, here are a few more things you'll want to avoid as you craft your item descriptions:

- Verbal stinginess as found in maddeningly brief one-liners like, "Item as pictured."
- Intentionally ambiguous language that sidesteps or otherwise avoids disclosure of pertinent details.
- Too much subjective language ("This is the best you'll find for sale anywhere") that often incites buyers to shop around.
- Criticisms of other sellers' goods or derision of the seller's themselves.

If ever you doubted the importance of good item descriptions, hopefully you'll recognize their key effect on your sales success as well as their impact on how well you and your business are perceived. If you'll take a bit of time to carefully consider how you'll describe your items, you'll be serving up perfect descriptions every time.

FORTUNE BOOST #7
TIMING IS (STILL) EVERYTHING

As the old saying goes, "timing is everything." Though maybe an overstatement when it comes to online auctioning, savvy sellers have found that strategic timing—in terms of *when* and *how long* an auction will run—can have significant impact on their ultimate success. But what is the best day of the week to list or end an auction? How long should an auction run? And which is the magical hour for ending an auction? If these are your questions, this Fortune Boost provides some answers.

The Long and the Short of It

Before listing, you'll need to calculate which day you want your auction to end (this in turn will dictate your auction's starting day). eBay offers several choices for auction length—anywhere from 1 to 14 days. Remember: If an auction is too long (such as the 10- or 14-day epochs), it might be forgotten during its lengthy duration, whereas if it's too short (as in the 1- or 3-day quickie), it might not generate any momentum before it disappears.

In general, it's best to let auctions run for a seven-day stretch. Granted, this can be a long wait for sellers anxious to close a deal; however, by having an auction encompass a full seven days you'll potentially reach people who browse the Internet and auction sites only on certain days of the week (believe it or not, some folks still have limited access to a computer). Most importantly, the seven-day listing will span both weekend days when auction traffic is generally higher. (Incidentally, the five-day duration is your next-best bet, but be sure to start the auction on Tuesday or Wednesday to ensure it that ends on one of the upcoming weekend days.)

What a Difference a Day Makes

Although opinions vary, Sunday is still considered to be the best day to end an auction. Start and end your auction on a Sunday and you'll tap a full week and weekend's worth of exposure. Again, Saturdays and Sundays tend to bring out bidders, accommodating those who don't enjoy the luxury of surfing the 'Net at their workplaces.

Are there bad days to end an auction? Well, Fridays can be challenging because your listings won't benefit from the weekend surge. And folks who sneak off for early weekends might be away from their computers on Fridays and Saturdays. By ending an auction on a Sunday, though, you can still entertain those folks who've been away for most of the weekend yet are ready to go online upon returning home Sunday afternoon or evening.

And how about those holidays? Most sellers agree that it's best to avoid ending auctions on a holiday (especially holiday weekends). Because most of us are either traveling or otherwise occupied by festivities, the traffic at auction sites will typically be light.

Rush Hour

Perhaps the most crucial consideration in timing strategy is the hour your auction will start and ultimately end. By and large, the best time to start or end an auction will be in the evening hours when potential bidders are better able to browse for extended periods of time, having a better chance to notice your new listings, not to mention allowing them to be "in attendance" to bid during your auctions' final minutes. Be sure to consider time zones in all this. Try to allow West Coast citizens enough time to get home from work without making East Coast citizens stay up all night (Hint: between 6 p.m. and 8 p.m. Pacific Time is the safest bet.)

International Know-How

Some sellers have wondered how to accommodate their global customers, those who literally live on the other side of the world. As all of eBay's listings are

Figure 7-1 Use eBay's scheduled listings option to set a future launch day and time that makes it easy to list for other time zones without staying up all night.

tracked in Pacific Time (because eBay's located in the heart of California's Silicon Valley), it's practically impossible to satisfy stateside bidders and overseas customers simultaneously. The solution: cater to the largest audience. That is, if ever you find your goods are of particular appeal (and therefore have greater earning potential) to customers elsewhere on the globe, position your auctions to end in the same manner previously discussed, yet on a different continent. You might even consider hosting multiple auctions for the same items concurrently, some timed to satisfy U.S. bidders and others that will cater to off-shore buyers. And, thanks to eBay's *scheduled listings* feature (see Figure 7-1), you can list your items at a time that suits you and instruct eBay to launch them at a later time that suits your customers.

Bidder-Friendly Auctions

You can see that smart auction timing takes your customers' surfing, bidding, and living habits into account, trying to be accommodating to their schedules by and large. In fact, many sellers have reported receiving kudos from their customers for running auctions that tend to be easy to bid on thanks to their customer-considerate timing.

FORTUNE BOOST #8
A WELL-SEASONED SALE

Although the online marketplace is open for business 365 days a year, many sellers wonder whether holiday periods (such as Memorial Day Weekend, the Fourth of July, or Christmas) are a boost or a bust for selling items. While it true that some buyers elect to take a break from online shopping during these seasonal periods, long-time sellers have found there's still plenty of customers to be served and sometimes even greater opportunities to increase sales amidst the festivities. Here are some points to ponder as you manage your holiday sales.

Rotate Your Stock

Perhaps the most significant key to maximizing holiday sales is to strategically position items of seasonal interest. If Memorial Day heralds the onset of fun in the sun, be sure to have those summer-related goods prominently displayed in your virtual store window. When July 4th rolls around, shift attention to patriotic and even election-related items. Whatever the holiday might be, expect that buyers will be inclined to purchase seasonal goods (either current or vintage) that embody the spirit of the moment. Of course, be sure to get a jump on the other sellers by placing and advertising such goods *before* the big day arrives. Because buyers have learned the importance of staying ahead of the crowds, help them with those holiday-related purchases by making such goods available several weeks ahead of time (and don't forget to factor in the time it will take to get those goods into your customers' hands). See Figure 8-1.

Holiday-Friendly Auctions

When buyers are looking for that certain something that will help them celebrate a calendar occasion, most will turn to eBay for a quick fix and a fast find. If you decide to list seasonal items in the big auction space, be sure to give special consideration to the duration of your auction. Strive to have your auctions end in plenty of time to complete the transaction and deliver the goods to your buyer before the holiday arrives. Also, give consideration to the desirability of shortened auction durations (such as a 5- or 3-day run) to entice buyers to bid on your items, knowing they can wrap up business quickly rather than wait out a 7-day or even those seemingly unending 10-day stints (ugh!). And don't forget the immediate drawing power of a Buy-It-Now listing that allows the particularly antsy buyer to grab the goods immediately.

Planning a Perfect Ending

A matter most puzzling to sellers is whether it's good business to attempt to wrap up fixed-price and auction sales on an actual holiday date. Are people logged on and shopping on December 25th? After pushing away from the Thanksgiving table, do folks settle in and surf eBay? Apparently, they do. (I actually took time last November and December to monitor eBay auction activity and was astounded to see so much active bidding on the respective holidays, finding that auctions ending in the evening fared better than those closing earlier in the day).

Though surf's up all year 'round, it's generally not prudent to target an actual holiday date in an attempt to close a high number of sales; the added holiday distraction can sometimes hamper timely response from your buyers and might only delay overall transaction times. A better approach is to straddle the holiday, so to speak, enabling shoppers to find your goods before, during, and after the day has past (for auctioning, this would suggest listing an item on, say,

Special Event or Holiday	Event Date	Best Dates to List	Popular Items Associated with this Event
Thanksgiving	4th Thursday of November	3–5 weeks prior	Pilgrims, turkeys, American history
Sporting Events (e.g. Super Bowl, Stanley Cup)	Varies according to event scheduling	2–3 weeks prior	Team merchandise, event tickets, tailgating supplies, memorabilia from past contests
National Elections	Varies according to election cycle	1 week–6 months prior	Campaign memorabilia (past and present), T-shirts, candidate appearance tickets
Major Film, Book, or Music Releases	Varies according to release date	2 months prior up to and through 2 months after	Advance advertising and marketing merchandise, 1st printings or pressings, opening day premiums, promotional-only material
Annual Awards Ceremonies (Oscars, Grammys, etc.)	Varies according to awards ceremony date	1–4 weeks prior	Movie memorabilia (current and related vintage), music (CDs, vintage LPs and Tapes), promotional materials, awards event tickets.
Weddings	Most common months are May, June, and November	2 weeks to 12 months prior	Bridal gowns and accessories, invitations, reception supplies, wedding party gifts, wedding services.
Halloween	October 31	1–5 weeks prior	Popular current year costumes and accessories, vintage costumes and accessories, decorations, music, related film material
Hanukkah	Varies from year to year, usually mid-December	1–5 weeks prior	Menorahs, dreidels, and gifts for each day of this 8-day holiday.
Christmas	December 25	1–5 weeks prior	Hard-to-find "hot gifts" of the current season, vintage items, anything else that can be offered as perfect or eccentric gift, spiritual or religious items, current and vintage décor.
New Year's Eve	December 31	1–8 weeks prior	Hats, horns, confetti, champagne, champagne glasses, tickets to popular celebration events
Valentine's Day	February 14	1–4 weeks prior	Jewelry, lingerie (for him and her), picture frames, fashion clothing and accessories, champagne flutes, silk flower arrangements.
Easter	(varies year to year)	1–4 weeks prior	Religious and spiritual goods, Easter Bunny baskets and goods (new and vintage), clothing (especially children's spring outfits).
4th of July	July 4	1–4 weeks prior	Flags, outdoor entertainment items.
Mother's Day	2nd Sunday in May	1–3 weeks prior	Silk flower arrangements, picture frames, whatever Mom loves.
Father's Day	3rd Sunday in June	1–3 weeks prior	Power tools, men's fashion accessories, outdoor grilling goods, hammocks and other outdoor relaxation items, whatever else Dad loves.
Start of School Year	Traditionally, end of August/start of September.	1–5 weeks prior	School supplies (organizers, calculators, backpacks, other electronic goods), current text books.
Springtime	~ March 30	1–4 weeks prior	Outdoor gardening items.
Summertime (Memorial Day)	May 30	1–4 weeks prior	Outdoor furniture and accessories, sports equipment, pool toys.
St. Patrick's Day	March 17	1–3 weeks prior	Anything green

Table 8-1 Event and holiday schedule and potential sales items.

July 1st with a closing date of July 5th or 7th). In this manner, you'll be more apt to catch the attention of shoppers who browse before the holiday, those who might find some surfing time during the holiday, and those who will resume their online hunting after the calendar event has passed.

The Need for Speed

Holiday shoppers (especially those purchasing during the annual winter gift-giving season) might be in need of fast service. Help take the stress out of their shopping by accepting instant payment (such as credit card purchases or accepting online payment) so the transaction can be completed in mere minutes. Then, consider offering special shipping services to these buyers (such as Fed Ex Overnight, UPS Second Day, or USPS Express Mail) if the goods need to be received before the holiday. The availability of easy payment and fast shipping options could determine whether a buyer will purchase from you or shop elsewhere. And be sure you and your buyer agree to the shipping method and delivery expectation *before* the package leaves your hands.

Post-Holiday Sales

And finally, consider this: just as retail venues seek to clear out holiday leftovers, so should you cater to the online post-holiday shopper. After a holiday passes, sellers can typically find a resurgence of buyers still interested in holiday-related goods or looking to get the jump on the next big celebration. Adjust your offerings accordingly, catering to the holiday just past as well as positioning for the holiday-to-come.

FORTUNE BOOST #9
UNDERCUTTING THE COMPETITION

Whether it's lower-priced air fares, free memory upgrades, or five months of premium cable channels at no extra cost, selling to today's overcourted consumers has become the new battleground. It's truly a buyer's market these days as goods become more available and more customizable to exact customer needs and desires (thanks largely to the Internet's ability to serve up near-myriad choices and comparisons at practically zero expense to the shopper). Sellers, however, are left to struggle with effective ways to stand out in the crowd and positively attract customers away from rivals without having to offer goods at unprofitable fire sale prices. Is there still hope for an online entrepreneur to make a fortune without giving away the farm? You bet, and it comes from discovering new ways to undercut the competition—and it's *not* all about pricing.

Sizing up the Competition

Before you can begin taking steps to confront your competition, you'll first need to recognize who (or what) that competition really is. You likely got a glimpse of those with whom you'll be batting for customers when you researched the activity of goods you're interesting in selling. Whether you searched eBay itself or the Internet in general, you likely encountered other sellers—some big, some small—who are currently at work selling the sorts of goods you hope to likewise profit from. But as you now seek to understand how your competition operates and what may be key to their success, pay special attention not only to the prices of their wares but also the "perceived value"—that is, the inherent benefit their customers expect to gain from purchasing the goods they offer. Look closely and you might find the following perceived value indicators:

- **Reasonable Pricing**—Well, look at the prices, of course, and see how they match up to others in the market.
- **Depth and Duration of Value**—Are the goods being presented in a way that suggests a purchase from a particular seller will result in a best-in-market experience (as opposed to inferior sellers' offerings), one whose levels of satisfaction will outlast those of others? Do you ever wonder why folks will pay $3.00 or more at Starbucks for a cup of coffee when the brew in their own home costs only 20 cents or less? What's the perceived value or enhanced experience that accompanies (or purports to accompany) a Starbucks cup-o-joe?
- **Service and Convenience**—Are other sellers offering an easy and pleasurable shopping "experience" that becomes part and parcel value along with the item itself?
- **Reputation**—Do your competitors have a solid reputation for quality, service, and general reliability that commands customer loyalty?

Consider each of the above perceived value elements when you explore and assess your competition. Most importantly, poke into their potential weaknesses, both those you might perceive yourself as well as those you may have heard others explain or complain about; those are your entry points to beat the competition. Sometimes it can be a simple matter of offering payment choices, shipping options, and fast customer response time. Every competitor has strengths and weaknesses; establish who your competitors are and the areas of opportunity you can exploit to get out in front of the pack.

Effective Price Strategies

OK. So there is a little bit about pricing that you should consider here. We live in a very price-sensitive consumer market these days, a time when even the promise of a mere dollar saved is enough to allow a competitor to lure away a customer you've been actively courting. There are ways, however, to attract a customer's attention through pricing strategy, hopefully long enough to establish the value of your nonprice (perceived value) benefits. Here are some pricing tactics to consider to boost your sales through customer attraction:

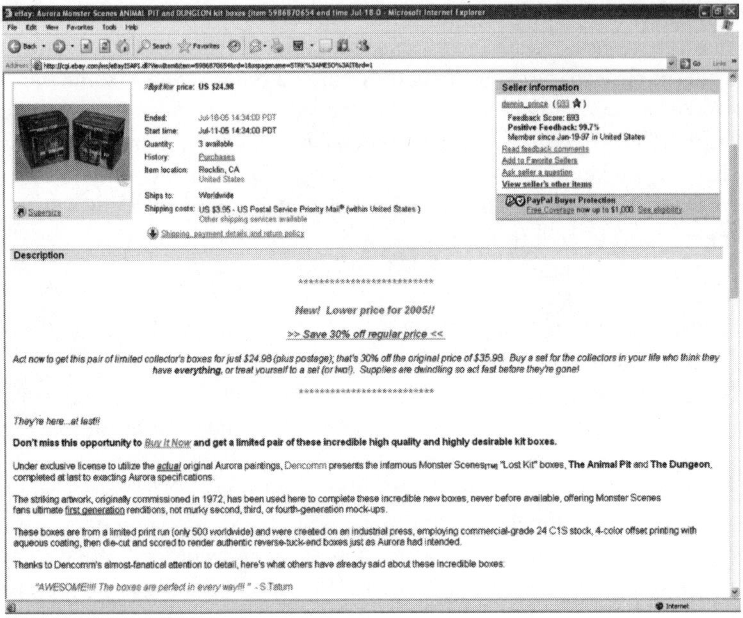

Figure 9-1 I used reference pricing in this eBay listing and watched my sell-through rate double immediately.

- **Reference Pricing**—*"Was $99.99, now just $69.99!"* The use of a reference to a former (and usually higher) price immediately communicates a valuable savings to be gained that prior customers didn't experience. (See Figure 9-1.)

- **Bait Pricing**—*"These prices good for a limited time—Act now!"* Sure, we've all heard it before and, somehow, the time-boxing of a price offering still manages to motivate many of us to make a purchase before it's too late.

- **Price Bundling and Multi-Unit Pricing**—Buyers will purchase more goods if they're given a value incentive for doing so, such as total sale price reductions when multiple items are bought. (This tactic doesn't necessarily apply to auctioned items, those with a final bid price established via the auction methodology, though you can offer other incentives such as reduced shipping, free shipping, or throw-in premiums.)

- **Penetration Pricing**—When you want to get quick attention, especially with a new item or as a merchant with a new angle in an existing marketplace, try "low introductory prices" to attract customers; it may be enough to show them the rest of your goods and also introduce them to your stellar customer-service methods.

Yes, pricing has much to do with attracting customers away from other sellers and into your virtual store but, as you can see, not all pricing strategies have to be particularly aggressive or loss-bearing.

Low in Cost, High in Value: How Well Do You Relate?

Finally, as you look to leap-frog over your competition, be sure you've carefully studied the customers you seek to attract and understand what it is they truly value. Believe it or not, many customers shop based on how well the seller caters to their needs (as noted before) and how much confidence that seller imparts in each and every transaction. Set yourself apart from the rest by learning how to relate to your customers in ways that will gain their trust, respect, and allegiance. Whether you cater to a select market and can show off specialization skills or you serve a global marketplace and can make buyers feel as if you're just down the street from them, understand your customers while you scrutinize your competitors, and you'll find you'll be able to undercut the competition without ever inciting a raised eyebrow among your peers.

FORTUNE BOOST #10
FIXED VERSUS DYNAMIC: WHICH PRICE IS RIGHT?

Back when eBay responded to buyers' desires for an alternative to the sometimes drawn-out auction cycle, sellers were faced with deciding which method would best serve their customers without impacting the businesses' bottom lines— dynamic (auction) or fixed (ascending bid) prices? The good news is both methods can successfully coexist and, if exercised to their fullest, the benefits to be realized are worth the effort of adapting to the buyers' desires.

Play the Game

Many buyers were originally drawn to the eBay auction experience not only by the goods they coveted but for the excitement and suspense of the game as well. Sellers found they could pull down some incredible profits as a result, whether offering up their otherwise unwanted castoffs or parading wares high in demand yet low in supply. Be it the goods or the game, here are some situations that favor the use of the dynamic bidding process:

- If items like yours are consistently selling at an acceptable price, allow the bidders to enjoy the back-and-forth bidding experience along the way.
- Items of seemingly little or no value to a seller might spark a "why not" or "I haven't seen one of those in years!" response from bidders, so let them decide whether it's trash or treasure.
- Items that are in high demand at a time when supply is low will generally spark an old-fashioned bidding war, generally bringing home a healthy final price.

- And if you're uncertain about the value of your item but aren't averse to letting the market decide, take the bidders to task and see what happens—you might be pleasantly surprised.

A Quick, Noncompetitive Alternative

But there's definitely a population of eager buyers who aren't interested in competitive bidding nor inclined to wait for an auction to run its course. Instead, they prefer a quick purchase, plain and simple. Likewise, some sellers also prefer the fixed-price format as a way to mitigate the risk of relinquishing items too cheaply, avoid use of the secretive and oft-maligned "reserve" price, and generally effect a rapid transaction.

When might you opt for a fixed-price format in your listings? Consider these situations:

- Your item is in demand and you've found the current market value to be acceptable; offer to let buyers take it at that price and be done with it.
- Your item is in *high* demand and you stand to gain above-market value from a buyer who doesn't wish to lose out in the bidding wars any longer.
- Your item is of "time-boxed" demand (e.g., seasonal or trendy goods) and a fixed-price sell ensures the buyer of receiving it in a timely manner.
- You're in no particular hurry and can afford to set fixed prices to see if the market will bear a potentially higher price.

What Else Is in Store for Your Customers?

Storefronts (like eBay Stores) have also gained greater traction, allowing sellers to properly present *themselves* as much as they present their merchandise. Challenged to develop truly lasting customer loyalty in the relatively transient auction spaces, sellers should now take full advantage of the opportunity to firmly establish a virtual shop to better attract repeat customers. Beyond merely presenting items for sale at fixed prices, storefronts allow sellers to preview future sales items, provide details of past sales and, most importantly, communicate knowledge and information that lets buyers see you're a seller who's in the know.

Let the Buyers Decide

In the end, your best bet is to give the buyers what they really want: options. Whether they choose to battle other bidders for your goods or elect to buy your items outright, give them the opportunity to decide for themselves. Though this doesn't imply *every* item you offer has to be presented in dual strategy, use the different methods in an effort to ultimately give your buyers the goods—and experience—they prefer most.

FORTUNE BOOST #11
PERSUASIVE PRICING

Though many sellers fear profit margins are shrinking and that the boom of online bidding is a thing of the past, the truth is that high bids are still up for grabs, and profits still abound *provided* sellers use sound and sensible pricing strategies. No doubt about it, competition is stiff, but don't throw up your hands in exasperation, believing the only way to lure bidders is by offering your great stuff at garage sale prices. Instead, consider the pricing options you might have overlooked or misunderstood—those that can restore your faith and land you a fortune, proving that online auctioning is still a lucrative pursuit.

Know Your Stuff, Know Your Market

Don't make the mistake of believing *all* your goods are gold, dreamily anticipating that hordes of bidders will pounce and pay handsomely for every item you put up for bid. The preamble to proper pricing is the understanding of how your goods will measure up in the competitive auction marketplace.

- **Supply and Demand:** Start with the most basic question: what's the current market demand for what you're selling? Are there scant few items like yours to be found, or is there a current glut? How well are other items like yours selling? Are they all gaining bids, or are they closing with nary a second glance?
- **Origin, Condition, and Completeness:** Verify provenance and authenticity of your items—and have proof. Then expect that damage, wear, or missing parts and pieces can often reduce the value of an item by half or more.
- **Recent Prices:** Study the actual prices that items like yours have been selling at. If you disregard current market prices, you'll either underestimate (and potentially undervalue) your items, or you'll overestimate your items with pricing schemes that appear unreasonable and unfounded.
- **Your Goals and Margins:** Don't forget the bread and butter of good business—ensure that your sales can support your income needs and goals. Sometimes you can't let an item go too low without taking a loss, and you'll need to sell other profit-bearing items in the meantime, waiting and watching for when trends and prices shift.

How Low Can You Go?

Now you're ready to bait the hook. And what draws bidders the fastest?—*low opening bids*. Expect that a key draw of online auctions is the lure of the bargain. Don't fear that your great stuff will go for mere pennies on the dollar. Though some bidders do sneak away with a real steal from time to time, most often sellers who've done their research earn respectable prices regardless of (and sometimes thanks to) a low opening bid. Here's why:

- **Low bids are easy bids.** You can always count on bargain hunters to drop a quick buck or two on an undervalued item, and that's usually all it takes to get the bidding going. Soon, others will find your low-priced treasure, determined that they can't let it go for next to nothing—*and it won't*.
- **Some bidders hate to lose.** When outbid, some thwarted bidders will come back to bid again, striving to reclaim an item they've taken "emotional possession" of, while bringing your item up to (and often beyond) present market value.
- **The fun is in the pursuit.** Many bidders enjoy the gamesmanship of auctions and low minimum bids offer plenty of opportunity for a back-and-forth price volley to ensue. By the time the auction's ended, you'll find those dependable bidders have done their duty well in bringing you a good value.

Is Higher Better?

Some sellers avoid using the garage-sale price tactics of low minimum bids. It stands to reason that some higher-quality or highly desirable goods might be undermined and misrepresented by a low opening bid, one that could suggest, "it can't really be worth much at that low of an opening price." Higher opening bids, then, do work well in these instances:

- **You get what you pay for.** A higher opening bid can communicate that your item is the real deal and deserving of a more realistic starting price.
- **Weed out the clientele.** "Bottom feeders" and "auction gamers" often bid on the cheapest stuff while not always being the best end-customers. If your item is worthy of a more serious bidder/buyer, raise the stakes in order to zero in on the bidders who know and appreciate what you're offering.
- **Show what you know.** An item with a higher opening bid can communicate that you're an astute seller who knows the value of what you're offering. Your confidence in a higher price can telegraph your knowledge and sincerity to bidders.

Even when using a higher opening bid, keep that starting price well below market value—don't stymie the bidding process or your profit potential with *too* high of a price. Try this: establish an opening bid price that falls between 70 and 80 percent of current market value. Bidders will see that you have an understanding of your item's value but aren't opposed to letting competitive bidding set the final price.

Reserve Your Right

There's nothing wrong with a little protection, and if you're unsure about recovering your investment or getting a reasonable price for an item, slap a reserve on it. Make no mistake, some bidders are immediately put off at the sight of a reserve price but sometimes, for you, it's the most prudent thing to do. But use reserves wisely: dropping a reserve on every auction will gain you a reputation of being a fixed-price-seller-in-auction-clothing who has little knowledge or faith in the bidding process.

But what should that reserve price be? Aim to set it around or just below current market value, giving bidders a bit of wiggle room to keep competitive bidding alive after the reserve's been met. If your reserve price is too high, though, expect that bidders will turn away when market value has been realized but the reserve price has yet to be reached.

Embrace the Early Bid

And what if the first bidder who happened by said, "I'll take it."? Some will if you give them the opportunity. When you have an inventory of goods that you can sell at fixed prices, use the "Buy-It Now" feature at eBay to help you pull down a quick sale. If you have a time-sensitive item to sell (such as trendy items or holiday fare), make it easy on your bidders to find and close a deal quickly.

Try One, Try All

And with the different pricing options available to you, be sure to sample them all. Experiment with different strategies to find which method brings the best prices and most reliable sell-through. Though you don't need to reinvent your business model with *every* auction, making judicious use of different pricing schemes can help you attract a greater number of bidders and hasten your path to fortune.

FORTUNE BOOST #12
TEN TIPS FOR IMPROVING YOUR FIXED-PRICE SALES

If you've been auctioning for a while, you've no doubt established or have considered starting up an online store, perhaps within eBay's own eBay Stores. While eBay Stores has tools available to help you build your fixed-price venue, the help runs short when you want some advice on *how to run* your online shop. Here are 10 timely tips to help you gain better visibility, greater customer satisfaction, and maximum return on your fixed-price sales efforts.

1. **Be seen in everything you do.** Whenever you list items for bid, be sure to conspicuously advertise your online store, too.
2. **Make your store inventory easy to browse.** Categorize your fixed-price goods in meaningful ways that will help customers zero in on exactly

what they're looking for. Don't just dump an unsorted inventory in a heap and hope visitors will have patience to comb through it all (many don't, you know).

3. **Be accessible.** Don't make it difficult for your customers—especially new ones—to get in touch with you. Be sure your contact information is clearly visible in your store area. If your contact information can't easily be found, you've likely lost another customer.

4. **Keep a customer list.** Once you've satisfied customers, keep the relationships alive by adding their names to your customer list. Allow an "opt in" opportunity for first-time customers to be added to your courtesy communications of future items to be offered.

5. **Make your terms known.** Be clear, concise, and complete when posting your business terms and policies. Shipping options, insurance, return policies, and guarantees all need to be clearly spelled out and easy to find.

6. **Diversify your listings.** Whether or not you specialize in a particular type of item, be sure to list items in multiple venues (there are other sites besides eBay, of course) and use multiple selling formats (fixed and dynamic). The more you can diversify your location and sales methods, the better chance you have of attracting an equally diversified clientele.

7. **Exhibit your expertise.** Don't be bashful. Make liberal use of the eBay "About Me" page and showcase your sales history, your related experience, your business credentials—everything that tells your customers why you're the seller with whom they can feel confident. Oh, and don't forget to post a picture of your most valuable asset— _you!_ Customers like to see whom they're dealing with.

8. **Give 'em more than just goods.** Most successful sellers offer generous amounts of additional information to their patrons. Post additional articles, images, and interesting information that will help your shoppers learn more about the goods they seek, the goods you're selling.

9. **Maintain customer "want" lists.** As you develop your customer base, get to know what else they're looking for. By keeping their wants in mind, you improve your ability to sell more goods faster (essentially, a _pre_ sale), and you further enhance your customer relationships.

10. **Post customer testimonies.** With their permission, visibly post the comments of your satisfied customers. (Don't expect they'll all make the extra effort to review your feedback profile). Not only will past customers feel special about seeing their names for others to see, you'll also help new customers get a better feeling about your commitment to total customer satisfaction.

Unlike auction listings, an online store should advertise more than just the items you're selling—it reveals the details of how you run your business, how you

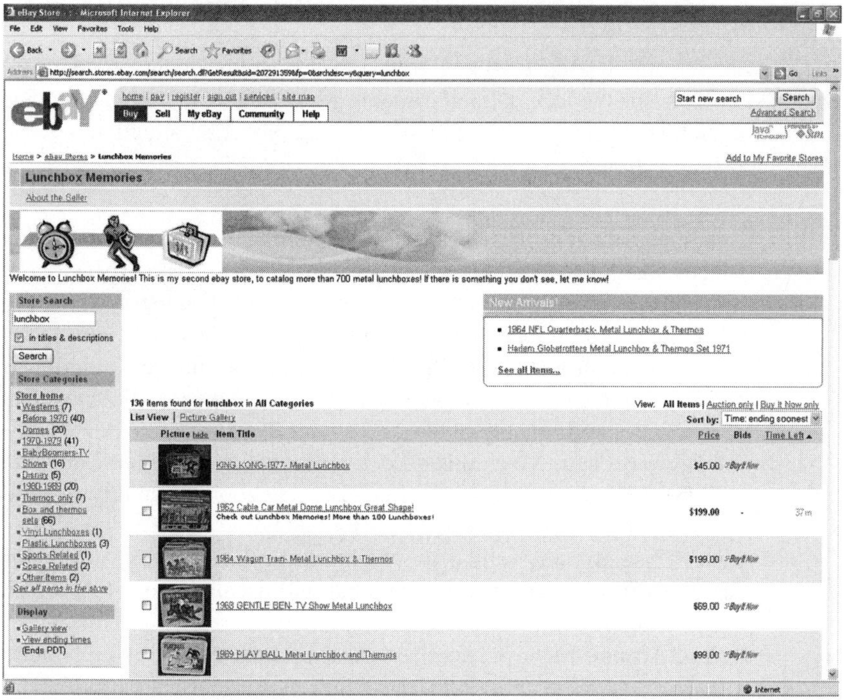

Figure 12-1 Still one of my favorite eBay stores is that of Lunchbox Memories. It always leaves me craving a peanut-butter-and-jelly sandwich.

manage your sales, and how you serve your customers. Make sure your online store incorporates these top 10 keys to success, helping your customers find an easier and more satisfying experience when visiting your nonauction offerings. (See Figure 12-1.)

FORTUNE BOOST #13
PICTURE PERFECT: FIVE STEPS TO BETTER PHOTOS

Often, good images are all it takes to convince buyers to take it now or bid it up, depending upon your sales method. Too often, though, great items never fail to earn their true value due to inferior images that poorly represent the item, coupled with a buying population that has become increasingly selective and justifiably leery of taking risks on items that are poorly presented. Even if you're an amateur shutterbug, the ability to take good photos of your items is easily within your reach. Here are five steps to taking better photos every time.

Step One: Get the Right Equipment

Before you concern yourself with how to take better photos, focus on how well equipped you are for the task. Digital cameras are definitely the tools of choice these days, and when shopping for a digital camera, pay close attention to these image-boosting features:

- **Image Resolution:** This is the most important factor in determining which camera you should purchase and how much you can expect to pay. You can spend hundreds of dollars (even thousands) on top-notch equipment, but all you'll really need is something a simple as a 2.1 megapixel (or better) point-and-shoot digital camera. Higher image resolution is certainly a plus, but beware of the overall image size (in kilobytes) that accompanies high-quality photos.
- **Lenses and Focus Mechanics:** Look for a camera that offers both auto and manual focusing, with a real bonus being zoom capability for illuminating tiny details with crystal clarity.
- **Ease of Use:** Simple is still better. Fighting and fumbling with a complex camera will not only be frustrating, but will usually result in less than stellar images.
- **Tripod Mount:** Most cameras have these by default, but be sure. Mounting your camera on a tripod reduces blur caused by a shaky hand.

Step Two: Instant Photo Studio

A photo studio—in deference to using your desktop or garage floor—doesn't have to be elaborate to be effective. Simply purchase one or two parson's tables (the inexpensive kind you find in the bed-and-bath stores) and situate them side-by-side, preferably covered with a fabric that provides contrast. This is tabletop photography, as many pros practice it (see Figure 13-1). If you'll be photographing larger items, get a piece of half-inch plywood that can straddle the two tables. It doesn't have to be fancy to be effective—just stable and sturdy.

Step Three: A Simple Background Check

With your studio surface in place, you now need to establish a background that will best compliment your items and provide a more professional appearance. A good choice for establishing background is a length of inexpensive material of a solid color (with white, black, or dark blue offering the best contrast results). Tack the material to a wall or in a corner to form a backdrop, and then drape it down and over your work surface (see Figure 13-1). You now have a consistent background color that will show off the item without showing it up.

Figure 13-1 Instant, easy, and affordable—here's a tabletop studio created with a single round parson's table and a remnant of crushed purple velvet. "Wahhl, thank ya' very mushhh..."

Step Four: Step into a Better Light

While it's not terribly difficult to establish good lighting, it's almost certain death for an image (and the auction) if the lighting is terrible. I caught up with sculptor and photographer Nelson Broskey to glean a few of his best-used lighting tricks to get the most professional-looking images on an amateur budget:

- **Go Natural:** Photos taken in natural sunlight usually bring the best results as far as illumination of detail and truer color. If the sun is shining, photograph outdoors.
- **If It Must Be Artificial:** Buy an inexpensive light kit for consistent quality if shooting multiple items. Otherwise, at the least, use incandescent bulbs (of no higher wattage than 60W) for best results; higher-wattage bulbs tend to give items a washed out look. And stay away from fluorescent lighting; it casts a yellow-green tint on your images and usually misrepresents the item's coloring.

- **Control the Light:** Aim the light where you need it to get the best results. If outdoors, use a reflector (something as simple as stark white poster board or a mylar auto sunshade) to direct sunlight at your item. If using artificial lighting, purchase three automobile work lights and suspend them above and on either side of the item (again, being careful not to blast too high a wattage at your item).
- **Glare:** This is a problem for natural or artificially lit photography. Avoid flash shots, and 90 percent of your glare problems will disappear. If glare is still a problem or you must use a flash, tilt the item in such a way that the light (or flash) doesn't strike its surface directly.

Step Five: Ask Your Customers Whether It Really Matters

If you ever doubt the negative impact of a poor image, ask your customers. Long-time eBay enthusiast Gretchen Hakala shared this insight: "I'm annoyed by sellers who post bad images—it's sloppy and shows the seller must not be too concerned with quality."

And with just five simple steps that will help you improve your item images, why risk lost sales and a damaged online reputation—that *would* be sloppy.

FORTUNE BOOST #14
PICTURE *IM*-PERFECT: 10 IMAGING MISTAKES THAT WILL COST YOU SALES

In Fortune Boost #12, you read the tips and techniques to ensure higher-quality images of the items you're selling at eBay. And while we're all prone to learn well when presented with a nice selection of "do's," it's sometimes as effective—maybe more so—when we're offered an equally enlightening list of "don'ts"—practices we'd be better off to avoid. To that end, here's a list of the top 10 photo faux pas that tend to afflict sellers' auction images and that you'll want to steer clear of as you continually strive for those "picture perfect" presentations.

Poor Lighting: If the lighting is dim, the image detail can be grossly underrepresented. Equally, an item too brightly lit will result in a severely overexposed image. And those darn fluorescent bulbs tend to cast a greenish tint to images. Whenever possible, use natural (outdoor) lighting or aim two 40-watt incandescent bulbs at the item, one from either side. (See Figure 14-1.)

- **Blurry Images:** Whether poorly focused or just too close to the camera's lens, fuzzy images are an annoyance to bidders and reflect lack of attention on the seller's part. Always check the focus before you shoot and, if a jittery hand might be the culprit, use a tripod for a true "still-life" image. (See Figure 14-2.)

Figure 14-1 If bidders are left in the dark over the details of your item, they probably won't bid.

- **Excessive Glare:** A close cousin to poor lighting, excessive glare can be the result of an overlit item, yet is usually caused by poorly managed flash usage. If your item catches the glare of the flash, shoot it from an angle (left, right, over, or under) to avoid those glare "hot spots." (See Figure 14-3.)
- **Lack of Cropping:** Buyers aren't concerned if you're the sort who works amid a messy desk just as long as they don't have to search its surroundings for whatever it is you're advertising for sale. Crop your images to cut out anything that distracts from the item—that includes the kids or the kitten, no matter how cute they may be. (See Figure 14-4.)
- **Reflective Surfaces:** Have you seen the now-infamous image of the chrome teakettle and its immodest proprietor that previously made the rounds on the Internet? If so, you'll know why you need to take care when photographing reflective items that might reveal distracting or even embarrassing elements opposite them. Shoot these items at an angle and across from a neutral background. (See Figure 14-5.)
- **Bad Backgrounds:** Forgo the fancy backdrops or the garish colors—they only distract from your item. Choose neutral or complimentary colors to really make your item stand out. Solid darks or lights are still the best bets to provide a clean and appropriately contrasting background. (See Figure 14-6.)
- **Confounding Combo Shots:** Some sellers think it a good idea to photograph multiple items in a single image; they should think again. Other

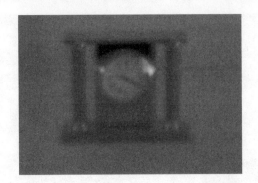

Figure 14-2 No matter how much you rub your eyes, you'll see it's the image that's bleary.

Figure 14-3 Unchecked glare makes it impossible to see the details of this clock's face.

items adjacent to the one you're selling will again distract the potential buyer away from what you're really offering for sale. (See Figure 14-7.)

- **Lack of Closeup:** Ever looked at images of jewelry or small collectibles where the item is too tiny to clearly discern? Avoid this frustration by getting closer to the item (watch the focus), taking full advantage of your camera's zoom function, or opting to use a flatbed scanner. Your buyers will appreciate the extra detail these image alternatives can provide. (See Figure 14-8.)
- **Overenhancement:** While there's certainly nothing wrong with touching up minor image imperfections, resist enlisting every image enhancement tool lest you render the image off-color, unnaturally sharp, and generally jagged and blocky looking.)
- **Excessive Image Size:** A fast way to alienate potential buyers is to make them wait and wait and wait for a huge image to display on their

Figure 14-4 Can you guess that it's the clock that's up for sale? Most bidders aren't interested in this sort of guessing game.

Figure 14-5 The photographer's hand is clearly reflected in this image—and it obscures the detail of the clock itself.

computers (many won't wait more than five or six seconds anyway). Set your digital camera to take moderate-sized pictures, looking to avoid any image that exceeds a 40KB file size.

- **Bonus Blunder! Borrowed Images:** Besides the fact that many images found online are actually copyrighted, sellers who "acquire" pictures in this way are truly misrepresenting the items they're selling—they're not showing the actual item that's being offered. This could lead to significant customer dissatisfaction and a possible cry of "fraud!"

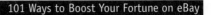

Figure 14-6 Surely there's a better background than this.

Figure 14-7 Is this an online auction or "Let's Make a Deal?" Don't make your buyers choose from Item #1, Item #2 or Item #3.

Certainly, none of these are truly *fatal offenses* and many can be forgiven by tolerant buyers. Still, take the opportunity to learn from past mistakes, committed by yourself or by others, to further improve your item images and overall marketing of the goods you sell. In short order, you'll find that your image-taking and

Figure 14-8   Can you see enough detail in this item to determine whether you'll bid on it?

presentation skills will be sharply improved and will likely lead to greater sales success in the process.

FORTUNE BOOST #15
COLOR YOUR WORLD…GREEN!

Now here's a bit of powerful science and psychology that can help you improve your eBay sales to ultimate profits—the power of color. With so many sellers concerned about what goods to sell and how to ensure that they'll have an endless stream of inventory, some forget to stop and notice the green, green grass they just trod across (figuratively *and* literally). When it comes to merchandising, most big marketing and other such PR firms have recognized the impact color can have on the shopping and eventual buying experience. At eBay, you should take note of this very important element of the shopper's psyche and understand how color strategies can help you harvest a rich green fortune for yourself.

How Color Comes into Play

If a picture is worth a thousand words, then what impact would color have over black and white? The biggest brains in marketing have long known that color has undeniable impact on shoppers. It evokes emotion, activity, and involvement. Some studies have concluded that, when marketing a product, color advertisements generate up to 50 percent more purchases or customer inquiries than do black-and-white ads. Further, the use of color has been documented in test results as responsible for accelerating learning, enhancing information retention and recall (as eBay's own colorful logo demonstrates), and inspiring participation.

Therefore, if you want to double your sales, you need to be sure you dabble in color when it comes to your eBay listings.

Colors stir impulses and promote responses in people, compelling them to take action to satisfy a want or need. In the world of food marketing (be it packaged or prepared in a restaurant setting), color is tantamount in ensuring customer satisfaction and satiation. According to statistics gathered by the folks at ColorMatters.com, here are some examples of how color use incites reactions or imparts perceptions in each of us:

- Elegance is often communicated through the use of shiny black.
- Mystery is often communicated through the use of violet.
- Neutrality is often communicated through the use of gray tones.

And, when it comes to serving the genders, the findings show:

- Women prefer red.
- Men prefer blue.

To this end, it makes sense to use the appropriate color, in various hues and textures, to properly market to a specific gender. Clearly, it's proven now that color can sway thinking, change opinions, and trigger desired reactions. Color is all around us in our lives today, and the savvy seller who harnesses its effects can gain impressive results through its use.

The Content of Colors

So with all that said about how colors can have a positive impact on your eBay listing designs, here's what the researches have found about the different colors and the impact each has.

- **Blue.** As already mentioned, this is the color preferred by most folks, especially men. It's a color that can suggest coolness (both in terms of temperature and temperament) and has an extremely versatile spectrum, from a soft baby blue to a mysterious and compelling midnight richness. Add a bit of boss metal flake and you have a preferred choice of muscle car owners, too.
- **Yellow.** This is a warm and advancing color and has been noted as actually being able to elevate blood pressure in humans. It's a pleasant color, though, suggesting warmth, brightness, cleanliness, and happiness.
- **Red.** If you want to know why police officers tend to pick out red vehicles from the multitude of cars, this is why: this color is the attention-getter.

Of course, it's the hottest of the colors and, along with blue, it's another top choice among men when it comes to their vehicles. Of course, it also embodies sensuousness and even sexual appeal and intrigue.

- **Green.** If good health and a fresh vitality are the order of the day, here's the color for your marketing campaign. Notice how green is liberally used in the marketing of health food products, fresh produce, and even environmental awareness.

- **Brown.** This one can go either way. It certainly embodies a sense of earthiness that can communicate naturalness, wholesomeness, and rustic appeal. On the other hand, it can also denote a grungy quality. As it is complimentary in nature to gold, it can also suggest an air of richness or value when used in conjunction with a soft dose of yellow (as in "golden brown").

- **Black.** As previously noted, black indicates richness, expensive appeal, and well-mannered sophistication. As a background color to provide the ultimate accentuation, black (and black velvet texture) is always a good choice. While a foreground color of white can be a bit too much of a stark contrast, yellow, red, and some lavender tones are nicely set off by black. Watch out for using dark blue text on a black background; the effect can impart a weird sort of 3D effect but can also cause quick eyestrain.

- **Orange.** Naturally, this is the color of autumn, of coziness, and of bountiful harvests. Orange is perfect for appealing to buyers eager for holidays, family gatherings, and a shared feast. Add a bit of brown to it to gain a golden rich appeal.

With that information, you can now begin to plan how you'll put color to work for you in your marketing efforts, both at eBay as well as in other venues you may explore. Take care, though, as you discover the excitement of using color through HTML coding in your product listings: too much of a good thing will quickly go bad. To prevent overdoing it, limit yourself to just a few key colors, set off against a black or white background. Use color as an accent in your eBay listings where a nicely designed color logo or a well-placed color splash can have dramatic effect among the standard neutral white palette of the site.

Most importantly, as you use color in your listings, try to establish a consistent color scheme—in a logo or other design element—that will help customers begin to identify you and your business. Look closely at other big businesses as well as the products you purchase every day or every week. See how color plays an important part in promoting the product and how it compels you to identify and purchase it. Use that same psychology of color in your sales efforts and you'll be coloring your world a vibrant green in no time. (See Figure 15-1.)

Figure 15-1 When you're ready to learn more about color and the effects it can have on your eBay sales, visit www.colormatters.com for some excellent insight and information.

FORTUNE BOOST #16
APPEALING TO YOUR BUYERS' SENSES

Sellers often overlook the importance of appealing to their buyers' senses. That is, in all the flurry of listing goods, managing transactions, and maintaining customer satisfaction, it becomes easy to overlook these small but significant nuances of the actual items sold and how, upon receipt, the item will communicate its value through the five senses. Therefore, here's a look at how selling to the senses, so to speak, will help you improve your customers' impressions of you based on how they experience the essence of the goods they purchase from you and how inclined they'll be to purchase additional items from you, too. Now *that* makes sense, right?

Sight

Clearly, first impressions are lasting ones. If an item you have to offer is dusty, dingy, or generally just a bit dilapidated in appearance, see if you can clean it up a bit. And while brushing off the dust and wiping away the soil is typically a good idea, take care in your cleaning. Some sellers have damaged items in their efforts to add a bit of polish (such as attempting to remove old price tags, stains, or what have you), and some buyers proclaim that removing an item's natural "patina" is a definite no-no. Therefore, clean when it makes sense—when there's no risk of devaluing the item—to give it the best possible appearance. (Find out how other sellers and collectors shine up similar articles.) If you're not sure, provide a full disclosure of the item's present state and the potential for polishing, then leave it for the buyer to decide if a cleaning is in order.

Smell

Then again, sometimes the nose knows long before the eyes ever get a glimpse of what's inside a package. Take special care to please this sense, as buyers are often more than disappointed when an item brings along a stench that wasn't bargained for. If an item has a musty odor from moisture exposure, let it be known. If you're a smoker and your items have absorbed the odor, let it be known. Whatever the situation, if your goods have a certain "air" about them that could be potentially offensive, be certain to state it up front.

Touch

Usually, touch isn't a sensation that proves too troublesome. Of course, items that are rough, sticky, or whatever—and shouldn't be—necessitate full disclosure. The same holds for furniture or other items that might have been worn smooth over years of use or could have the telltale rippling or warping that comes from moisture damage; these situations should also be properly explained at the outset. Many buyers will close their eyes and run their hands over an item to detect variations or imperfections that their eyes might miss. Be sure there are no tactile surprises in store for your customers.

Sound

Naturally, when you're selling audio-related items (such as old records, tapes, radios, and so on), you'll want to fully describe the aural qualities of the goods. But, beyond these obvious sound-related items, give consideration to any sounds *any* of your items might make. If it rattles, is something broken? If it squeaks, does it need to be lubricated? Again, no sense is to be overlooked when selling to and satisfying your customers.

Taste?

Taste is the one sense that you might not need to cater to as carefully as the previous four. Still, some rock, gem, and coin collectors have stated that their taste buds can offer the final determination about an item's authenticity and lineage. Go figure.

Making Sense of It All

Though it might sound a bit far-fetched, appealing to your buyer's senses is just another factor to consider as you mine your eBay fortune. Remember the limitation that selling online prevents buyers from fully experiencing an item as they would in person. Work to present as much sensory information as possible when listing your goods, and then be doubly certain that there will be no sensory surprises when the goods arrive.

FORTUNE BOOST #17
KISS: KEEP IT SIMPLE, SELLER

Sooner or later, sellers must confront the temptation to jazz up their sales listings to the point of excess. Whether you've just learned HTML, found a great bunch of animated gifs, or simply feel you have to have the nicest display on the cyberstreet, it's not uncommon to...well... get a bit carried away. Unfortunately, overdoing the eye-candy will too often shoo away the prospective customers you're trying to impress. Take a lesson, then, from those who have overdone it before you: keep it simple, keep it quick, and keep those eBay sales moving ahead.

Back to Basics

The earliest eBay listings consisted of only simple titles and plain-text descriptions, and time has shown that these simple pleasures are still the best. Put your efforts into crafting effective item titles (incorporating the most frequently used search keywords), and follow with useful descriptions that offer full disclosure of your wares. Often, expressionistic sellers get so caught up in virtual neon that they fail to give the basic item details shoppers are seeking.

Next up, be sure to provide clear and true images of the item, depicting as many angles and details as possible. Crop out unnecessary background clutter and only enhance the image in order to brighten or correct color. Beware of overenhancing an image to the point that it no longer looks like what the buyer will ultimately receive—that leads to customer dissatisfaction.

Finally, make sure your sales policies and methods are easily found and clearly stated—something else you don't want hidden within an onslaught of fancy formatting.

A Bit of Personality Still Helps, Though

But don't think all your listings need be as bland as tapioca. On the contrary, a bit of well-placed style can effectively enhance your item's presence as well as the customers' shopping experience. Use some simple HTML to add special fonts, colors, simple backgrounds, and interspersed images in a way that compliments your items and showcases them in a visual theme to entice visitors to stop, shop, and buy. It's the same subtle tactic used by the big marketing brains, and it works. When used in moderation, your custom listing designs can lure otherwise apathetic shoppers off the street and into your virtual showroom.

Time Is Money—Theirs and Yours

There's no denying it: the more you adorn your listings, the longer it will take them to fully display. Bidders and buyers are a busy lot—they don't have all day to wait for twinkling lights, clever animations, and blaring muzak to download to their monitors. In fact, research has shown that few Web surfers and shoppers will wait beyond five or six seconds before they decide to bolt for another destination. And not every potential customer has the benefit of viewing the Internet via DSL, cable, or other high-octane connections; yes, some *are* still using a 56K dial-up line.

To you, the ultimate loss of excessive designs could be threefold: the loss of the sale, the loss of your listing fees, and the loss of your valuable time spent overdecorating what could have been a simpler and more enticing listing.

Perfect It, Then Project It

Once you've designed and perfected your efficient listing design, save yourself additional effort over the long run by capturing it in a template that you can apply time and again. It's definitely a time saver when you only need to "plug in" item-specific information in your chosen format. Yes, there are plenty of template providers out there, eager to help you achieve a similar result, though you might unwittingly be advertising their service more than advertising yourself and your items. However, when you invest in developing your *own* unique template, you stand to make yourself and your listings more identifiable to repeat customers who will soon recognize *you*—and that's a design that's good for gaining a fortune.

FORTUNE BOOST #18
A LITTLE HTML GOES A LONG WAY...TO PROFITS!

Now that you're duly sheepish about adding too much glitz and glimmer to your eBay listings, let it now be known that using *some* HTML niftiness can excite your bidders and bring home a boost to your bottom line. It's all about exercising moderation and, when you make strategic use of HTML enhancements, you'll find that many of those would-be looky-loos can be converted into energetic bidders. Here are some pointers on the best listing recipe that makes tasty use of graphic enhancements in a way that won't needlessly increase your listing time and, more importantly, won't hopelessly alienate your potential bidders and buyers. With just a "pinch" of font and a "dash" of images, you'll see how well-placed embellishments can boost your earnings potential.

It's Easier than It May Look

If you've never seen HTML code before, chances are it will look like another foreign language at first glance (actually, it is a language and if you've never seen it, well, it's foreign to you). Understand that all HTML, at its most basic, is a collection of special *tags* that tell the Web browser how to display the actual content, be that text or images. These formatting tags, then, are housed within the right and left carat brackets.

The text within the tags are HTML commands that can perform wondrous things to your eBay listing, bringing it to life in a dazzling and enticing way. The key, of course, is not to overdo it. Too much tagging will have your bidders gagging. Practice a bit of constraint when you use HTML formatting to really make your listings look professional. Here is some of the easiest and most effective formatting you can do:

- Create a slightly larger and stylized title font.
- Introduce color to set off your title text or to highlight specific words within the title.
- Vary the font style, size, and color to maximum effect.
- Embed images into your listing without incurring additional listing fees.

For example, take a look at the HTML-enhanced listing shown in Figure 18-1. This is a simple yet effective listing that provides visual interest to compliment the accompanying descriptive text.

Certainly, there's more you can do with HTML, but remember to *keep it simple*.

An HTML Template That You Can Use Today

To help you make immediate improvement to your listings today, feel free to make use of the actual HTML code that generated the example in Figure 18-1. Work with this one a bit and look at your local bookstore and elsewhere online for additional resources regarding HTML tags and techniques. Enjoy, but do so in moderation; your bidders will appreciate it.

```
<HTML>
<P align=center>
<FONT face=impact color=green size=10>How to Sell ANYTHING on
<FONT color=blue>eBay <BR>
<FONT color=green>...and Make a FORTUNE! <BR>
<FONT color=black size=5>by Dennis L. Prince <BR><BR>
<FONT color=blue><I>- Autographed First Edition! -</I>
<FONT face=arial color=red><BR><BR>
```

Figure 18-1   A little bit of HTML helped me add appropriate visual appeal to this special charity auction listing.

```
<I>Charity Auction Benefiting</I> <BR>
<IMG height=100
src="http://my.starstream.net/dlprince/auctionpix/TFT.jpg" width=220
align=center> <BR><BR>
</P>
```

```
<IMG height=400 alt="Front Cover"
src="http://my.starstream.net/dlprince/auctionpix/ebayfortune_auction.jpg"
width=325 align=right>
<P align="LEFT">
<FONT face=arial color=black size=3>
```
Here's a great opportunity to gain a collectible signed first edition book, learn how to use eBay like a pro, and help underprivileged children this holiday season.
```
<P>
```

```
<P align="LEFT">
```
Best-selling eBay authority Dennis L. Prince offers his insider tips and insight into the ways and means to sell anything on eBay...and make a fortune!

Author of more than a dozen eBay and e-commerce books, Prince provides professional yet personable guidance to help you make the most of your eBay experience. From learning how to effortlessly navigate the site, bid like a pro, and sell like a seasoned veteran, this book is your short-cut to eBay expertise. Prince has been an avid eBay user, seller, and advocate since the site's inception and he's ready to give you the fast track to fortune. At over 250 pages in length, this book is ready to help you in your eBay endeavors or it will make a unique gift for that eBay enthusiast on your holiday giving list.
<P>

<IMG height=220 alt="D.L. Prince and friend" src="http://my.starstream.net/dlprince/auctionpix/dprince1.jpg" width=200 align=left>

<P align="LEFT">
With over 40,000 copies of "How to Sell ANYTHING on eBay...and Make a FOR-TUNE!" already sold, here is a rare chance to grab a rare first edition of this best-selling book, autographed by Prince and even personalized for you, if you like. All proceeds from this auction will go directly to the Toys for Tots organization, an important program successfully run by the U.S. Marine Corps Reserves since 1947. In the 57 years of the program's operation, Marines have distributed more than 332 million toys to over 159 million needy children. Here's your opportunity to make your contribution to this valuable program while gaining a terrific resource and collectible for your own personal library.

<P align="LEFT">
High Bidder will please pre-pay, plus postage. Insurance will be additional upon request. High bidder will also be sent a copy of the Toys for Tots donation receipt. If you have any questions, please send contact Prince via e-mail at dlprince@bigfoot.com (or use the "Ask seller a question" link within this listing).

<P align="LEFT">Check Prince's eBay
<A href="http://cgi5.ebay.com/ws/"http://cgi.ebay.com/aw-cgi/eBayISAPI.dll?ViewFeedback&userid=dennis_prince"">feedback
</A>
and bid with confidence.

<P align=center>
<P align=center><IMG height=150 alt="Prince Autograph"

src="http://my.starstream.net/dlprince/auctionpix/dlpauto.jpg" width=250
align=center>

</FONT></FONT></P></FONT></FONT></FONT></FONT></FONT>
</HTML>

FORTUNE BOOST #19
CH-CH-CH CHANGES: HOW TO HARNESS THEM FOR YOUR OWN GOOD

Those who have been around eBay for very long have seen the site go through numerous changes, not only in its layout but also in its offering of buying and selling feature, its usage policies, and its costs. Many have bemoaned the rate of change that has become inherent in the site and, on some occasions, a very vocal portion of the using base has threatened to leave the site for good. Change is inevitable at eBay, just as it is throughout the Internet and to overall e-conomy. For sellers who are looking to keep traction—even improve it—during times of change, here are some key considerations to ponder as you strive to deflect any potential negative impact of change, harness any benefits of change, and ensure that your customers always feel a steady rate of satisfaction when they shop your goods.

Help Your Customers Navigate the Site Changes

Practically every Web site that survived the dot-com crash of the 1990s has undergone significant change and redesign, and eBay is no exception (as you can see from the proof of evolution shown in Figure 19-1). As the site has undergone cosmetic changes (sometimes many significant changes within a single year's time), sellers have struggled to maintain their presence and visibility among it all. In order to maintain your virtual presence—to continue to be seen and known to your customers—here are some proactive steps to take to lessen any negative impact that may arise when the landlord changes the foundation underneath you:

- **Promote your eBay ID:** When you choose an eBay User ID, be sure you choose one that your customers can easily remember and find when they search for you directly. Whether it's your own name, your store name, or some other sort of name that easily identifies you and your products, be sure that ID can be remembered and can be distinctly searched by customers eager to find you when the site's home page or search pages change.
- **Recommunicate your location:** Whenever you engage in direct customer communication, whether before, during, or after a transaction, be

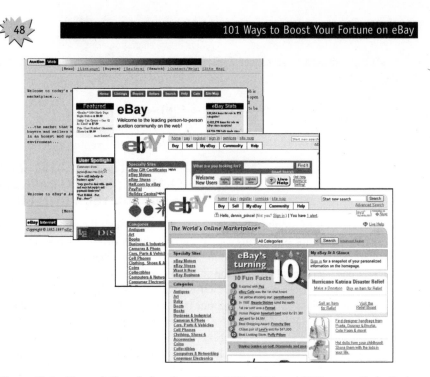

Figure 19-1 The evolution of eBay, from 1995, 1997, 2004, and 2005, respectively. You've come a long way, eBay.

certain to always note your eBay ID and be sure to communicate with a list of past customers (if you've been keeping a clientele list) to forewarn them of upcoming eBay changes and how you can be easily found amid any site alterations.

- **Keep a keen eye on your keywords:** Regardless of any changes that eBay makes, their search functions will always remain tops in bidder usage. When the site changes its layout or tinkers with its search tools, your best bet for helping customers find you—both existing as well as new customers—is to ensure that your listings contain all the right keywords.

Anticipate Changes Coming Your Way

You can either take a passive approach and let change afflict you or you can take an active stance and anticipate such events. One of the best ways to stay abreast—and in front of—changes at eBay is to maintain a regular viewing of eBay's own announcements area. Just click on the "Community" box from the main tool bar (located at the top of most every eBay page) and then navigate to these two key information areas:

- **eBay General Announcements Board:** Visit this hub of news and information (navigate from the home page to Community and on to General Announcements) from eBay's leaders and administrators to learn the latest about site changes, programs, and other service-related topics. Savvy sellers keep a regular watch on the announcements posted here (as well as the ensuing user feedback to such announcements) to spot and prepare for upcoming changes.
- **eBay System Announcements Board:** Visit this area of eBay (navigate from the home page to Community and on to System Announcements) to stay up-to-date on planned system outages and how to manage your listings and customer interaction around this brief service disruptions. eBay *will* interrupt their availability on a regular basis (usually weekly) for a couple of hours to perform regular maintenance and backup protection. Sometimes the main site will be unavailable while other times only certain functions will be affected (such as searches or viewing individual listing pages). Your best bet is to avoid having auctions end during this period of time.

Whether you agree with or approve of the announcements you'll learn about in these information areas, it is important that you stay informed and make any necessary adjustments (such as altering your listing schedule if an outage is planned during a time when your auctions would be ending) to ensure that neither you nor your customers will be affected by planned site changes. A little knowledge and action up front will help you ensure that your bottom line doesn't suffer as a result.

FORTUNE BOOST #20
MAINTAINING A CLIENTELE

Not long ago, there was a time when a good variety of merchandise was the only hook needed to attract the eager to eBay. Those days, however, are long gone. Today, more and more eBay sellers have recognized the equal importance of the "customer experience": how well the customer is served, how comfortable the customer feels, and how often the customer returns. It's no longer a matter of goods alone—serving your customers well and gaining their loyal and repeat patronage is crucial to the long-term health of your business.

The Staggering Statistics

Today, online shoppers are interested not only in *what* they will be served but equally *how* they will be served. If you invest your efforts only in the particular merchandise you offer, ignoring your responsibility for the customer's shopping experience, you'll soon find you're lagging behind your competitors. Don't believe it? Here are some revealing statistics previously presented by Vicki Henry, CEO of Feedback Plus, Inc., on why customers *don't* return:

- 1 percent die
- 3 percent move away
- 5 percent buy from friends
- 9 percent prefer competitors
- 14 percent judge by first encounter
- 68 percent leave because of rudeness or indifference

Remember, with the millions of items online up for sale or bid on any given day, it's highly likely that another seller will be offering the same sort of thing that you have on the block. If another seller greets the customers with a bigger smile and a more attentive policy than you, that seller may well win the customers that you just ignored.

It's the Little Things

Delighting customers and gaining their loyalty doesn't require grandiose efforts that are difficult to sustain. Your consistent attention to the simple elements of customer service is often all that is needed to build a devoted customer base. Here are a few things you can do to keep that customer satisfied:

- Always follow up after a transaction to ensure that the item your customer purchased was received intact and as expected.
- Ask for your customers' feedback (and really want it) regarding how they felt about their transaction with you.
- Listen to your customers—they're the ones telling you if you're doing well or not.
- Sweat the details—look for ways to continually improve your correspondence, packaging, product appearance, quality, and so on.
- Underpromise, overdeliver. Customers should be delighted at how well the product and service have *exceeded* their original expectations, not the other way around.

It doesn't take a Herculean effort to show your customers you care. In fact, some small-business owners are discovering that they're better equipped to establish and foster good interpersonal relations with their customers when compared to the often distant and prerecorded personalities of the larger firms.

Customer Satisfaction—Their Words, Not Yours

"Sure my customers are satisfied—just ask me and I'll tell ya." Though that comment may sound funny, there's more truth in that seller-centric sentiment than many would want to admit. It's a trap that's easy to fall into: believing your *own* praises. Experts often remark that to truly excel in customer satisfaction, a seller needs to have a passion to serve customers, leaving it to them to decide when they've been satisfied.

"Real customer service comes from the heart," notes a veteran seller. "If you don't truly and deeply value what the customer means to your business' health, you may as well not bother." These comments underscore the need to let the customer—not yourself—determine what's satisfactory. It's one way to ensure that you remain totally customer focused. For better or worse, you don't give out the grades here, the customer does; the wise seller keeps a pulse on her customers' satisfaction as a way to understand which direction the business is going.

And at the end of the day, it's an undeniable truth that customer service should become and remain a seller's top priority in the effort to develop lasting customer relations.

FORTUNE BOOST #21
GET TO KNOW YOUR NEWBIE

It's a dilemma for the new age: on the one hand, sellers want to actively attract the interest and patronage of online newcomers, while on the other, they know there's the possibility they'll have to work harder with these uninitiated buyers in the cyber-market.

While not all "newbies" are problematic, many eBay sellers agree that working a sale with a first-timer can require some extra effort, extra explanation, and occasionally extra patience. However, if you're prepared to assist a neophyte through the sometimes-perplexing world of online buying, you'll find yourself in a prime position to adopt a long-term customer for your efforts.

Communicating with Your Newbie

When you encounter someone who's "new in town," put your best foot forward and mentally prepare yourself to help them through a process that could be quite foreign and even intimidating to them.

For starters, be prompt in all of your communication and be prepared to answer additional questions regarding your terms, methods, and policies. Then remember that some of these new shoppers might find conducting long-distance business with complete strangers quite a daunting and uncertain undertaking. Your punctual responses and polite answers to their questions will assure them that you are there to assist with their purchase.

Of course, be on the lookout for the occasional dark cloud—you know, the buyer or bidder who's looking to scam and scamper. The undesirable elements are out there, and if your newbie turns out to be an unethical person, be sure your sales policy clearly outlines your expectations of timely payment and so on. If the newbie ne'er-do-well is trying to be clever, cut that one loose and move on.

Most of all, when sizing up and making first contact with newbie shoppers, remember that you're going to make an early impression upon them about how this online marketplace works.

A Newbie's Shopping: Under Control or Out of Hand?

Of most interest to sellers should be the shopping habits of a new bidder. Though it's difficult to evaluate a newcomer's activity in venues outside of eBay, within the site a seller can quickly ascertain whether the new shopper is adopting one of two common buying styles:

- **The Super Cautious:** Some new shoppers won't buy much at all (either in dollar amount or in the number of items concurrently bid upon) until they can gain a certain level of comfort and familiarity with the online process. If they have good first encounters and believe the cyber-market to be a venue of success for them, they'll typically loosen up and get a bit more active in future pursuits.
- **The Super Shopper:** Other new shoppers, however, find online bidding and buying to be a veritable playground. Although their enthusiasm is appreciated, a quick check of their current and recent bidding activity (use eBay's Advanced Search page and search on bidder ID) might reveal that they're committing to a hefty tally. So what? So you'll want to act fast to ensure that your item will be quickly and fully paid for, lest your new customer finds that he's overcommitted his present bankroll.

Of course, these are pretty much the two extremes, and you can expect a good many newbies to fall somewhere in between. And though some might argue it's not a seller's business to know about how, when, and how much a newcomer bids or buys, those who've been selling on a regular basis understand that it's worth noting how newbies are shopping and how to engage them to ensure the deal comes to a successful close.

A Seller's Golden Opportunity

It's wise to recognize the special opportunity to aid and build rapport with new shoppers. There's certainly little time for intense hand holding of newcomers (a seller *must* attend to other customers, after all), but consider these methods of engagement and approach, which will help to ensure a win-win situation with a newbie:

Set the Tempo: Many new buyers aren't exactly savvy to the protocol of online buying; they might be overanxious; they might be undercommitted. Working with good e-mail communication and an even better sales policy, promptly get the exchange in motion once a sale has been decided. Demonstrate your tried-and-true professional business process, and newbies will know they're working with a real pro—someone who'll reliably guide a smooth transaction.

Be Their Guide: It's also good practice to help newcomers (*your* new customers) better understand how eBay auctions and fixed-price sales work. Remember, if you're there to assist them, chances are they'll remember you, your products, and your good business style. That's usually the recipe for earning repeat business.

Customer Care

At the end of the day, a seller's bottom line is determined by the amount of care extended to customers. Though it's certainly not just newbies who frequently require additional attention, the opportunity to lend a hand to a wide-eyed newcomer is where lasting customer relationships are formed. Take the time to understand and assist newbies and they'll likely find that you're their new seller of choice.

Taming the Technology—Cutting Costs While Pumping Up Profits

Assuming you've been working online auctions for awhile, you're probably somewhat familiar with the different *auction management services* available. These are suites of tools that have been designed to help small, medium, and larger businesses manage and maintain their flow of item listings and closed transactions. This occurs within a collection of integrated functions that smoothes out the process and streamlines a business's ability to conduct fast and efficient transactions. Their promises and appeals are enticing as they explain how their suite of tools will take you to the next level of online auction fortune and will take the time and burden out of the process. Proceed cautiously: yes, some of these tools can offer some excellent aids to your activity, but they can also needlessly siphon off your profits and leave you with a collection of "extra stuff" that you don't use but for which you are being regularly billed. In the interest of boosting that bottom line of yours, here's some insight to help you decide if you need more tools and, if so, which ones will be the best to keep your fortune floating along.

Do You Need Additional Tools?

First things first: determine if you really need additional tools to help you maintain and grow your eBay fortune (and remember, the level of fortune you aspire to depends on your own wants, needs, and intentions). Essentially, the key to effectively using auction management services is to understand just how much *service* they'll actually provide to you. Without sounding like a commercial, if your business can be properly supported by it, stay with the tools within eBay itself;

you'll be certain your tools are fully integrated into the site's other workings and you'll likely save money because most eBay tools are free. If, however, you find third-party tools that offer features you see as truly beneficial to your sales and business growth, look to the provider of that service as a good place to invest some of your business capital to help boost your fortune.

A Look at the Top Two Third-Party Services

Many of the numerous auction management service sites have dissolved in recent years, but two very strong companies have remained and have developed some tools that truly are effective and efficient. In short order, here's a look at the two most prolific tool vendors around today:

- **Andale (www.andale.com).** First on the list is Andale, an auction management service company founded in 1999 and one that's been around to ride and survive the dot-com boom and bust. Created with small businesses in mind, Andale offers a compelling *a la carte* offering of services, including listing tools, image hosting, checkout functionality, and e-mail services. Andale offers even more services, but the one that is most intriguing to sellers is the variety of research and analysis tools the site offers. Although eBay has reduced its stable of closed items from 30 days old to just 14 days old, Andale has the rest of the historical data that can help you in your market research efforts. In well-organized fashion, Andale research provides telling statistics such as average selling prices of specified items, category statistics, one-year trending graphs, and even comparison data that will tell you how your items' pricing will stand up to retail prices. By far, this is a differentiating feature Andale has to offer, what with eBay pretty much having provided all the other tools your business needs. And because you can "use only the products you need—and as much as you need," it's relatively easy to pick and choose among Andale's tool set, keeping the services that you truly like and avoiding others that don't provide the results your business needs. (See Figure 22-1.)
- **Vendio (www.vendio.com).** Formerly known as AuctionWatch.com, this is the most venerable of the auction management sites still around today, originally launched in 1998. At the time, AuctionWatch.com quickly became the premiere auction service site, not immediately for its toolset offered but for the incredible amount of useful auction information, articles, and analyses of the online auction industry. Couple the strong editorial content with the most active online auction forum (even rivaling that of eBay's own community forums), and AW became the first and last destination for auctiongoers seeking real-world insight and information. Of course, AuctionWatch grew to provide listing services, image hosting, and even payment services to help buyers and sellers get the most from their

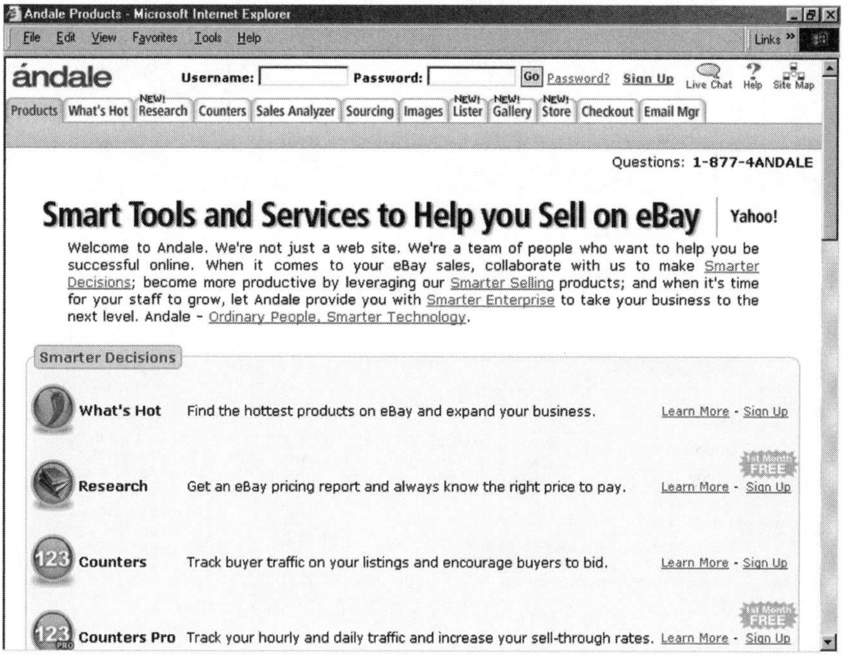

Figure 22-1 *A la carte* pricing and tight integration into eBay makes Andale.com my first choice in auction management services.

online auction efforts. In 2003, the company renamed to Vendio Services, Inc. and further focused its services to help businesses "through the entire online sales process, including inventory management, online store creation, merchandise placement on both fixed price and auction marketplaces, customer communication, and order fulfillment." With their long-standing experience in the realm of auction management services, Vendio definitely deserves a look. (See Figure 22-2.)

Of course, there are numerous other auction management services out there to review and perhaps use. Study all sites' prices carefully and calculate those costs as you work to accurately project your operating costs. Whenever possible, cut costs where they don't provide a noticeable (and calculable) positive impact to your business. Depending on how well organized you already are and how well you're using the built-in features of other computer-based tools (including e-mail tools, file folder tools, and even spreadsheets), you may find you're able to manage your business quite well without having to include a third-party management service in your process. If so, that's terrific news for your fortune potential and a testament to your business prowess. Bravo!

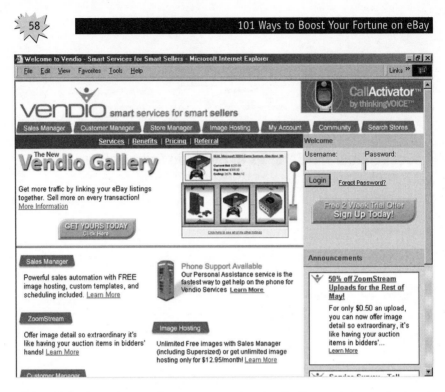

Figure 22-2 Long-time auction management service Vendio.com has your business's branding and market proliferation in mind to help grow your results.

FORTUNE BOOST #23
FREE (AND NEARLY FREE) EQUIPMENT TO OUTFIT YOUR AUCTION BUSINESS

Continuing the quest for the best auction tools at the best possible prices (read: free or near free), take a look at your current collection equipment to determine if you have what you need to run an efficient auction business. Much of the equipment you think you need to create stellar listings that beget high bids is likely readily around you and doesn't require a trip to the local computer or home equipment store. So while we're working in this part of the book to boost your fortune by cutting your costs, here's a look at where you can find free or nearly-free equipment that will have the greatest impact on your bottom line.

A Look around the Office

Begin your quest by looking around your own home office. If you've established a place where you regularly list, sell, and ship goods, chances are you have a good collection of the equipment you already need for success on the path to fortune. If, however, your computer is becoming something of a collectible in its own right, maybe struggling along with a paltry 10GB of storage or less, consider these ways to upgrade on the cheap:

- If you have a heavily tech-centric friend or family member (most of us have a lovable "geek" in our lives), always check to see if they have former equipment that you may be able to snag outright or snatch away cheap. Techno-philes' castoffs are often more powerful and resilient than much of the "current" equipment of other folks.
- Check your newspaper for local police auctions, usually disposing of seized assets or recovered property that couldn't find its way back to the original owner. Upgraded printers, scanners, and even digital cameras can be grabbed cheap in this way and still be suitable to help you stage winning listings.
- Clean up what you have. That's right—sometimes the only upgrade your equipment needs is a good bit of housecleaning. Run the system tools on your PC (such as the disk defragmenter) and remove any unneeded programs that might be eating up precious memory. If your digital images aren't looking so hot anymore, maybe the camera lens or scanner glass just needs a wiping down (to the embarrassment of some, this sort of thing occurs more often than you might think).

It's easy to get caught up in believing you can't compete in the online auction realm because your eight-month new equipment is now "horribly outdated and inadequate." Baloney! Do a bit of clean up or see if there's some free or cheap equipment you can clean up on and see how well you do.

A Look around the House

When it comes to noncomputer auction equipment, many folks are surprised to find that many of the commonplace items stored in their back rooms, garages, and basements are just the tools useful in running an efficient auction enterprise. Take a look around your home for the following:

- If you have a folding card or dining table or even a large sheet of plywood and two waist-high crates or saw horses, you have an instant package preparation table. Don't go buy a spiffy-clean new table but, rather, find a tablecloth to spread over the top (some sellers have bought an inexpensive roll or two of contact paper) and you'll have a clean and spacious surface upon which you can comfortably prepare and pack items for shipment.
- Remember the discussion of good photo tips from Fortune Boost #13— find an old parson's table and a length of solid-colored fabric and you have an instant photo studio (refer back to Figure 13-1 in Chapter 13). Check the garage for hanging work lights or make use of some handy floor lamps to get the lighting you need when photographing indoors.

- And how about securing a working space to begin with? Some sellers have pondered whether they should rent an actual office space in town to ensure the proper focus on their eBay work. Save the monthly expense and set about to convert a spare room, a dark corner, or a spacious garage into your own auction office. And, if you do, check with your tax advisor because you may be able to claim a portion of your monthly home mortgage and utility costs as deductible business expenses. There's even more savings added to your bottom line while you simultaneously outfit your auction business for near nothing.

A Look around Your Community

If you've combed through all the nooks and crannies in your home and have pestered your family and friends for any unwanted equipment you need but are still coming up a bit short, hop in the car or walk the neighborhood to the closest garage sale or flea market you can find. Again, as technology continues to inundate us these days with newer, faster, and fancier goods and gadgetry, last year's purchases are the sorts of things that others are eager to off-load for just pennies on the dollar. Granted, some folks will try to ask more than the item's worth in such a setting, so you may need to haggle a bit or keep looking, but the dirt-cheap deals are out there and they're often not too hard to find. Keep your eyes peeled.

A Look around eBay

Of course, don't forget to poke around eBay itself, as often you'll find the final pieces of equipment you need within the auction site itself. Look for office supplies, postal scales, packing peanuts, and other items within the listings, and many times you'll find much better deals than what you might pay in retail prices. And don't forget that whenever you upgrade any of your equipment, list the previous equipment (hopefully kept in good condition and with all original manuals, paperwork, and whatever) on eBay so other sellers just like you can find the bargain they need to boost their auction business.

FORTUNE BOOST #24
AUCTION AIDS: DOWNLOADING SHAREWARE AND FREEWARE

Sometimes you need some additional computer tools that are not already resident on your hard drive and aren't offered within eBay's suite of auction goodies. Whether you need a simple image editor, a font finder, or other programs that aren't readily in reach, it's time to go shopping. Of course, your first step is to go on a shopping excursion where you leave your wallet behind. The Internet is absolutely brimming with software tools that can help you in your auction efforts and come to you absolutely free of charge. If you're interested in getting the tools you need at a price that is free, read on.

Defining "Freeware" and "Shareware"

With so many talented and technically inclined folks rubbing shoulders in Cyberspace, many who designed and developed useful software applications (some large, some small) wanted to have others try out the functionality to see if the design served its purpose. To that end, many developers have created programs that they offer as "shareware" or "freeware," that is programs that others can download and use for free. Sometimes these are limited-feature versions of a program, but other times they consist of the full banana. The authors of these programs will typically ask for a satisfied user to make a purchase (using the honor system) or an in-kind donation to help fund the next version of a program. Some shareware and freeware will only operate to full functionality after an actual purchase has been made or will actually cease to operate after an allotted period of trial use (known as a "time bomb"). Most programs of this sort were designed and offered to be of true use to others, yet a few shady developers have less-beneficial intentions in mind (read the next section regarding cautions to exercise when downloading shareware and freeware). The best and usually safest collection of shareware and freeware programs can be found a numerous Web sites including www.tucows.com, www.shareware.com, and www.download.com. There are so many other sources of these programs that you may want to start searching from your favorite Internet portal site (e.g. Yahoo, Google) and see what you find. (See Figure 24-1.)

Cautionary Advice

Upon learning there are free software programs just awaiting you on the Internet, it's easy to be lured into gobbling up every one you find that might help your auctioning efforts or would otherwise be fun and entertaining. Take heed, though, that there are a few things you should do before you download any shareware or freeware:

- Find out as much about the program authors as you can, especially any other programs they've developed (just for point of reference and to determine true applicability to your immediate needs).
- Determine if the downloadable program is an in-progress effort (often called a *beta version*) or if it's a final, completed program.
- Determine the system requirements, especially supported operating systems (Windows 98, 2000, XP or MacOS) and the amount of memory required to store and run it.
- Determine if you're receiving a full-featured version or a stripped-down free version.
- Determine if the program has time bomb (expiration) logic and will cost you if you wish to continue use of it.
- Most importantly, take care where you find and download software and elect to use screened sites such as those mentioned previously in this

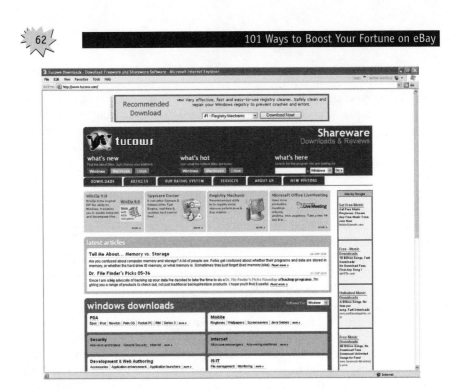

Figure 24-1   A long-time favorite of shareware and freeware junkies: www.tucows.com.

Fortune Boost (these sites will screen out the damaging programs posing as useful tools). If ever you download a shareware or freeware program and then experience troubles with your computer's normal operation, remove the program immediately.

Protecting Your Investment

Although you haven't actually invested money in the programs you've downloaded, you have invested time and effort to locate and acquire them; why not protect that? When you find truly useful shareware and freeware programs (and there are many out there), take the time to keep a copy for future needs. When you download a program, your operating system will typically present a pop-up window that asks if you want to save the downloadable program to your hard drive (for future installation and activation) or "run" it immediately, effecting an immediate installation and activation. While the latter approach makes sense to those who want the program installed and ready for use as quickly as possible, there is no backup in case the program is ever corrupted, lost, or if you upgrade to a new computer and would need to install the program again (provided you'll be able to find your now-favorite version some time down the road). Therefore, it becomes prudent to elect to save the downloadable file, preferably in a specially designated system folder (e.g. "Downloads") to keep on your hard drive or to occasionally copy off to a CD-ROM or other external storage for archival purposes.

A Head-Start to Finding Some Useful Auction Tools...for Free!

OK. So here are a few shareware and freeware programs that you might find of immediate use in your auctioning. Each of these can be readily be found at www.tucows.com:

- **Ipswitch WS_FTP:** Here's an easy-to-use image upload utility that helps you quickly upload auction image files to your personal Web space provided by your ISP.
- **AdTemplate:** If you're looking for a little assistance with designing auction listings, this program can give you a creative boost.
- **Honesty.com Counters:** Although you can use the Andale counters for free when listing at eBay, you may want to take advantage of Honesty.com's free counters when designing your own commercial sales sites.
- **LviewPro:** Still one of the fastest image editors around, this program allows you to make quick light/dark adjustments, color tweaks, and crops fast so you can get your images up and visible in your eBay listings.

And there's so much more. Take some time to explore the other auction-related shareware and freeware programs available and choose those that will make that greatest impact to improving your listing efforts. And, remember, they're free!

FORTUNE BOOST #25
THE ART OF COLLECTING PAYMENTS

It's difficult to conjure up any other notion that might be more pleasurable than happily collecting money that sits around you. For some, this is just an enjoyable daydream, but for successful eBay sellers, this is their reality. Of course, the joy of collecting payments for items sold can be all the more satisfying when it comes as more of a pleasure and less of a chore. The speed and efficiency with which you can collect payments due you will immediately translate to the healthy growth of your fortune. And if you can ultimately collect larger payments (thanks to higher final bid and sale prices) and collect them easier, the more opportunity you'll have to seek out additional profitable opportunities. Here are some keys to collecting larger payments easier, and hassle-free.

Start with the Payment Type

Buyers like choices, and if you can provide payment choices that suit their needs *before* the purchase, you'll positively position yourself to make a fast collection after the listing has concluded. Though it may be a bit of review for some, here is a list of payment types that prove to yield the best results when it comes to offering choices and being able to successfully collect on a sale:

1. **Online Payments:** Although the notion of using an online payment system back in 1999 was something of a "risky endeavor," the service, protection, and speed this option offers today makes online payment the top choice among online buyers and sellers. Payment for an item can be completed in mere minutes (or less!) following the close of a listing, and sellers can see their financial assets increase just as quickly. As buyers are generally quite eager to receive their winnings, accepting online payments allows the seller to ship an item just as soon as the money's in the (virtual) bank.

2. **Money Orders and Cashier's Checks:** Formerly the top choice among buyers and sellers before online payment took hold, money orders and cashier's checks come in a close second in payment preference. The plus here is, because they're purchased with actual cash assets on the buyer's end, sellers know they're as good as cash when they arrive. Therefore, shipment of goods can occur as soon as the payment arrives. The only drawback here is the waiting period associated with the buyer purchasing the money order (although some are using Western Union's BidPay online money order purchase site to speed that up a bit) and the snail-mail delivery time until the check arrives to the seller.

3. **Personal Checks:** Personal checks are still very much in use in this digital society. Be it force of habit or what have you, some folks prefer to use personal checks when they pay for online purchases. This method is certainly the exception and not the norm today, but it's wise to announce your willingness to accept this form of payment. The processing time will be considerably longer as you wait for the check to arrive via snail-mail and then wait for it to clear your bank before you ship the goods (be sure to clearly stipulate this waiting period in your sales policy).

4. **Cash:** Few sellers will encourage the use of cash payment but it *does* occur that greenback dollars might appear in the mail from a buyer (usually for very low-cost purchases or for some payments received from international buyers). If you receive cash, follow it up with an e-mail to confirm receipt and ship the goods right away.

It's important to offer payment choices to your potential bidders and buyers to let them know you're ready to cater to their unique needs and wants. When you do that, you will have successfully set the stage to make an easy collection on the backside of the transaction.

Fast Action Translates to Fast Cash

When it comes to action, remember that the seller sets the pace and, therefore, sets the stage to determine how quickly and easily payment can be collected. Here are the steps to take to hasten—without harassing—the action on your buyer's part:

- Establish your payment expectations in your sales policy that is included in each of your eBay listings. You've established the payment methods you accept, but also establish when you expect payment to be received. Successful sellers will stipulate online payment is to be received with 24-72 hours, and snail-mail payments are to be received with seven days following the listing's end.
- When the listing ends, eBay will send a notification to both buyer and seller to indicate the transaction should now commence. Follow up that e-mail message with either an eBay invoice (or third-party tool's invoice, if you use one) or a direct e-mail to the buyer, congratulating her on her purchase and recommunicating the payment procedure. Communicate with the buyer within 24 hours of the listing's end to better ensure fast action from her end.
- Communicate directly to the buyer when payment is received and when the item ships. While this doesn't directly apply to the collection of payment (you've already received that now), it will go a long way to helping you encourage a future purchase from the buyer and ensuring that future transactions can flow as smoothly as the first.

Payment Troubles?

And what happens if the payment is late? Sellers are frequently befuddled over what to do when the money doesn't arrive quickly (if at all) and what they can do to successfully close a transaction that may be going awry. Here's a list of steps to take if your buyer seems to have lost the motivation to pay up:

- If there has been no response to an end-of-auction (EOA) notification and no payment received, send a follow-up e-mail message to reiterate that the listing has closed and the obligations of the buyer.
- Review the high-bidder's feedback rating and actual user comments posted to determine if others have experienced difficulty with the buyer or if, perhaps, this is a unique case. Be patient if there doesn't seem to be a trend for poor behavior.
- If response is still lacking, use eBay's contact information request (available by clicking on the User ID from the auction listing) and, discreetly, attempt telephone contact.
- If still no response, consider reporting the user as a deadbeat bidder to eBay's SafeHarbor. Be sure to forewarn the user that you'll take this

course of action—allow a 24-hour notification before you file the complaint with eBay (the user just might be motivated to respond).

- Make note of the user's ID and watch for it in any upcoming auctions you'll list (you can even visit eBay's site map and block the bidder ID from participating in all of your future listings).

Clearly, deadbeat bidders are the exception and not the norm for most successful sellers at eBay. If you do find you're attracting more troublesome buyers to your listings, revisit your sales policy and be certain your terms and expectations are clearly stated. Do as much work as you can up front and you'll find that collecting payments can be easy and highly rewarding.

FORTUNE BOOST #26
SMILE! THESE PHOTOS ARE FREE

There's no doubt that adding photos to your listings will not only increase your chances of making a sale the first time around but it can also increase the ultimate price you receive for your items. While it's true that many items can and do sell without accompanying photos, successful sellers have learned that adding a photo is not only easier than ever but often serves as the little "nudge" that turns a mildly interested browser into a highly motivated bidder. Beyond the fact that ensuring each listing of yours has an accompanying image will boost your profits, you'll also find that adding more than one photo to your listing can further enhance your profit potential and can be done so without incurring a cent of incremental cost—if you know how to include photos the free way.

Reviewing eBay's Photo Hosting Service

For starters, probably the easiest way to add images to your eBay listings is to use the site's own Basic Picture Services, found during step 3 of the item listing process, "Add Pictures & Details" (see Figure 26-1). This is great for listings where just a single photo is needed but what if your auction will benefit from multiple photos, perhaps those needed to depict critical detail and multiple angle images? Well, eBay's Basic Picture Services will suit your needs *at a cost*. That's right, the first image is free but each additional image will tack on 15 cents to your listing fee. And, if you want the option to show those images in a larger size upon the prospective bidder's request, that will cost an additional 75 cents. Suddenly, your profits are being eaten away before the first bidder has even seen your listing.

Save Your Profits by Taking Image
Matters into Your Own Hands

Here's the simplest answer to the dilemma of how to add multiple (and sometimes "supersized") images to your listings at no additional cost: HTML. Recall the

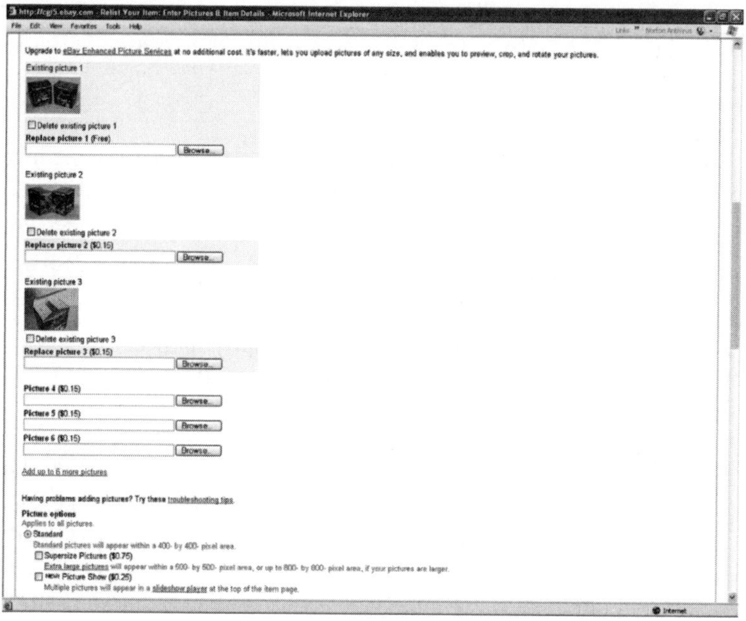

Figure 26-1 If you have just a single excellent photo to upload, consider the ease and no-cost option of eBay's Basic Picture Services.

discussion in Fortune Boost #18 where basic HTML coding structure was introduced and the example of a more stylized listing was shown, *one that included three images*. The images in that listing were free, that is their inclusion did not cost a cent in accumulated eBay listing fees. In case you missed it, adding images using HTML is simple and easily repeated when you use the following "tag" syntax:

```
<IMG height=220 alt="D.L. Prince and friend"
src="http://my.starstream.net/dlprince/auctionpix/dprince1.jpg"
width=200 align=left>
```

When you use the "IMG" tag, you can specify the location of an image that you want to include in your listing. What location? Well, you'll need to store the images you intend to use in your listings somewhere on the Internet and, as you can see from the actual example here, the image is stored in a personal Web space, one that was provided *free of additional charge* by a hosting Internet Service Provider (ISP). When you sign on with a provider that gains you access to the Internet and provides you with one or more e-mail addresses, you're usually offered 10 megabytes or more of Web space; that's where folks can build their own personal Web sites or can store photos and other data. Upload your auction images to your free ISP Web space, call to the address of each photo as you want to use them in your listings and, with that simple IMG tag, you'll be able to include one, two, three, or more photos in your listing at no charge.

Big Images at Big Savings

Next, consider the times when you want to display a particularly large image to clarify detail within an item photo. Rather than pay to supersize a photo, simply add a single line of additional HTML tagging, the "anchor" tag. It looks like this:

```
<A HREF= "http://my.starstream.net/dlprince/auctionpix/dprince1.jpg">
<IMG height=220
SRC="http://my.starstream.net/dlprince/auctionpix/dprince1.jpg"
WIDTH=200 ALIGN=left ALT = "Click image for a larger view.">
</A>
```

Notice how the anchor tag—the "A"—in the first line of HTML above is used to start the whole process, followed by the reference tag, HREF. The reference denotes the actual Web location of the full-sized image you want your bidders to see. This is followed with the next line of HTML that begins with the familiar IMG tag, but this one serves as a smaller version of the full-sized image (known as a "thumbnail") and provides an embedded image in the listing while also serving as a clickable link to the full photo. The ALT tag was also used to provide useful text when a bidder rolls the mouse over it; after a second or two, a small text box will appear instructing the bidder to "Click image for a larger view."

In essence, use of the anchor tag in HTML is serving two very important purposes: first, it allows you to offer full-sized images to your bidders without your incurring additional eBay fees; second, it allows you to display quick-to-load small images (thumbnails) within your listing without having to make bidders wait around for a large image to load. Many shoppers won't wait around for an image to load, especially if it takes more than five seconds. If, however, you provide a thumbnail and the option for the bidder to view a larger image, then they can make the conscious choice to see the bigger photo and will expect to wait a few extra seconds for the image to load.

And, best of all, smile because these photos are free!

FORTUNE BOOST #27
FIVE FATAL AUCTION OFFENSES (AND HOW TO AVOID THEM)

If ever you take lightly the importance of maintaining a professional business attitude and upholding the promise of unfailing customer service, then give this little list a read. Selling at eBay and elsewhere online is work, lots of work. Some days you're in a groove while other days you may feel you've fallen into a rut. To truly boost your fortune potential, you need to watch out for the creeping up of unsavory actions and attitudes, those that might try to infiltrate your own thinking and lead to the self-destruction of all you've worked for up to this point. Following is a list of the five most fatal auction offenses committed by sellers, possibly some of which you've experienced when you were in the buyer's role. Take careful note of these fortune failings because the seller who exhibits these behaviors usually hasn't been selling for a very long time, and any notion of fortune to be made is but a distant fantasy.

- **Ignore Your Customers.** Ever walk up to the "customer service" desk only to be summarily ignored by the representative sleeping there? Online, it can be even more maddening: when buyers are sending e-mail inquiries regarding the details of an item they've won, the status of a payment they've sent, or the whereabouts of an item they're expecting, it is stressful enough without the added frustration of having to wait endlessly for an answer from a seller gone AWOL. Sellers who ignore the all-important *interactivity* of online auctioning are rarely destined to make a fortune much less succeed on any level at all. A buyer or potential bidder wants fast answers, and the conscientious seller will respond as quickly as possible to encourage a bid (especially considering these auctions are controlled by the clock).
- **Be "Too Busy" to Complete a Transaction.** Some sellers have shown that they're highly attentive when listing items and collecting money. After the item has shipped, however, they're off to court other customers and don't have the time to go back and deal with a "closed deal." The problem here is that the deal *isn't* closed until the customer has received the goods. There might be an issue with the merchandise sent or the overall satisfaction of the customer who received it. But that's old news, right, and who's got time to tend to that when there are more high bids out there to collect? Of course, such a seller doesn't recognize the need to tend to customer needs even after the sale, especially if there appears to be a problem. And, sadly, this leaves many honest buyers out of luck or on the far back burner, at best. Of course, that buyer will never return to the seller's auctions again and will likely post a negative feedback message to warn others of this too-busy seller. Successful sellers recognize the need to follow the transaction right up until the very end, the point when the mutually satisfied buyer and seller post positive feedback for one another. Take your eye off the ball too soon, and you'll wind up with a virtual shiner.
- **Be Erratic in Your Policies and Procedures.** Every seller has the right to set terms and conditions as they see fit. However, customers get pretty cranky if a seller advertises a friendly sales policy only to change it after the "bait" has been taken. The high bidder has emerged only to find that the shipping costs are far more than was advertised or payment *will only be accepted* in a single method or shipping will take weeks longer than the buyer was originally led to believe. Sellers need to stay true to the words of

their policies because many bidders use those terms to decide whether they'll bid here or bid with the competition. A change to the policies mid-stream will cause the buyer to wonder if the item itself is going to likewise make a sudden change between the time its been paid for and when it actually arrives. Profitable sellers stay true to their posted policies and will only make changes to those terms *before* listing new items for bid or sale.

- **Be a Grouch.** Had a bad day? Who cares? Your customers certainly won't be in any mood to withstand your bad temper, that's for sure. Things will irk you, stress will visit you, and some customers will try your patience to the very end, but you've really got to maintain the image of being in control and ready to serve, or else your customers will sneer and go buy from your competitor—you know, the other seller who understands the true value and profit potential of maintaining regular patronage. While it's perfectly understandable (even expected) that the auction business can wear you thin at times, keep all of that to yourself and never let your customers feel the brunt of your bad day. Use form responses and a well-managed and repeatable process to cover for you when you're simply not able to smile. The customer will never know the difference and you'll be much happier too when the tough times subside and you're still entertaining a very satisfied customer base.

- **Be a Cyber-Pest.** Keep people informed but don't mass-mail to all your customers' in-trays. Follow up after the auction but don't harass a buyer day after day until the payment arrives. Ask someone to post feedback, but don't deluge them with demands that they comply. Let them know what's next up for auction, but if they don't' seem interested, stop; just stop. It's one thing to be interactive with your customers but entirely different—and unacceptable—to be virtually hyperactive.

While this list of five auction offenses may seem extreme to you, the facts stand that they've been encountered more times than not within eBay and other online transactions. Some folks seem to believe that customer engagement and satisfaction principles don't apply to the online realm; if you can't see the customer, why go to the extra lengths? Those would be the famous last words of a seller whose about to go out of business fast. Your opportunity is to do just the opposite when it comes to these five fatal flaws and be there to scoop up the sour sellers' dissatisfied shoppers and treat them to the excellent experience that will keep them coming back for more.

FORTUNE BOOST #28
SALES POLICIES THAT REALLY PAY OFF

Often, one of the best ways to grow your profit potential is to keep a steady pulse on your customer base and their ever-changing needs and wants. As the eBay marketplace continues to evolve, wise sellers recognize the value of keeping their sales policies evolving as well. If it's been awhile since you've reviewed the effectiveness of your terms of service, take this opportunity to make sure you're still in touch with the purchase provisions that mean the most to your customers and that will yield the greatest possible returns to your bottom line.

The Guiding Principle

In the eBay marketplace your sales policy will set the ground rules and expectations for your customers. You're in the driver's seat here and your bidders and buyers will look to you to lead the way regarding how to successfully complete a sale. While this is a powerful position to be in, it's also one of significant responsibility and not to be taken lightly. Always remember that you're in business to *serve* your customers and, hopefully, your sales policies will embody that sentiment. Though many sellers have been unfairly treated or downright burned by the occasional "bad apple" buyer, it's important to be sure a sales policy does not become overly rigid or unfriendly as a result. If it does, you'll be losing potential sales right and left to other sellers who have learned how to deftly delight their customers (perhaps those who were formerly *your* customers) through sound and sensible sales policies. If this happens, your fortune potential has just shifted into reverse.

Shipping and Handling

Though it's the long-standing protocol that high-bidders and buyers will be expected to pay the costs of delivery, determining *how much* to charge can often be a vexing proposition. The safest bet is to always charge exact shipping costs plus any additional costs for insurance, delivery confirmation, professional packaging, or special services requested by the buyer.

Using a fixed shipping cost can serve you and your customers well, especially if you sell the same sort of item on a regular basis. If the items you sell vary in size and weight, it might be best to lean towards charging the exact fee—you'll avoid the risk of having your fixed cost sway too far one way or the other, either overcharging your customer or undercollecting at your own expense.

And how about that contentious "handling fee?" Only you can decide if it's right to charge your customers additional fees for your time and effort to package and ship their purchases. Some sellers consider this an inherent cost of doing business while others claim they will take a loss if they don't collect handling fees. Whichever you decide, be certain that you've clearly explained how you'll levy shipping and handling fees within your sales policy. Don't blind-side your buyers with additional fees they never saw coming; chances are good they'll never come back to you again.

Payment Options

Many online buyers need to know how they'll be expected to pay for their purchases, so let them know, plain and simple. And with so many changes in payment methods lately (especially in the online realm), this is one area of your sales policy that you may find requires frequent updating.

Online payment services—such as PayPal and BidPay—have gained significantly favorable status with buyers. Though some of these services have instituted usage fees and commissions (something that has many sellers grumbling), denying acceptance of online payment could result in lost business. Because these services allow buyers to pay using their credit card, the statistics still prove that credit customers will generally spend more than their cash-carrying peers.

Of course, the more payment options you can offer to your customers, the better your ability to suit their specific needs and desires. While some still wouldn't think of submitting their credit card information in cyberspace, the time-tested money orders or cashier's checks are as good as cash in the seller's hands. And personal checks are still preferred by some buyers, despite the typical check-clearing waiting period (a delay you might consider waiving for repeat customers in good standing).

Refunds and Guarantees

With online competition continually heating up, refunds and guarantees seem to be the newest lure to attract buyers. The more cavalier sellers boldly proclaim, "We'll take back anything and gladly refund your entire purchase price" and often enjoy higher sell-through rates for such a no-risk policy. Some sellers, though, may be in the business to liquidate certain merchandise and might conversely state, "all sales are final." Naturally, the best place to be is somewhere in the middle.

If you fear offering the "no questions asked" refund, consider a fairly balanced policy such as, "Returns gladly accepted within 30 days of purchase. Please notify your intent to return before shipping an item back. All items are subject to inspection, with refunds being issued within five days of item verification."

Of course, *not* accepting returns or offering refunds can still be reasonable, as in the case of goods being offered "as is." But whether you offer refunds or not, the key to success is the crystal clarity of your policy, one that customers will understand and can agree to *before* they make a purchase.

Tone and Delivery

And regardless of the terms you'll include in your sales policy, be sure they're stated clearly to avoid misinterpretation. And, while you do so, try to ensure that your policy doesn't read too abruptly, unfriendly, or even condescending. Though done so unintentionally, some sellers have been surprised how combative their policies have turned out. Read it back to yourself or have someone else read it to ensure that it properly projects your desire to serve your customers in every possible situation.

FORTUNE BOOST #29
SLASHING YOUR SHIPPING COSTS

In a slightly different take on how cutting costs will improve your eBay profits, take a look at how the costs you save in your own operation can be passed along to your customers. Whenever you can control and reduce your operating costs, you have the opportunity to offer better value to your customers, who will recognize, appreciate, and reward you for such efficient operation in the form of repeat purchases and word-of-mouth promotion. This all sounds great for your business outlook, so how can you slash your shipping costs and add to your eBay fortune? Glad you asked.

Freebies, Freebies, All Around

Although it's been doing business online for years now, it's interesting how many online sellers (and potential fortune-makers) aren't aware how many free and much-needed shipping supplies are available for the asking. Visit the USPS Web site at www.usps.com and navigate to the shipping supplies area (easiest to find when you click on the "Business" button on the home page and then select the "Supplies" link). You're now in the Postal Store, where you can click on "Shipping Supplies" to choose from the five different subcategories. For example, when shipping domestically, click on the Priority Mail link and you'll be whisked to several pages where you can select from dozens of free boxes, cartons, envelopes, sealing tape, forms, and more. This is all free and, to the online seller, this is like being set loose in a candy store.

The supplies you select to order are yours for the asking and they'll even be delivered to your doorstep within a week or so—*also free!* Immediately, you've virtually eliminated the expense of buying shipping, packing, and labeling supplies. Be sure to check out the other major carriers (such as United Parcel Service and Federal Express) as they, too, offer free suppliers to their customers. Is there a catch? You have to use the delivery service designated on the carrier's packaging (such as Priority Mail, ExpressMail, and so on), but it has to get from here to there anyway, so how is that any sort of drawback? (See Figure 29-1.)

Choosing Postage Costs Wisely

Next, look at the costs of the different delivery methods being offered by your carrier and determine which service will provide reasonably fast delivery and the lowest-possible cost. For example, notice from Figure 29-1 that USPS provides boxes for Priority Mail delivery in both "as weighed" and "flat rate" cost options. Here's where sellers who deal in consistently sized items can shave some shipping cost. If you're shipping heavier items like printed matter or some types of home décor, you may find it's cheaper to pay the flat rate of $7.70 using the Flat Rate box rather than paying even more using a similar sized "as weighed" Priority Mail

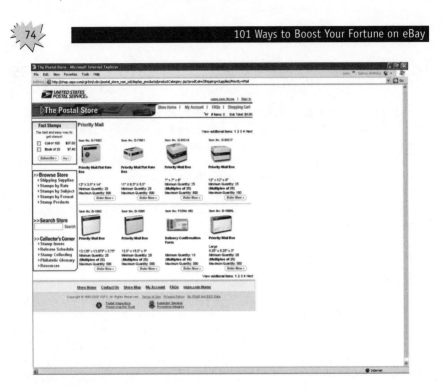

Figure 29-1 Navigate to the Shipping Supplies area of U.S. Postal Service Web site for free supplies that provide safe passage of goods to your waiting customers.

box. Weigh your items and then weigh the potential cost savings. Of course, be sure that whichever packaging you choose, the item inside can be guaranteed to arrive intact and undamaged. While you're at it, be sure to compare the services and costs across carriers, determining which has the best rate and can provide a high level of customer satisfaction, too. Remember, if anything happens to an item you send, be it damage or an unusually lengthy delivery time, your customer will blame you, *not* the carrier, for the nuisance. Keep this in mind as you weigh your cost-savings potential.

Saving Time, Every Time

Then cast a very time-frugal eye on the amount of effort and legwork required of using one carrier's service over another. If you have a carrier drop-off station nearby where you'll be managing your eBay business, give that one a bit of an edge over another that could require extra travel time and fuel cost. Better yet, look to USPS, UPS, or FedEx, who offer free pickup of packages at your home or place of business. All you need do is have the goods packed and ready to go; the carrier will visit and collect your items to be sent for you. Meanwhile, you're able to save time and travel expense while you continue working your eBay business.

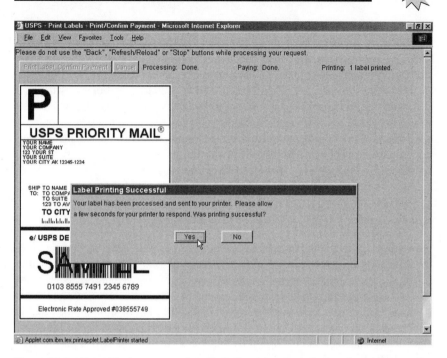

Figure 29-2   Your shipping costs and applied effort just got slashed again thanks to online postage purchase and printing.

Online Postage—Stamping Out Inefficiency for the eBay Businessperson

Perhaps one of the best developments in shipping methods (next to free supplies) is the advent on online postage purchase and printing. If you haven't already, you must harness the cost-slashing value of printing preposted shipping labels from your eBay office, whenever you need. Both USPS and UPS postage purchase is already integrated with eBay itself. When the listing has concluded, you can collect your payment from your buyer and click a link (from within the actual item listing page or from within your My eBay page) and purchase and print the shipping label; your buyer's name and address are already prefilled into the label, saving you even more time. Print the label on an attached or network-accessed printer and you're done (see Figure 29-2). Oh, and don't forget to select the "economy printing" mode on your printer properties to save on ink consumption, too.

And It's Still OK to Recycle

Don't overlook the cost savings when you recycle shipping supplies. Boxes that contained items you purchased and received can be reused to ship goods to *your* customers. Be sure the box is sturdy and still clean (remember, the appearance of the shipping package is your customer's first impression of your business' integrity) and never reuse a box that looks like it's been used more than twice itself. Of most value to you in recycling shipping supplies is the packing fill *inside* the box. Because the carriers don't provide filler peanuts or bubbles or what have you, store up the clean fill you find in the packages you receive. Extruded foam peanuts and air-filled polybag "pillows" are lightest and can provide the appropriate amount of protection while keeping the overall package weight (and shipping cost) down. Recycling is still good for the Earth, too, so do you part to reuse, repurpose, and reap the rewards of slashing your shipping costs.

FORTUNE BOOST #30
WHEN BUYERS HAPPILY PAY YOUR FEES, YOU WIN!

Now you're entering the realm of careful price setting and operating cost recovery. While there's no doubt eBay is probably the least cost-intensive entrepreneurial effort you can undertake when it comes to merchandising, wouldn't it be better still if you could erase the remaining fees that accompany listing goods, accepting online payment, and paying sales commissions? This is the land of walking the fine line between skillful cost control and burdening customers with your costs of doing business. If you can walk the line carefully and know when to ease up at just the right time, you'll find you can successfully pass your selling expenses on to the customer without unnecessarily gouging or otherwise exploiting them in the process.

The Honesty of It All

First, understand that this isn't some underhanded, sneaky scam to dupe customers into paying more than they should for your items; just the opposite. The secret to recouping your selling expenses is all in the calculation of your profit margin and determining if you can nudge it up a percentage or two to offset your selling costs. There's nothing wily or wrong with that, right? Actually, this is the sort of careful cost control tactic practiced by upstanding businesses, large and small, the world over. The key is to ensure that your profits exceed your expenses (duh!) and then further refine those figures to erase your expected costs of doing business. In the meantime, if you can run your operation as efficiently as possible, you can realize additional cost savings in a way that allows you to pass along special offers, either temporary or long-running, to your valued customers. If you're running lean enough to, say, be able to offer free shipping to your customers *while* having your selling costs covered by your profits realized, then everybody wins!

First Things First: Calculating Markup and Profit

Before you can begin rubbing your hands together in anticipation of recapturing your selling costs, you have to determine at what price you need to sell to achieve a profit. Sounds obvious but so many sellers today tend to leave profit up to chance. Instead of the passive approach, consider the following as you determine a necessary profit margin:

- **Actual Item Cost:** If you acquire your inventory via onesey-twosey purchasing, your average cost per item might be higher than you think (this is especially true if you deal in a wide range of goods). On the other hand, if you purchase the same sort of item in a onesey-twosey fashion, determine an average acquisition cost and apply that as your base item cost. If you purchase resellable goods in bulk, use your supplier's standard net cost as your acquisition cost. When special deals or discounts come your way that reduce the per-unit cost, consider that immediate addition to your profit potential *without* altering your recorded average unit cost.
- **Acquisition Cost:** Next, determine how much it costs you to acquire the goods, factoring in transportation or delivery costs, travel costs on your part, storage or other inventory care costs, and so on. Carefully track these costs, especially over an extended period, to arrive at an evenly distributed/attributed per-item acquisition cost.
- **Listing Costs:** Now, factor in your eBay listing costs including listing fees and final value fees based on your average expected (and hopefully *sustained*) selling price. When you arrive at this final number, sum up the three and you have your most basic cost of goods sold.

Now comes the matter of determining the achievable selling price of an item such that will gain you the level of profit you desire. For example, if you want to achieve a 30 percent markup on an item, you would need to manipulate a simple formula as follows:

$$\text{Selling Price} = \text{Total Cost} \times (1 + \text{Markup Percent})$$

Using that formula, then, if you have an item that bears a total cost of $5.50 (that includes per-unit cost plus transportation, storage, listing, and any other costs incurred to get it to the point of sale) and you wish to earn a 30 percent markup, your selling cost would be calculated:

$$\$5.50 \times (1 + 0.30) = \$5.50 \times 1.30 = \$7.15 \text{ Selling Price}$$

Once you figure your total item cost, you can then work with various markup scenarios and compare those to the current market price (the demand for the goods where buyers will indicate the price they're willing to readily pay) to establish your per-item profit potential. Again, the more efficient and stable your acquisition costs, the better chance you have to determine if the selling price that gains you the profit you want is attainable.

Now, On to Gross Margin Profit

Markup percent isn't the same as profit margin. If you crack open your collegiate accounting tomes, you'll recall that *gross margin profit* is that remainder when total cost of goods sold is subtracted from revenue. The actual *gross margin percent* is then calculated from that remainder. It's a bit more math but it's not too difficult:

Gross Margin Percent = (Selling Price – Total Cost) / Selling Price
Using our previous example of the item you'd sell for $7.15, then:
Gross Margin Percent = ($7.15 – $5.50) / $7.15
Gross Margin Percent = $1.65 / $7.15
Gross Margin Percent = 23%

Ah! Now we have a working gross margin percent that's clearly different (and leaner) than a mere markup percent. At this point, you can use the gross margin percent calculation to experiment with setting the selling price of an item. If you want to achieve a 30 percent *gross margin percent*, the calculation would look like this:

Selling Price = Total Cost / (1 – Gross Margin)

So…

Selling Price = $5.50 / (1 – 0.30)
Selling Price = $5.50 / 0.70
Selling Price = $7.80

Take your selling price based on desired gross margin percent result back to the online marketplace to determine if the demand is such that you can achieve this sort of selling price (or higher?). Now you're doing business.

But What about Having the Fees Paid For?

Absolutely! Back to the discussion of getting buyers to happily pay your fees, when you can find a gross profit margin earning that actually exceeds your profit-over-expense goal, sometimes only by two or three percent, you stand to cover the cost of your selling expenses through the prices earned when you sell your items. When you establish an offering that further boosts your gross profit margin, you can explore the possibility of making special offers (limited free shipping, buy-one-get-one-for-half-price) that will lure more customers and hopefully keep them as recurring patrons.

All the while, your shrewd calculation of cost and profit is enabling you to earn well beyond your point-of-sale placement cost and begin to cover your selling expenses.

If that sounds simple, well, it is. The hard part is *sustainability*. Big businesses wrack their minds and wring their hands trying to maintain profit margins as the economy swings and sways. In an eBay business, you'll be likewise challenged to stay ahead of the curve, to anticipate upswings in demand or downturns in desirability, always ready to apply your profit calculation to maintain an achievable selling price while continually looking for ways to further reduce your listing expenses. This isn't an endeavor for the faint of heart or weak of spirit but for those who are seeking to boost their eBay fortunes, it's just good business sense.

FORTUNE BOOST #31
RESISTING THE TEMPTATION TO TAMPER

Listen up because this won't take long: don't attempt to tamper with the outcome of your eBay listings. Oh, sure, it seems that it would be so easy to help along that listing that's seemingly sitting without anyone taking notice, nobody stopping by to bid. Perhaps if you could somehow get a first bid going, folks might take another look. Or maybe the item you thought would earn you thousands has been sitting around with a mere 10-dollar high bid on it and the auction clock is quickly winding down. Maybe if you could find a way to nudge it up a bit, others who may be silently watching will recognize it's time to start bidding, high and fast. And maybe you see an active auction for the same sort of item you intend to list and its high-bid value is shooting through the roof. Knowing your item is a better specimen, maybe you could discreetly tap the high bidder and a couple of underbidders on the shoulder to let them take a peek at yours, one that they may want to buy after bailing out on the current listing. If any of this sounds tempting and tenable to you, STOP. This is bid tampering and it's in direct violation of eBay's rules.

But What's Wrong with Just a Bit of Involvement?

With over 150 million registered users about and tens of millions of items up for bid or sale every day at eBay, what's one little episode of tampering going to hurt? The fact is, its affect will be centralized but its impact could be far reaching. When you attempt to tamper with the outcome of an eBay listing, be it your own listing or that of someone else (yes, that means the buddy who slyly asks, "hey, would you mind placing a bid on my listing just to get the activity going?"), you engage in fraud; that's right, *fraud*. Those who routinely work with one another to effect such tampering are known as being in "collusion," an illegal and prosecutable offense that has afflicted auctioning since their earliest days, centuries ago.

More to the point, though, here's what you really have to lose if you give in to the temptation to tamper:

- You can lose the active status of your eBay account, possibly suspended for a period of time or permanently banned from using the site.
- You can lose your base of customers, those who have traded with you successfully over the years and who have come back to you because of your commitment to good, honest dealings.

- You can lose the trust of buyers and sellers, those who have dealt with you in the past, be it at eBay or offline, and who might be reticent to engage in transactions with you upon learning you've been suspended or banned from eBay.
- You can lose your fortune and your freedom. Yes, the news has chronicled the downfall of scammers and schemers who have been severely fined and even incarcerated for engaging in online fraud tactics.

Yes, sometimes is seems all too easy to just slip into eBay and give a listing or two a bit of a boost, but the downside of such activity could cost you your fortune and so much more. Keep to doing good, clean business and you'll find your fortune soon enough.

FORTUNE BOOST #32
SALVAGING AN "UNSUCCESSFUL" AUCTION

When you're in the midst of selling at eBay, it's natural for you to step into the auction arena with high hopes for high bids, and most sellers can usually achieve a high level of success at the auction sites. However, when your hopes are high but the bids aren't, you might wind up with an occasional "unsuccessful" auction. Whether your reserve price wasn't met, your Dutch auction had a quantity left over, or even if nobody bid at all, there might still be a way to drum up a sale even after the final gavel has struck. Here are a few things you can do to bring success to your "unsuccessful" eBay auction.

Calling In the Reserves

Believe it or not, one of the easiest postauction sales to make is when your auction's reserve price isn't met. Whenever you have an auction close without the reserve price being met, it's good customer courtesy to contact the high bidder as a form of closure. But, as you're thanking a bidder for his interest in your item, you might ask if he's still interested in making a purchase. Often, bidders are willing to make a deal. In a polite e-mail, ask the high bidder if he would like one more chance at your item:

"Thanks for bidding on my item. Unfortunately my reserve price of $40 wasn't met (you were only $5 away). If you're still interested in the item at this price, just let me know before I relist it. Thanks!"

Divulge your reserve price to let the high bidder know how close they might have been to winning. The bidder may take you up on your reserve price (try throwing in free shipping to help clinch the sale) or the bidder may counteroffer a lower price. Don't get greedy here—if the counteroffer is reasonable and you're truly interested in making a sale, work with the bidder. If you have enough profit margin to work with and are willing to negotiate, you still might make a decent profit.

Note: eBay is rather protective over the notion of transactions occurring outside of its virtual walls. In fact, eBay policy suggests this is a prohibited practice if ever the buyer might feel coerced or otherwise pressured into a purchase. The fact is, if a sale is missed and both parties are still interested in completing the transactions, they can, if in mutual agreement, proceed outside of eBay and without any eBay protections (and *many* successful transactions occur in this manner every day). As a seller, take care in such solicitations and, if a buyer contacts you first (and they do), consider the opportunity to make the sell provided the buyer agrees to your sales policies.

Suggestive Selling

When selling to your Dutch auction winners, let them know if you have a few extras that have gone unclaimed. Sometimes, buyers might take you up on a second unit at the same or a slightly lower price as the one they won. Don't push—just offer.

As a footnote, suggestive selling is also a great way to sell items you haven't even listed. If you're selling a vintage movie poster to an enthusiastic high bidder, it might be wise to mention you have additional material from that same film (avoid the direct suggestive sale by including a form e-mail that may contain small images or links to other products you have available). Collectors often look for items related to the ones they've just won. Mention what else you have for sale and you might knock off two auctions with one bidder.

Don't Resist—Relist!

Remember that, at eBay, if your first listing was unsuccessful, you can relist that same auction a second time and, if the item sells, your second round of listing fees will be refunded. There's much to be learned from an unsuccessful auction and you'll want to carefully determine why the item didn't sell the first time before you relist. For more details on the best approaches to relisting an unsuccessful auction, see Fortune Boost # 36.

When You Least Expect It

And sometimes the buyers will come to you. If a buyer contacts you after your "unsuccessful" auction has ended, asking if you're interested in making a sell, give the buyer a listen. Though some buyers might try to swoop in and take advantage of you (offering an offensively low selling price perhaps), many are legitimately interested in striking a reasonable deal. Reply promptly and be prepared to negotiate a bit—remember that if the buyer was interested in paying your original price, she would have bid so during the course of the auction. And don't be surprised if a high-bidder gives you the suggestive selling routine in reverse: *"Got anything else like this?"* It's a real bonus when the bidders start knocking on *your* door.

FORTUNE BOOST #33
COURTING YOUR UNDERBIDDERS

Following on the heels of Fortune Boost #32 comes the situation of when you've just witnessed a spirited round of bidding on one of your items and you wish you had more to go around to satisfy those who were knocked out of the winner's circle. Well, sometimes, you *will* have more of the same item and you might be able to save yourself some time and listing cost when you elect to inform your underbidders. It's a fine line to walk, though, when you do this and you want to be certain not to get yourself into the bad graces of eBay. Therefore, in all fairness, here are a couple of ways to keep from letting those outbid buyers leave dejected and dispirited.

Note: It bears repeating that eBay is quite sensitive to transactions occurring outside of its marketplace. Be cautious in any and all contact with underbidders and assure them of your offer to them is only being made as a sign of good faith. If the sellers say "no thanks," indicate you won't contact them again.

Consoling the Losers

Nobody likes to be outbid at an auction, and if you have the same kind of item that just got sniped at an auction site, you might be able to help out one of the less fortunate bidders. You can easily drop a quick e-mail to the second-highest bidders to see if your item might be just what they're looking for. Essentially, you've saved them the legwork of having to find another themselves, and you might find an enthusiastic *"I'll take it!"* coming your way. (Again, beware of eBay's prohibitive policy that would attempt to block such acceptable seller-buyer interactions.)

Can the Spam!

Now, before you get too excited, understand that when you're e-mailing bidders to make a postauction sale, you're essentially making unsolicited contact. Treat this with the highest degree of sensitivity. Though some folks you'll contact could be quite receptive, others might consider you a nuisance. Keep your message short and clear, and be sure to let the recipient know this is only a message of courtesy. Try something like this:

> "Hi. I have another of the item you were just outbid on. If you're interested, I could give you more details. If not, please disregard this message. I won't contact you again. Thanks."

Understand again that eBay discourages such unsolicited contact, partly in an effort to ward off spammers but also because there are no commissions earned on off-site sales.

Expect that some buyers will be leery of an unsolicited offer, knowing they're not protected by eBay's antifraud programs when they deal outside the auction space (hopefully your good reputation and reasonable sales policies will allay any doubts in this area). And, never *contact other bidders during the course of an auction—that's called* bid siphoning *(attempting to sell your item to bidders currently engaged in a similar auction). Bid siphoning could get you suspended (and rightfully so) if you're ever caught doing it.*

It's okay to make occasional unsolicited contact; just use good judgment and good timing when you do.

Using eBay's Second-Chance Offer

Recognizing the good business sense of courting those would-be winners while also seizing an opportunity to collect some additional commissions for their own coffer, eBay introduced the "Second-Chance Offer" where sellers can *legitimately* contact underbidders to offer an item for which you have multiple units or even in the case where the high bidder skipped town. Essentially, the second-chance offer covers the following:

- It's a one-to-one offer between a seller and a selected underbidder.
- Notice of the second-chance offer is managed by the seller using the appropriate link from either the item listing page or as found in the seller's My eBay page.
- A second-chance offer is made to a particular seller and is valid from 1 to 60 days (the seller decides the duration of the offer).
- A second-chance offer, if accepted by the buyer, will be covered by eBay's usual site policies and will result in a final value fee being levied to the seller.

If you don't feel comfortable making the direct approach and would prefer to keep your transactions within the eBay space, consider the second-chance offer as an easy way to save an unsuccessful auction or sell additional identical items you may have without the trouble and expense of relisting.

FORTUNE BOOST #34
LISTING YOUR LOSS LEADERS IN ALL THE RIGHT PLACES

The days of a business owner or employee walking about in a sandwich board—both front and back sides heralding a great new store, product, or incredible deal—are all but gone. Still, the concept behind the sandwich board is *very* much a part of today's marketing sensibility, especially when it comes to the Internet.

Every day you surf the 'Net, you'll be bombarded with pop-up ads and flashy banners that attempt to capture your attention and draw you in to take a closer look. When it comes to eBay, your ability to easily (and affordably) manage this sort of "splash advertising" can be limited but you can use the time-tested technique of catching buyers' attention and encouraging them to further peruse your wares: the use of loss leaders. When you're looking to catch customers' eye and guide them into your virtual store, sometimes a killer deal can lead you closer toward some killer sales.

Loss Leaders Defined

Before going any further, let's be sure we agree on the definition of the term, "loss leader." Classically defined, this is the designation of one item (possibly more) that you position to sell at a significantly reduced price, perhaps even below your own cost. While this may sound as heresy in relation to everything discussed so far about amassing profit and securing a fortune, the loss leader is merely a tool used to act as the *lead element* in your marketing approach. The idea is that customers will be drawn to the crazy bargain you're offering and step in closer to determine if this is a real opportunity. Once the customers have determined the deal is for real, you now have their attention and "presence" in your virtual store (being your eBay Store of fixed-price offerings or within an auction listing where you can tout other tantalizing items concurrently up for bid). It becomes likely that customers will see other "regularly priced" items of interest, and the loss leader serves the seller by generating more traffic and the potential for additional sales.

Managing Loss Leaders to Ensure You Don't Take a Loss

The key to getting the most from a loss-leader strategy is to know how to properly implement and manage it to the benefit of your business. Follow these principles and you'll see how near-giveaway items can give a big lift to your auction income:

Loss leader marketing works best when applied to an item that has wide appeal to a large customer audience. Focus on an item that is desirable to multiple market segments and not focused on a niche base.

As you prepare a loss-leader campaign, be sure to have adequate stock on hand to support increased demand. Customers get cranky when they find your super bargain has already dried up by the time they notice and rush over to snag a ridiculous deal (often this will backfire on sellers, creating the impression in customers' minds that the deal was never legitimate and was merely a cheap ploy or blatant bait-and-switch bamboozle).

As you prepare your loss-leader inventory, investigate if a higher-than-normal inventory acquisition will secure a lower-than-usual acquisition cost. If so, you can hedge your margin of loss on the item or you can reduce the item purchase price even lower. When you can price super low, you'll often attract bargain hunters who'll make a purchase even if they're not particularly interested in the item itself; it's just such a great deal that they can't pass it by.

Most importantly, coordinate the availability of a loss leader item with as many other complimentary items (available at regular profit-bearing prices) as possible to help ensure additional purchases and level off the profit loss of the loss leader item. This is key to making a loss-leader strategy pay off—more sales to more customers who are drawn to your gamut of offerings after pursuing the terrific bargain you've offered.

More Ways to Profit from Your Loss Leader Strategy

Certainly, the value of gaining a bulge in your customer base is not to be understated; buyers drawn in by the loss leader who can be converted into repeat customers are pure gold to sellers. Here, though, are some additional gains to be made from loss-leader campaigns:

- If you specialize in seasonal or holiday-themed merchandise, plan loss leader campaigns around the key events because customers will be actively pursuing such goods. This helps draw even more customers in to purchase the bargain, then they proceed to select among the other seasonal goods you offer that they desire.
- When you encounter an opportunity to acquire a quantity of inventory at low, low acquisition cost, consider the potential of offering that merchandise as a loss leader. You may be able to establish a good relationship with a supplier of goods such that you can secure additional low prices on inventory down the road.
- If you're overstocked on some goods that you need to move out, use the loss-leader approach to deplete your stock without having to be stuck with it or attempt to return it to a supplier and possibly incur restocking fees.

How Non-eBayers Use eBay Loss Leader Marketing

Finally, recognize how some non-eBayers use the auction site solely for loss-leader marketing. Some businesses, be they entirely virtual or an extension of a brick-and-mortar presence, see the low-cost advertising potential in offering loss-leader items to eBay's swelling user base of over 150 million. Given that doing business on eBay is extremely cost-effective (as compared with traditional advertising and promotion costs), a loss-leader offering, temporary or ongoing, can help promote a business. When customers come to take advantage of the great deal, the business makes full use of the opportunity to provide more information and direction to its commercial existence elsewhere.

FORTUNE BOOST #35
BREAKING DOWN BULK LISTERS

There comes a time in your eBay sales effort when you need a bit of help getting all of your great items up for sale or bid. While many sellers have managed to maintain a tidy profit using eBay's standard listing methods (along with the ease of relisting, covered next in Fortune Boost # 36), others simply need to be able to list more in less time and with less effort. The good news for these folks is "bulk listers." eBay pioneered the method of bulk listing with their own Mister Lister, first unveiled in back in 2000, and has gone on to supplant that tool with their spiffy new "Turbo Lister." But eBay's not the only one in the bulk lister game. Other auction-centric service providers have also ponied up their own bulk listing solutions, each with a set of features and each with a price tag attached. Which lister is best for you and which will give you the most for your money? Here's a quick rundown of the key bulk listers available and how to tell what you need (and what you don't) out of a bulk listing tool.

Which Lister Is Right for You?

With so many similar and some different toolsets being offered, you need to assess if your business would truly benefit from the expense of a bulk listing tool, especially one that will take a regular bite out of your bottom-line profits. Here are a few questions to ask as you try to determine which listing tool would best suit your needs.

- What is the cost of the tool, either for a single download purchase or for ongoing costs to list items through the tool's manufacturer?
- Is there a support team available that can help you with questions or problems you might encounter as you use the listing tool?
- How many screens do you need to navigate in the tool before a listing is complete? (The fewer, the faster.)
- How much freedom do you have in scheduling the starting times of your collection of listings? Take note that it's preferable that not all auctions start—and subsequently end—at precisely the same time; allow your bidders to play in multiple auctions of yours, especially those folks who like to bid at the last possible moment.
- How tightly integrated is a bulk listing tool into other elements of the manufacturer's suite of tools? If the tool is too tightly integrated (that is, the manufacturer is working to convince you to purchase additional tools you might or might not want or need), you might find it's not possible to effectively use *just* the bulk lister if you prefer only that tool.
- How compatible is the tool to different computer operating systems? Check this carefully against the OS you're running now. The last thing you want to do is have to go to the time, effort, and expense of upgrading your computer platform just to satisfy the needs of a bulk lister (then again, if you're looking for an excuse to finally upgrade your system, maybe this is the push you've been looking for).
- Again, where will you list items? Naturally, Turbo Lister is targeted solely for eBay use, but what if you want to list items at Amazon Auctions, Amazon Marketplace (fixed-price items) Yahoo Auctions, or at a Yahoo Store? If this will be your situation, then you may need to consider a third-party listing tool.

- What happens if the third-party bulk lister you'll use becomes unavailable? Remember that busy holiday season of 2002 when Andale services were suddenly interrupted for 16 hours, affecting sellers' listing capability; this can be an area of risk to your business. Again, this sort of situation is the exception and not the rule, but it drives home the point that you also want to strive to make your business as interrupt-proof as possible by eliminating reliance upon too many other systems, servers, and other such third-party tools that may go "clunk" when your business least expects it.

But when it all comes down to making a final choice, you'll need to test drive the various tools to really be certain how (and if) they'll benefit your increased volume of selling and if they're worth any cost they might incur. Of the three major tools described below, each offers a free trial period. Take advantage of that and work with each for about a week to see which suits you best.

Sifting through the Bulk Listing Services

Many of the former bulk listers out there have dissolved in recent years, but a strong few have remained and have developed some tools that truly are effective and efficient. In short order, here are the top services that rise above the fray today and that have the best suite of services to help you in your business.

- **eBay's Turbo Lister (http://pages.ebay.com/turbo_lister/):** This one tops the list because it's free and it seems to be free of defects (mostly). Because it was developed by the eBay team, you can be assured it will work within the realm of the site and its various listing features and options. It's easy to install and you can be creating your first listing "collections" within minutes. The tool also accesses eBay every time you launch to check for updates and will automatically refresh your installation when updates are detected. You can upload collections of items (up to 300 at a time!) and either launch them immediately or store them for a couple of weeks for later launch. All in all, it's a great tool and it's of no cost to you. (See Figure 35-1.)
- **Andale (www.andale.com):** Andale, as you recall from Fortune Boost # 22, is a full-featured auction management toolset. Its bulk lister, Lister Pro, is beefy and can deliver some great-looking results, but it'll cost you. Ten listings a month cost $2.00 and you can purchase service levels up to 5,600 listings a month for about $225. Lister Pro has an HTML editor, an image manger, a listing scheduler, and even a nifty relister. This tool also supports listings at Amazon and Yahoo sites. Still, depending on how many items you intend to list, how consistently you'll list at that volume, where you'll list them, and just how spiffy you need them to look (less dazzle is better, remember), then you'll want to cast a cautious eye on any tool that adds to your auction costs. (See Figure 35-2.)

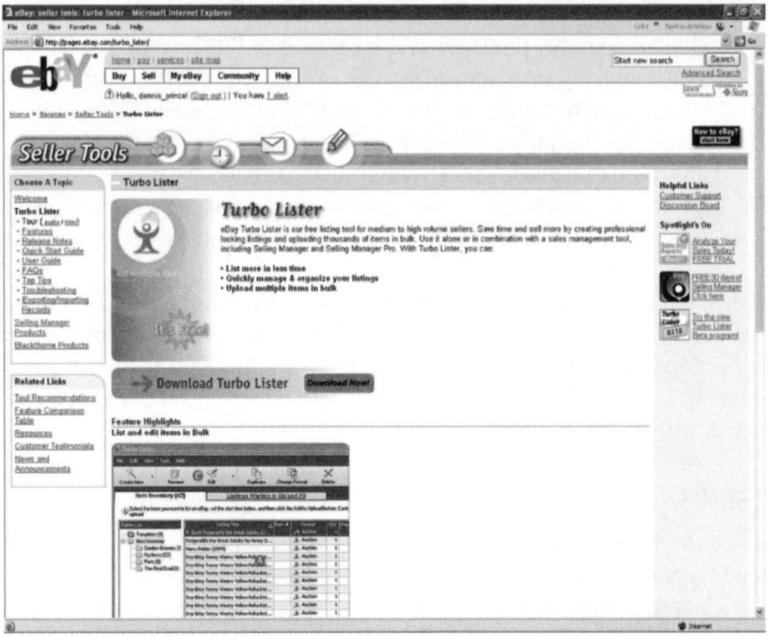

Figure 35-1   Ebay's Turbo Lister provides you the ability to list up to 300 items at once.

- **Vendio (www.vendio.com):** Vendio's bulk lister, Sales Manager Pro, supports the major online portals of eBay, Yahoo, Amazon, Froogle, and its own suite of Vendio Stores. As far as pricing goes, Vendio uses a variety of tier-payment plans and varied service offerings that are a bit pricey and even cumbersome to navigate. You can elect to simply use their bulk lister at a rate of $0.10 per item plus one percent of the final sales value. That seems a bit steep considering it can still be had for free at eBay. If, however, you want to use their full suite of auction management services, you might find some value in the overall offering. Oh, and their online community forum is just as active as ever and brimming with great interactive auction information. (See Figure 35-3.)

Of course, you'll likely encounter some other bulk listers out there, those created by some rather inventive entrepreneurs, so you'll want to give the rest of the 'Net a look (if, for nothing else, just to say you did). With any bulk listing tool you may consider, study any attached pricing carefully and calculate those costs as you work to accurately project your operating costs. Whenever possible, cut costs where they don't provide a noticeable (and calculable) positive impact to your business. Remember, when it comes to auction costs, any you can eliminate will immediately boost your eBay fortune.

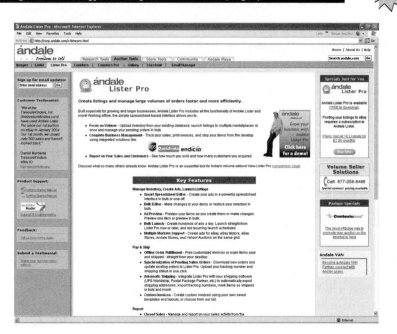

Figure 35-2   Andale's Lister Pro isn't free, but it offers service and support to help you manage bulk listings at eBay and elsewhere.

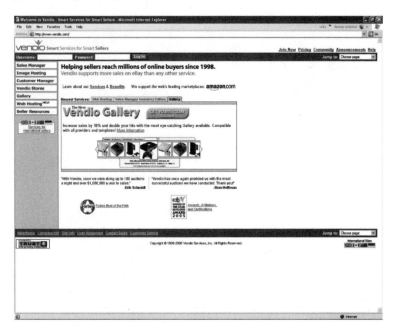

Figure 35-3   Vendio offers bulk listing as well as a whole host of other auction and inventory management solutions.

FORTUNE BOOST #36
RELISTING FOR REWARDING RESULTS

Even the most successful online auctioneer admits that some items don't sell the first time around. Undaunted, these seasoned sellers have learned that relisting such goods is not only easier than ever, but typically yields a successful sale when aided by some simple remarketing strategies. If you've been discouraged when your item doesn't sell (either no bids or reserve price not met), don't lose hope. Of course, there are no guarantees that a relisted item will sell, but by understanding eBay's relisting process and incorporating a few simple adjustments, a successful and cost-effective sale may be waiting for you on a second go-round.

How Much Rework Is Involved?

First, get familiar with the mechanics of relisting items. The best news is that, at eBay, relisting is a breeze. When your listing has ended, visit the item page and you'll see that the relist function is just a click away (see Figure 36-1).

As if relisting from within the original item page wasn't easy enough, you'll also be glad to hear that it only takes one click to relist items from within your My eBay page. Simply click on the pull-down arrow on the item area noted, "Action" and select the "Relist" option (see Figure 36-2).

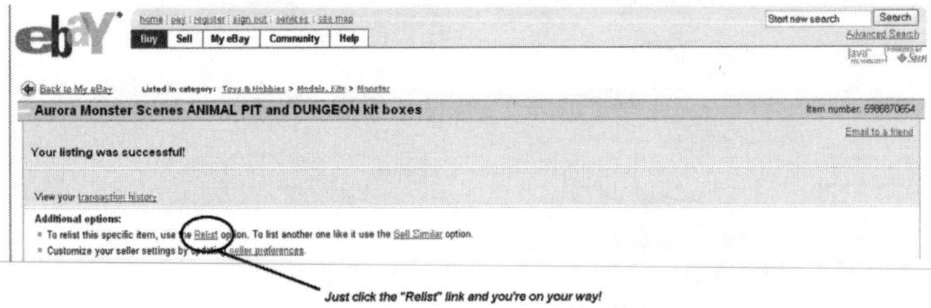

Figure 36-1   Relisting takes just one click from your ended item listing page.

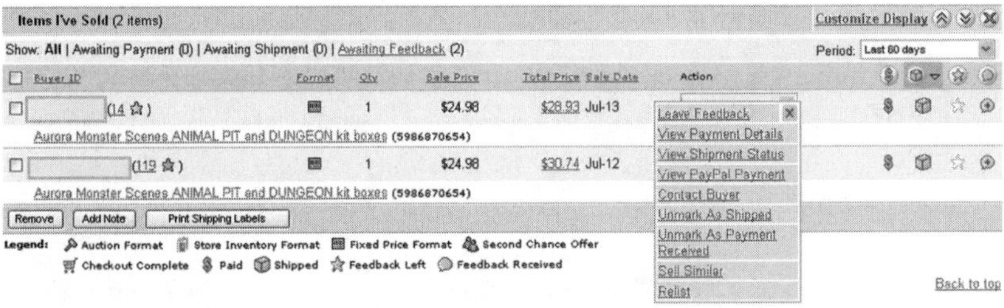

Figure 36-2   Relisting is easier still from within the My eBay page.

When you relist in either of the above ways, you'll be guided through the original listing pages as when you first created your listing. Here you can make changes or simply click the "Submit" button and your auction is running again.

Review, Revise, and Remarket

As noted in the previous paragraph, when you relist an item, it's your opportunity to make a few adjustments to improve your sales potential the second time around. Here's your opportunity to learn from your unsuccessful auction and determine what alterations you might make to improve your profit potential upon relisting. Perhaps you need a change in approach and strategy as you prepare to relist. Consider these key relisting opportunities:

- Review your auction title for clarity and maximum "hit" keywords (for buyers' searches).
- Review your auction category and determine if it was the best choice, the only choice, or if there's a better choice available.
- Review your auction description to be sure it's informative, accurate, and enticing.
- Did you offer images of the item?
- Was your minimum bid price or reserve price set too high? Can you adjust it down or forgo the reserve, trusting the current market to bring you a reasonable price?
- Was this the best time to list? Review the time, day, and season of your auction and determine if an adjustment is in order.
- How many times have you relisted (if this isn't just your second go-round)? Is it possible there's simply no interest in your item at this time? (Yes, this is a rare but plausible conclusion at times.)

An unsuccessful auction does have a value: it communicates that your approach, somehow or somewhere, didn't quite work. Be very open, perceptive, and flexible with each of your auctions. In many cases, it's a matter of fine-tuning your procedure as you're stabilizing your business approach and adjusting your offerings. Relistings allow you to "tinker" with your sales process until you can lock into your customer base in a way that has you bringing in the bids at a maximum fortune-bearing rate.

FORTUNE BOOST #37
WHY THE *ABOUT ME* PAGE MEANS
MORE THAN YOU MIGHT THINK

In it's earliest conception, eBay founder Pierre Omidyar envisioned an online community of Utopian measure where people would come together to trade in an open and boundless hub of commerce. His belief in the power and inherent goodness of community was immediately translated into eBay's Feedback Forum, the place where traders would post comments about their experiences with one another in eBay transactions, furthering a transparent marketplace where the eBay users would exist in a visible way conducive to fostering good business and better interpersonal relations. To a large degree, the Feedback Forum has achieved its purpose as serious buyers and sellers have learned to conduct themselves responsibly to protect their good name (and good eBay rating).

In addition to the Feedback Forum, though, eBay also introduced the "About Me" page, where registered eBay users could post even more information about themselves, serving as a virtual Yellow Pages listing of who they are, what products or services they provide, and why they're to be considered upstanding members of the eBay community. If ever you've scoffed at the value of an About Me page, thinking it would have little to contribute to your bottom line, think again. About Me says an awful lot about *you*.

Determining What to Include in an About Me Page

While no one is truly interested in a voluminous dissertation of your full life's history, your personal peccadilloes, or your political aspirations (well, a *few* folks might be), here's what you should consider including in your About Me page (you'll find the easy-to-follow instructions when you click on the eBay Site Map link, then locate and click the "About Me" text link under the "Community" column):

- Your name or the name of your business. Let folks know who you are and, if you're using a business name, make sure it clearly and compellingly communicates what sorts of goods you deal in.
- A welcome message that immediately imparts your tone and style in doing business (preferably friendly and inviting) and that also indicates something about your eBay history, business experience, and any relevant special skills or hobbies.
- Additional information that might impart your goals at eBay and how you'll work to earn and retain customers by nature of your goods, services, or other value-added elements.
- Useful information or articles (excerpts or permissible reprints) that will help visitors learn more about the sorts of items you sell, the sort of commodity you specialize in. These can be of use to them as they make decisions about purchases, both from you as well as elsewhere within eBay and on the 'Net.
- A photo of yourself, your business place (skip the messy office if that's where you're working), and a company logo (if you have one). Again, these are the elements that will add to the ability of customers to remember you and your wares.

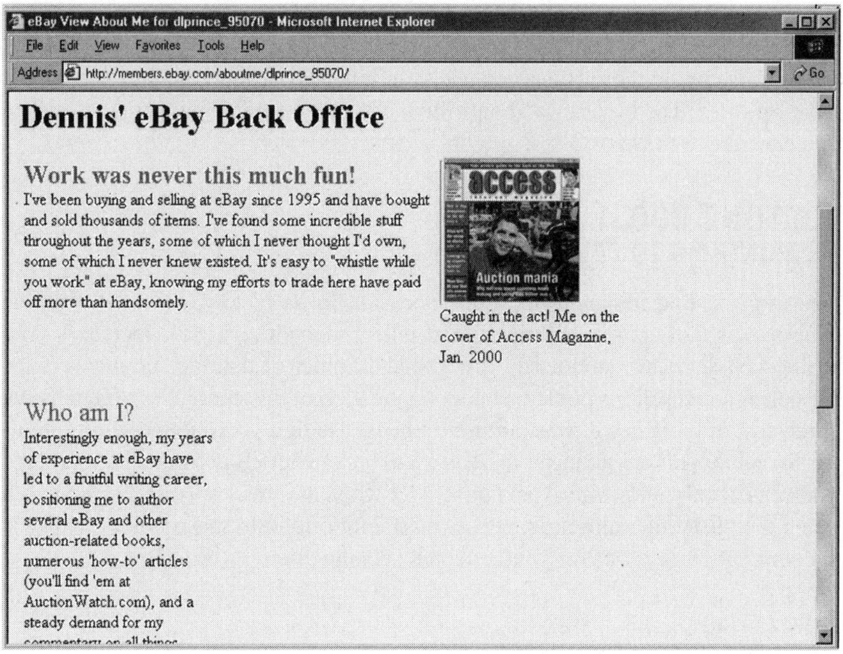

```
eBay View About Me for dlprince_95070 - Microsoft Internet Explorer          _ □ ×
 File   Edit   View   Favorites   Tools   Help
 Address  http://members.ebay.com/aboutme/dlprince_95070/                        Go
```

Dennis' eBay Back Office

Work was never this much fun!

I've been buying and selling at eBay since 1995 and have bought and sold thousands of items. I've found some incredible stuff throughout the years, some of which I never thought I'd own, some of which I never knew existed. It's easy to "whistle while you work" at eBay, knowing my efforts to trade here have paid off more than handsomely.

Caught in the act! Me on the cover of Access Magazine, Jan. 2000

Who am I?

Interestingly enough, my years of experience at eBay have led to a fruitful writing career, positioning me to author several eBay and other auction-related books, numerous 'how-to' articles (you'll find 'em at AuctionWatch.com), and a steady demand for my commentary on all things

Figure 37-1 This simple About Me page was created in about 10 minutes, but it lets folks know who they're dealing with and helps establish a rapport that could translate into more purchases.

The best news is you can create an About Me page as simply or elaborately as you like. However you like, just create one (and you can revise it later as you see fit) and let your prospective buyers get to know who *you* are. (See Figure 37-1.)

Recognizing the Value of an About Me Page

OK. So you've created an About Me page; so what? Well, if you doubt it's an effort that could provide payback to your profit goals, look at what's communicated directly and "between the lines" on your About Me page:

- It provides a more human element to the auction experience (and there are *many* buyers who are still jittery over the idea of engaging in a transaction with a perfect stranger within Cyberspace).
- It puts a face to a name, that is if you include a photo of yourself, buyers can actually see who their dealing with rather than relying on merely an eBay user ID.
- It can engender a greater sense of trust as buyers see you're willing to provide more information about yourself within the eBay community, showing your commitment to doing good business without any secrets.

Every day, big businesses work hard and spend big dollars perfecting and promoting their company image to the masses. At eBay, you'll want to act in kind, letting folks know more about you and your business beyond the great items you have for offer. The best news about About Me is it's free. Now there's a savings you can take to the bank.

FORTUNE BOOST #38
RESPONDING TO FEE HIKES

The truth be told, on more than one occasion in its history, eBay—*the* online auction portal of choice—has infuriated sellers with sweeping fee increases. And while such acts have summarily inspired all manner of outrage and outcry from the beleaguered seller's pool, the better application of this energy, exhibited by the shrewdest of the shrewd, was putting it to best use in ways to improve profitability. So, while you're looking at these ways to boost your eBay fortune, look at how you can buffer your profits from taking a hit when the site costs rise. Oh, and even when the costs are enjoying a period of stability, look to these tips to help you squeeze out more profit for your personal accumulation of fortune.

Time Is Money

For starters, begin your profit refining by closely examining your most valuable and nonrenewable resource: time. Take two to four weeks to carefully log your time (be diligent here) to see what you're really getting accomplished each day. You might learn you're surfing the 'Net too much or are chatting the day away with friends. And if you're sitting around waiting for that ancient PC to chug its way through your listings, it might be time to upgrade. The overall goal here is to ensure that you can reduce the time it takes to complete your auction tasks. Set firm working hours, use listing and e-mail templates, carefully schedule trips into town, and whatever else you do as you tend to your auction business. Develop an efficient work plan that keeps the profits rolling in and makes the best use of your working day.

Selective Selling

Though you may be feverishly listing hundreds of items (or more) each week, beware of venturing into the land of diminishing returns. If much of that inventory consistently goes unsold, you may be spinning your wheels trying to move items that folks simply aren't interested in—and for which you're racking up listing fees. Consider, instead, selectively marketing your most profitable goods, concentrating on offering the most popular, desirable, and reliable items. Then thoughtfully rotate your inventory through the auction venue to take advantage of the best listing seasons for certain items, to create anticipation for the next great piece you'll offer, and to harness every trend and craze that may boost demand for the goods you'll offer.

Trim the Fat

Take another look at your various operating expenses and thoughtfully investigate where you can shave a few dollars off here and there. Quit paying for packaging supplies you can get free from carriers and dump those costly Internet access features you're simply not using. Comb through your monthly expenses to see if anything you're paying for today can be had cheaper (or for free) tomorrow.

Venturing to Other Venues

Though it wouldn't be prudent to completely walk away from eBay's millions upon millions of potential bidders, recognize that fixed-price venues like eBay's Half.com as well as Amazon.com's Marketplace are viable venues to be used (and don't forget to investigate penetration into Amazon Auctions as well as Yahoo Auctions). To this end, seriously investigate whether you can begin listing items in an alternate venue. Some sellers find the books they want to sell also do quite well at Amazon Auctions. Here's your opportunity to diversify a bit, so make the most of it.

Promote Your Nonauction Presence

Don't forget that it's still an open marketplace out there. Though you'll have to carefully tiptoe around eBay's sometimes oppressive policies regarding off-site advertisement, seek to promote your own commercial sales site (if you have one) with your established customer base. For every new winning bidder you deal with, you have the opportunity to build upon your clientele. Serve them well and tell them of other goods you might have available. Do this discreetly (no spamming or hard sales) and you'll find you can boost your eBay profits both within the site's realm as well as outside its boundaries.

FORTUNE BOOST #39
A SMALL PRICE TO PAY

At this time, after so much has been discussed regarding increasing profits through the cutting of costs, take just a moment to consider what it all boils down to—finding a marketplace where you *can* boost your fortune at perhaps the lowest cost around.

eBay—A Wise Investment

Perhaps the most important concept in this Fortune Boost is that of recognizing the value of staying with the eBay platform (though not necessarily *entirely* if you have sales activity concurrently managed elsewhere online or off) and how cost-effective it is to be able to reach over 150 million potential customers (and growing) every day. To those who have always wanted to explore starting up a small business operation of their own, eBay has been the answer to that prayer. And, to those who have a small business but have wanted to significantly grow it—even globalize its reach—eBay has enabled that, too, without intense and risky levels of financial and personal investment.

Let's just wrap this one up by considering what you get for your money when you list at eBay. Just as the realtor says "location, location, location" is what matters most in a home investment, the same can be said for where you decide to establish your business. When it comes to online business, eBay is the teeming Megalopolis of the cyber shopping realm. More importantly, eBay is practically a business-on-demand that's easy to use and always ready to apply. Consider what you gain when you choose eBay as a foundation for your business:

- No overhead or up-front costs to launch your business (sell from your garage immediately).
- No sales staff or distributors to manage at the outset.
- No Web site of your own to develop, manage, and fund.
- No initial investment beyond insertion fees to begin marketing your product to a vast audience of potential buyers.

You likewise profit from the fact that eBay leads the online auction industry with a more than 60 percent share of the market, while its closest competitor (if you can call it that), Yahoo! Auctions, is only half that size. Amazon.com Auctions follows at a distant third. eBay has dominated the online auction and fixed-price market for over a decade now and is only getting bigger. That translates in stability and security to virtual shopkeepers who are looking for firm ground upon which to build their own empires. And, when it comes to boosting your fortune, nothing does it better than having built your business on a rock-solid and well-regarded market foundation.

FORTUNE BOOST #40
PROTECTING YOUR BUSINESS FROM VIRAL VANDALS

Just as brick-and-mortar shop owners need to protect their establishments against the disruption of vandalism, virtual shop owners have also found the need to be equally vigilant against cyber-vandals. With literally tens of thousands of known computer viruses and worms proliferating online, it's just a matter of time before your PC—*your virtual business place*—is exposed to a digital disease. Online sellers must step up their preparedness from these surreptitious attacks or else risk going offline at a moment's notice and possibly (*gulp*) until further notice. If you're uncertain whether you're online endeavor is adequately protected, review these safeguards, guidelines, and countermeasures that will help ensure that your eBay venture can withstand these unannounced and unexpected cyber-assaults.

Assess Your Risk

Despite ongoing warnings, many PC users simply aren't using antivirus software or have not kept their virus definitions current—these users are at high risk of contracting and redistributing viruses to their friends, family, and customers. Because new viruses are being unleashed all the time, it's up to you to keep your PC properly protected to avoid disruption to your business and ensure that you don't unwittingly infect others' systems.

If you suspect your hardware isn't duly protected, your first step should be to get your hands on an antivirus (AV) application and scan your hard drive. AV tools such as Norton AntiVirus, McAfee VirusScan, and Trend Micro's PC-cillan can identify any virus it recognizes and allow you to isolate, repair, or quarantine and delete infected files (these applications have been updated for MacOS compatibility as well).

Expand Your Virus Vocabulary

The good news is that you can often spot a virus on sight if you know what to look for. As most viruses are spread via e-mail today, be suspicious of e-mail attachments that seem unusual and come from senders you don't quickly recognize. Avoid opening file attachments that bear the following file extensions: VBS, WSH, SHS, WSC, JS, PIF, CMD, BAT, SCR, LNK, and REG. Also be wary with files that have COM and EXE extensions. But that's not all! Recognize that many more viruses infect files that use applications containing *macro languages* such as Microsoft Word and Excel. When an infected document or spreadsheet file is opened, the concealed virus is enabled as if it were a macro definition. This means you can contract such a virus by sharing infected files via floppy disc and CD-ROM as well as via e-mail distribution.

Take Preventive Action

Just as virus authors continue to hone their skills of ill intent, antivirus tools are likewise evolving to protect your data, your assets, and your business. Therefore, be certain to make full use of the virus screening and containment tools available. Here are the key safeguards you should have in place to gain the best protection:

- Scan your PC files on a regular basis; scan boot files on each power-up and conduct full system scans on a weekly basis.
- Update your virus definitions weekly (Symantec updates their Norton AntiVirus definitions every Wednesday).
- Keep the automatic virus shield enabled at all times.
- Ensure that the virus checking function is set to scan downloadable (Internet) and e-mail files upon receipt.

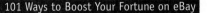

Ensure that removable media scanning (floppies, CD-ROMs) functions are enabled. If you use MS Outlook, install the Security Updates to prevent infected files from automatically executing (Outlook 2003 offers this as a standard security feature).

Keep up-to-date on new virus threats by visiting. www.sarc.com.

Backup and Disaster Recovery

After you've scanned your system and ensured that it's virus-free, create a recovery disc set as instructed by the AV application; it will allow you to boot up and scan your PC from floppy or ZIP media if a future infection ever occurs. That being done, it's time to perform a complete backup of your system, copying files to either removable media or to a separate hard drive (and many of today's newer computers have internal disc "partitions" devoted to serve as a backup storage area).

More pertinent to your business now, be sure you have safe and clean backups of the following:

- Customer and key contact lists
- Inventory data
- Sales data (pending and historical)
- Templates and other selling tools
- Image files

Be sure you have all necessary program and driver files for any add-on hardware (such as modems, accessory cards, printers) safely stored away on removable media as well the recovery disc that likely accompanied your system (this would be used in extreme cases where a full disc reformatting would be required).

Pay Now or Pay Later

Without question, adhering to a virus maintenance and system backup plan is time-consuming. Your best bet is to perform such routines on a regular basis (virus updates weekly; system backups biweekly or monthly) to keep the task manageable. If you will faithfully take steps to ensure the health and recoverability of your system, you'll stand the best chance possible to recover quickly should a virtual disaster strike. Don't put it off until tomorrow; protect your business today.

The Goods that Garner Higher Gains

FORTUNE BOOST #41
HOW TO KNOW WHAT'S HOT AND WHAT'S NOT

Here's probably the most-asked question of any seller-to-be and online fortune finder: "What should I sell online to make the most money possible?" Well, that's the same question that's being asked by every merchandiser, large and small, in every product market and in every locale around the globe. The fact of the matter is, sellers *can't* know and will never know what's best and most lucrative to sell *unless* they closely watch and listen to buyers (all buyers, not just those whom a seller has previously served). Buyers are very deliberate in communicating what they want and, when you look and listen closely enough, you'll soon be able to make some well-calculated guesses as to what buyers will want to buy next. When you can do that, you'll be on your way to knowing what's hot and what's not.

It All Goes Back to Market Research

While it would be nice to find the answer to some super secret that would guide you to the most popular profit-bearing goods, such an e-commerce elixir just doesn't exist (and beware those who will offer to *sell* to you such a foolproof plan; they'll only tell you what you're about to read here). Simply enough, start by looking over the details of offerings within the eBay categories and subcategories. When you search all categories in this fashion, you'll see a listing of category headers and subcategory headers that include parenthetical numbers indicating how many different listings are currently available within (see Figure 41-1).

Scanning category listings is a useful exercise because it gives you a view into where sellers are concentrating their efforts, working by the assumption that

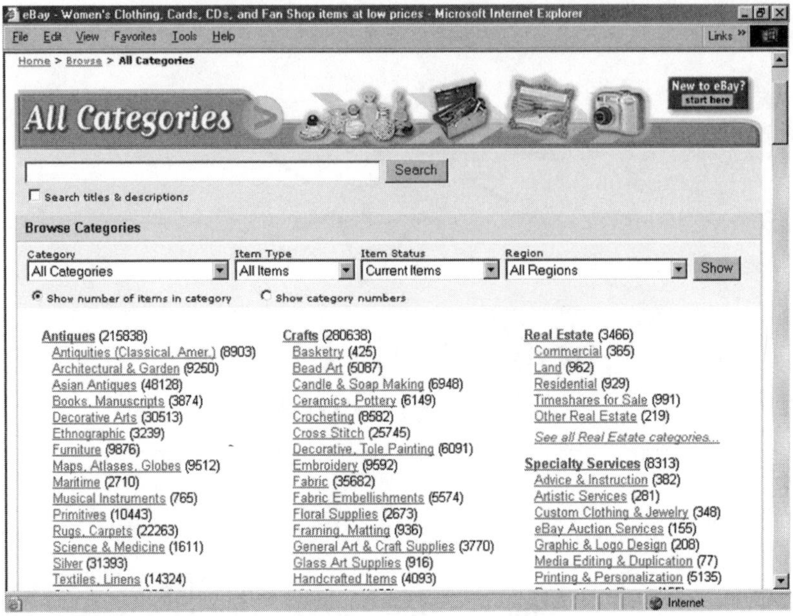

Figure 41-1   Good research of buyer trends begins with an aggregate view of where the action is. Review the category overview page at eBay to see where all the goods are first.

they wouldn't be offering it if it wasn't selling. Even though the number of listings doesn't directly equate to the actual number of items sold, you can gain an immediate pulse of where the action is, what categories seem to be up-and-coming by account of their numbers of active listings, and which areas are either less active or (pay attention here) prime for development.

Investigate Completed Items

Having investigated what's currently available by searching the category listings, refine that search by looking at what has recently *completed* at eBay. For this analysis, you'll need to narrow your search using keywords, terms, and phrases that will deliver results—lists of the items you're interested in marketing yourself. Completed listings are hugely useful in your research of what's hot and what's not at eBay in that they allow you to determine how well particular items are selling, what prices buyers are earning for these items, how many bidders seem to be bidding on these goods, and how much room there is for another player to offer similar goods (that would be you).

Popular Searches

Because only the buyers themselves can reveal what's hot and what's not, turn your attention now to peering into the sorts of searches the buyers are using.

Figure 41-2 The Sell by Category page leads you to learn the most popular and "In Demand" search terms for a particular category of goods.

Thankfully, eBay has provided a snapshot of this critical data that you can scan whenever you like. Although it's a bit difficult to find, here's how to navigate to this treasured information. Begin by visiting eBay's Site Map, then click on the *Seller Central* link you'll find on the Site Map page. From there, click on the *Sell by Category* link and you'll advance to a page that provides information on a category-by-category basis (see Figure 41-2).

In the Sell by Category page, you'll see various category headings and links to more information. Most pertinent to your quest now is the link, *In Demand*, as you see the pointer positioned in Figure 41-2. Clicking the In Demand link advances you to a listing of search terms that eBay has compiled for you and that is based upon buyers' search activity. Congratulations! You've just stumbled onto the fabled gold mine of how to determine what's hot and what's not at eBay. The key to tapping the fortune of any gold mine, of course, is to take the raw treasure you find and refine it into understandable and actionable information that will guide you in how you seek out items to offer and how you'll position them in front of the eBay masses.

A Breakthrough to Sell-Through

Next, to ensure you've sifted the best data from all directions in determining what's hot and what's not, your last step is to confirm you haven't missed any opportunities

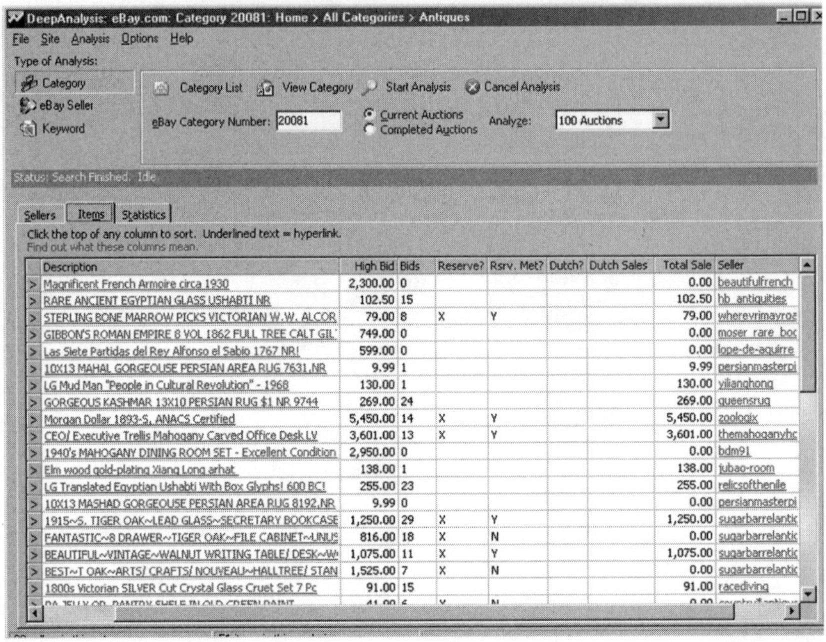

Figure 41-3 The Sell-Thru Stats found on HammerTap's Deep Analysis tool depict item activity, by category, and the rate at which they were bid on or purchased outright.

by looking back at what buyers have been *recently* purchasing. Recall you were looking in eBay's completed items to see what buyers have bid on and how much, yet eBay's only able to offer two weeks worth of this valuable information. Therefore, to mine deeper into past sales history, you'll need to enlist the help of a third-party tool such as HammerTap's Deep Analysis tool (see Figure 41-3). This tool was developed to sift through data of eBay auctions—active or completed—and extract information regarding items sold, selling price, number of bids, and seller. This is a tool that you can really sink your teeth into, as it provides the final level of detail for your market research.

What's Hot According to eBay

Finally, hoping to provide more useful information to sellers and keeping them from straying too far away, eBay has also offered their own compiled list, "Hot Items." To find it, visit Seller Central again (navigate from SiteMap to Seller Central), then choose the *What's Hot* link along the left-side column of links. In the next screen, select the *Hot Items by Category* text link to launch the Adobe Document Viewer (it's free from www.adobe.com if you don't already have it on

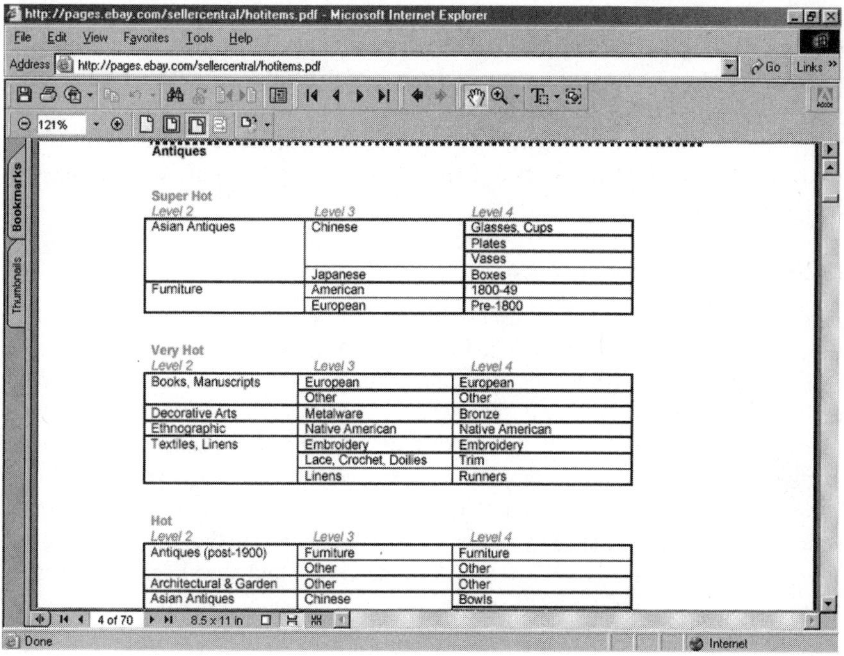

Antiques

Super Hot

Level 2	Level 3	Level 4
Asian Antiques	Chinese	Glasses, Cups
		Plates
		Vases
	Japanese	Boxes
Furniture	American	1800-49
	European	Pre-1800

Very Hot

Level 2	Level 3	Level 4
Books, Manuscripts	European	European
	Other	Other
Decorative Arts	Metalware	Bronze
Ethnographic	Native American	Native American
Textiles, Linens	Embroidery	Embroidery
	Lace, Crochet, Doilies	Trim
	Linens	Runners

Hot

Level 2	Level 3	Level 4
Antiques (post-1900)	Furniture	Furniture
	Other	Other
Architectural & Garden	Other	Other
Asian Antiques	Chinese	Bowls

Figure 41-4 eBay's Hot Item list is an Adobe (.pdf) document you can easily download and review from eBay's Seller Central area.

your computer) where you can review the detailed statistics of what eBay has culled as being the most popular items recently sold on the site (see Figure 41-4).

With all this information now at your disposal, you'll see there is no secret hiding place where you'll find magic answers to the question, "What should I sell at eBay to make the most money possible?" The fact is, the information is all around and the real magic to boosting your auction fortune is to determine that you'll carefully and thoughtfully analyze the information, watch and listen to buyers, and make your move based on what you've learned along the way.

FORTUNE BOOST #42
THERE'S STILL GOLD IN THEM THAR' GARAGE SALES

During eBay's early days, garage sales were the target supply source for online auctioneers, their virtual auction skills still unknown to many. When eBay became better known and more folks were ready to try their hand at making a fast fortune, garage sellers opted to list online rather than take paltry coins for their items. Soon, all the really "good stuff" that was formerly to be found on the driveways of

America and elsewhere was being held back. To some sellers, this meant the end to their eBay businesses, but times have yet again changed. Here's some refreshing insight for your savvy sellers: garage sale bargains are back in fashion. Read how your opportunity to cash in on garage sale gold has returned and how you can subsidize your eBay offerings with goods available as near as your neighbor's front walk. So dig out your fanny pack and sharpen your haggling skills; garage sales are hoppin' once again.

Only the Strong Have Survived

Although eBay is clearly a household name, most one-time sellers realize they won't be pulling down an immediate fortune with just a weekend's worth of listings; there's money to be made but, with an increasing supply of all sorts of odds-and-ends items, it takes a committed sellers to make those profits. Many sellers who quickly turned to eBay during the 1990s quickly realized that selling at the online auction site took work and commitment. For that reason, many have bailed out, considering the whole "eBay thing" just another of those dot-com fads. Seasoned sellers like you stand chance to cash in once again, thanks to those aforementioned fly-by-night sellers who have gone back to the garage and have begun offering up good stuff once again; it's just too much work to sell on eBay. Consistent sellers, that's great news because the goods are getting good once more.

But Are the Goods Any Good?

Of course, an astute seller will wonder if returning to the garage sale source will really yield much benefit (the thought being that all the really good stuff was already sold). While it's true that many excellent treasures have traded hands, the core operating principle behind second-hand selling still persists—the current owner of those whatever-they-are-items might now need to unload the goods. Few will intentionally take a loss, yet many former buyers are eager just to remove the clutter from their lives. To that end, there are some great items out there even today, many of which will yield some tidy profits.

Refreshing Your Approach—Skillfully Mining Garage Sales

So, if you had turned away from garage sales of late, look again; there's plenty of great bargains and good finds out there. Plus, now that eBay has been around a decade (and is still going strong), the castoffs that folks lug out to their driveways are the sorts of items that will appeal to the next "prime collecting" generation. Therefore, as you ready to return to the suburban trails that still lead to treasure, recall these key tenets of successful garage sale shopping:

- Check your local newspaper or online classifieds for listings of upcoming garage sales and plot out a course that will allow you to hit as many as possible on a time- and fuel-efficient route.

- Remember that upscale neighborhoods often have nicer items, but you'll likely be paying a bit more than at older neighborhood sales.
- On the other hand, older neighborhoods often are treasure troves for vintage goods that may have been stored away for 30, 40, 50 years or more (and there are still plenty out there). If you're hunting for vintage items, homes in these long-established neighborhoods will often have the goods you seek.
- Once at the sale, make a fast tour of the goods to spot key treasures quickly and pick up anything that looks to be of immediate value (if you don't, the person behind you will). Then, make another slower pass to look deeper for hidden treasures lurking in boxes or underneath other items.
- Check all items for condition and completeness and be sure to ask if you can plug in electrical items (this is especially important of vintage items from the 1960s and 1970s; gaudy goods that are in high demand *provided* they're in working order).
- Don't be afraid to haggle. Ask if the seller will take a slightly lower price for an item (most items are marked up an extra dollar or two by sellers who anticipate this negotiating game) or offer to purchase multiple items for a reasonable discount. Be reasonable, though, to avoid offending the seller.
- Be early! Some listings wave off "early birds" but arrive at least 15 to 30 minutes ahead of time to swoop in for the best items.
- Being late can be advantageous, too. Visit sales at the end of their run and see if the homeowner is willing to allow you to take a boxful or clear a table for cut-rate prices (the goods probably next winding up in the trash, otherwise).

If you've stayed away from the garage sales of late, believing their time of fruitfulness has come and gone, look again. There's some great stuff showing up these days, just the sort that can help fuel your eBay fortune.

FORTUNE BOOST #43
BUYING ON SPECULATION

Many sellers are also very active buyers, hoping to nab overlooked eBay treasures that will later bring in a king's ransom. Whether a hot new collectible or a timeless favorite, seller-buyers are constantly on the lookout for that diamond in the rough, anxious to quietly snatch it from the virtual parlor (or wherever) without much fanfare. However, when you look into buying goods speculatively—with the clear intention to resell at a profit and not add to your own personal collection—you need to be clear about what you're investing in, how much you'll invest, and how and when you'll turn it over for a profit. Here are some tips that will assist you in your speculative inventory purchases and future sales, helping you separate between true gold and commonplace clutter.

Know Your Stuff

Knowledge is power and it will be the strength of your speculative purchases. If you'll be speculating on items of which you're already an expert, you're ahead of the curve. If not, be sure to fully research what you'll buy.

- Use trade papers, collector's guides, the Internet, and even the auction places themselves to acquaint yourself with the item of investment.
- Become well versed in the history, manufacture dates, variations, and reproductions (if any) of the items you will invest in.
- Then research the seller—especially if this is to be an online auction speculation. Determine how long the seller has dealt in this sort of item and what expertise she has.
- If you're purchasing from a dealer at a show, responding to a classified ad, or standing at someone's garage sale, you'll need to be prepared to make quick assessments of authenticity and potential value your-self. If the item's inexpensive, you might not have much to lose in making the purchase. However, if it seems costly and you're just not sure, you might wish to pass or at least get the seller's contact infor-mation for chance of a later purchase—after you've done a bit more homework.

Know Your Limits

Regardless how desirable an item is or its profit potential, you'll need to ensure you buy it at a price that allows a profit to be realized. In general, you're best served when you can purchase an item at sort of "wholesale prices," that is roughly 50 percent or more below the current retail value of the item. This doesn't mean you'll always get this sort of price, but it should be your goal—how you relax that depends on how much profit you intend to make.

Of course, good haggling skills are a must in situations where you'll be buying directly from the seller. Quickly assess how much the seller knows about the piece and how fairly the item is priced. Never insult a seller with an obnox-iously low price—remember that seller might be trying to make the same profit you might have in mind.

If you're speculating at online auctions, your best bet is to set maximum bids—and not exceed them—that will allow you the profit margin you desire. While it's true that sniping (last-second bidding) often brings in good prices, it might also incite impassioned bidding on your part, causing you to exceed your bid limit. A good alternative is to bid early in an auction and then forget about it. Although you might be outbid often, you might also find end-of-auction notices coming your way, bringing tidings of great deals that you've won, too. But, if you have the willpower to stay to your limit, snipe whenever possible.

Finally, try to avoid rampant speculative buying. If you're grabbing everything in sight, you might forget how much you're spending. Even if you are getting great deals, your outgo could quickly exceed your income. Try to keep a balance between sales and purchases, with the best situation being where auction profits are reinvested in future speculative purchases.

Flow, Show, or Stow Your Stuff

When buying on speculation, you need to be shrewd about when to time your selling, when you merely give potential buyers a glimpse of your goods-in-waiting, and when to store away your goods so they can age to a fine profit-bearing ripeness.

- **On Flowing Your Stuff:** Obviously, the key to profiting from an invested buy is selling when demand (and prices) will be highest. Look for events (historical, film, media) that will make your item particularly sought after—then sell! Sometimes the best time to sell is immediately after purchase. If you're holding a trendy item that is virtually impossible to obtain, demand will be high. However, if you hold on too long, the demand might bottom out and you'll be stuck with a fad gone bad (anyone want to buy some Pokemon cards or a talking Furby right now?)
- **On Showing Your Stuff:** Some of your best sales happen when you're not actively selling. If you have some great items that you're holing up, pop them up for view on a Web site. Frequently, visitors will ask if the items are for sale, which could spell great profits for you.
- **On Stowing Your Stuff:** Some items you speculate on will need time to "mature" to reach their highest value potential. If you're buying items like limited sculptures, Christmas ornaments, character icons, or whatever, you might need to sit on these awhile before the true value comes out. Figure that most pop-culture items need around 20 years to reach maturity—the point when younger folks of that day have also matured and now feel a tug of nostalgia for reminders of days gone by. Therefore, find good storage for these items—someplace dry, dark, and solid. Believe it or not, the time will click by sooner than you realize and suddenly, you're sitting on a nice nest egg of the things people are now clamoring for.

Many sellers have found great success in their speculative purchases, especially those who use the tactic as another one of many inventory procuring and positioning strategies. Be sure to consider speculative purchases of this sort as you seek to broaden your eBay offerings. Who knows—someone might be offering you a fortune for one of your speculative buys.

FORTUNE BOOST #44
BACK TO SCHOOL, BACK TO BUSINESS

Though it's highly unlikely you would take the summer off from selling and auctioning, the return of the fall season brings opportunities to reinvigorate your sales results. As students return to the halls of higher education, sellers have the opportunity to become a part of the bustle, starting with offering the sorts of things students will need as well as some nostalgic fare past students may wish to reclaim. And if you're eager to list where the students will be looking, autumn's the time to jump into the flurry of buying and selling that will help prepare you for a richly rewarding back-to-school promotion.

A Quick Study in Better Bargains

Every year, students tally up a laundry list of items they'll need for the coming semesters. Whether seeking out computer equipment, wireless communication devices, backpacks, clothes, or even dorm-room decor, more and more students are turning to online outlets for the things they need.

"I purchase supplies for school online," shared a returning student. "I have bought a laptop, textbooks, graphing calculators, and other necessary items at online auctions."

Recognizing today's students as adept online bargain hunters, auction and fixed-price venues are visibly catering to the scholarly crowd's needs. eBay regularly devotes attention to this annual selling season, giving front-page placement for all manner of listed goods generally found on students' shopping lists while also offering additional promotions including sweepstakes and giveaways. But beyond eBay, Yahoo Auctions likewise offers up home page real estate to their back-to-school promotion, citing this and Christmas as two of the most active selling seasons of each year. Sellers, then, have the opportunity to add their student-supportive goods to the pool, taking full advantage of the increased site traffic during the back-to-school season.

The Context of Texts

Of course, students are on the lookout for good reference books and current textbooks that they'll need for the coming year and which are traditionally priced at exorbitant rates in campus bookstores. Here again is where the online destinations are stepping up to offer students another option. For example, Half.com is boasting "millions of textbooks" for sale within their fixed-price listings. Of course, textbooks intended for classroom use must be current, a challenge in itself as many publishers update material practically every year. Still, even recent textbooks are of use to students, "I used to look for recent but not new books in my major," recalled a student. "That way, when I wrote up my labs, I had references the other students didn't have." (See Figure 44-1.)

Figure 44-1 Beyond eBay, be sure to make full use of the eBay-owned Half.com for listing student textbooks for fast fixed-price sales.

The Student as Seller

It stands to reason that the educated crowd is smart enough to see a business opportunity at their fingertips. Though students typically aren't interested in becoming bona fide online entrepreneurs (they're busy with their education), they have found the online circuit to be a great place to recoup some of last semester's expenses. Some part-time online sellers have found a market in the new batch of interns and students. Older students sell all sorts of items, from paperback books, video games, and music CDs, working to put a bit of spending money in their pockets.

Of course, for the full-time seller, it's useful to pay close attention to what the students themselves are selling and at what prices. It amounts to the kind of market research that better defines the demographics, needs, and desires of the campus.

Remembering the Class of 19-Something

But if you're not bent toward selling school-related supplies, there's still room for the collectibles dealer to get in on the back-to-school rush. The in-touch seller recognizes how this time of year stirs up feelings of nostalgia in yesteryear's student body. As we send off our young adults for the college campus or escort our

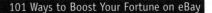

grade-schoolers to the bus stop, parents often yearn for the trinkets that embody memories of school days past. Naturally, as this currently includes the 30- and 40-something crowd, the prime bit of nostalgia in demand is the lunchbox. With its large collector base, lunchboxes are heavily traded year-round but especially so at this time of year. If you're tending an inventory that includes these treasured totes, be sure to get them within buyers' reach right away.

Beyond lunchboxes, recognize the nostalgic appeal of other such school-related items like pencil boxes, backpacks, character binders and notebooks, and even pencil-top erasers. Chances are, if it's something that makes you drift back to your blackboard memories, there are many buyers also eager to take part in the back-to-school ritual, whether they ever set foot on a campus or not.

FORTUNE BOOST #45
ROTATING YOUR MERCHANDISE
FOR YEAR-ROUND SALES

Whether due to seasonal appeal, a sudden and unexpected peak in interest, or a premeditated hype intended to drive a new trend, items in your inventory will likely have a "best time" to be put in front of your customers. To understand the ebbs and flows of product popularity and to shift attention to the various items in your inventory when the time is just right is what could be referred to as the "art" of *product rotation.*

And while some sellers prefer to spill out every single item in their inventory on the front table, others have found that careful flow and selective positioning of their wares is a better way to attract buyers at peak periods, keep them returning time and again to see what might show up next in your online front window, and keep that fortune steadily building every step of the way.

Keep Your Stock Current

First, here's a note for those who keep an online store: Although product rotation is a strategy that you might or might not choose to adopt, there is one tenet you simply cannot ignore: you can't sell what you no longer have. How many times have you visited online Web sites, eager to purchase some promised goods, only to be greeted by the words "SOLD OUT" stamped across many of the items prominently displayed? Further, have you ever been frustrated when you inquire about an item shown as available, only to find it was sold weeks ago? If so, you know that such a seller is clearly not minding the store. The point is, if an item is sold, get it off the virtual shelf and replace it with something you *do* have.

'Tis the Season

Naturally, seasonal items should be placed prominently in your virtual store window or featured in your current batch of eBay listings just prior to their annual peak period. The same goes for trendy items or those goods that are "all the rage" at the moment. If you have goods that herald an approaching holiday or are affiliated with the current public frenzy, get 'em to the front of your offerings, fast.

If you've come to anticipate certain times of the year when your top-dollar items tend to languish a bit, consider increasing your offering of lower-priced goods. Though it's natural that folks will shy away from big purchases at certain times of year (with annual tax time being one of the most notable), they're generally always in the mood to purchase something, right? Be sure to bring forth your low to mid-priced wares so there's still temptation to for your customers to find something affordable they'd like to bid on and buy.

Position, Then Reposition

If, despite your best marketing efforts, some goods still seem to elude your customers' desires, consider setting up a "sales table" in your Web store or listing a batch of marked-down auction items. Using the appeal of loss leaders (see Fortune Boost #34), remember how applying the label "sale" to an item can be enough to generate interest in an item without the need to drastically slash prices. And, to that end, you might consider procuring and rotating items for the sole purpose of keeping such a bargain area stocked at all times. Again, the lure of the good deals is often enough to get customers into your store, where they can stroll the rest of the aisles once they've come inside.

Take a Lesson from Your Customers

Finally, the key barometer of your overall product placement prowess will be determined by your customers. While some sellers get caught up into thinking they know how to best market their goods, the truth is that actual bids, wins, and sales will serve as the irrefutable report card. Monitor your eBay bidders' activity as well as that of the patrons who visit your online store, then be attentive to their wants and needs and be ready to shift your featured inventory at a click of the mouse when you see what's really hot—and what's really not—in your online inventory.

FORTUNE BOOST #46
MASTERING THE CRAFT OF CROSS-SELLING

Here's an effective sales strategy that, while quite simple, is too often overlooked by sellers as a fast and easy way to boost sales and increase end-of-the-day profits. *Cross-selling* is another of the time-honored marketing tactics that have long been used in consumerism and that some (but not enough) sellers have successfully employed in their eBay efforts. Here's how simple cross-selling can be in feeding your eBay fortune.

Leveraging from Your eBay Efforts

First, consider the work you put into your listing titles, ensuring that each and every word will provide the greatest potential to either be represented within the most common buyer keyword searches or will provide the additional amount of information to communicate more about the item (such as condition abbreviations) in a way that will compel a buyer to click in for a closer look. Considering that you have that potential bidder-buyer's attention now, why not take the opportunity to show off a few more of your great items that are up for sale? Yes, this is often known as placing a "commercial" in your listings but, so long as the commercial makes sense and could be considered of value to the customer, it's simply a good business tactic to use.

The Mechanics of Cross-Selling

It's true that in every eBay listing there's a link that allows lookers to "View Seller's Other Items," and that by itself is a method of cross-selling. However, a bland textual link like that sometimes isn't enough to really motivate some additional purchases by your customers. Many sellers aptly add this line to their eBay listing descriptions: "Be sure to click the link to see my other great items up for bid now!" That works, sort of, but the success rate of getting the potential buyer to actually peruse the seller's other goods by way of the eBay-provided text link relies, again, on the looker being motivated by a compelling written appeal.

A better approach leverages what eBay itself has learned: pictures are the best motivators of all. Recall how eBay discovered its sellers could get more looks and more purchases if a small thumbnail image preceded an item title in a search hit list. Savvy sellers have applied that tactic forward (though many were doing this prior to eBay ever offering the thumbnail image) by including images of other concurrent items up for bid *right in the description area of each of their listings.* Look at Figure 46-1 to see how a listing for a single movie lobby card (that's one of those 11"-x-14" pictures you often see in movie theater lobbies) includes thumbnail images of other lobby cards for the same film that are currently up for bid too.

To achieve the technique you see in Figure 46-1, all you need to employ is a bit of simple HTML. There are two methods to this technique:

1.   Insert a simple thumbnail image of other items you have up for sale that would be especially interesting to those looking at the current item. Your description text could read, "Be sure to see these other great lobby cards up for bid now. Just click on the "View Seller's Other Items" link to place your bids."

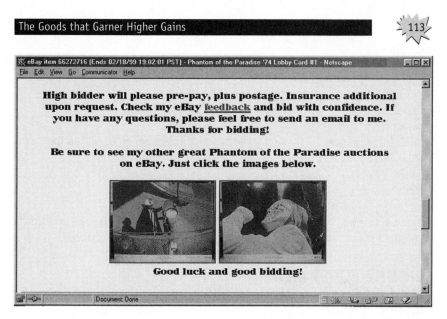

Figure 46-1 Including thumbnail images for similar concurrent item offerings within item descriptions is one of the best ways to succeed in cross-selling.

2. A more direct method would be to insert an actual link to the other item listings within eBay, represented with referenced images as you see demonstrated in Figure 46-1. This takes a bit more work, but for potentially popular or high-dollar items, it's worth the extra effort. You'll need to launch all similar listings within eBay first to obtain the actual URL reference of each item's listing page. Once you have the URLs, go back to each item listing page and click on the "Revise item" link where you can insert the HREF tag, along with thumbnail images, that will serve as clickable links to help bidders navigate quickly and easily to your other items.

For your convenience, here's the HTML code that was used to enable the anchored cross-sell images you see in Figure 46-1:

```
Be sure to see my other great Phantom of the Paradise auctions on eBay.
Just click the images below.
<P>
<A HREF="http://cgi.ebay.com/aw-
cgi/eBayISAPI.dll?ViewItem&item=58888495">
<IMG HEIGHT=150 WIDTH=200
```

```
SRC="http://www.geocities.com/Hollywood/Boulevard/8785/potp5.jpg"
ALT="Lobby Card #5"></A>
<A HREF="http://cgi.ebay.com/aw-cgi/
eBayISAPI.dll?ViewItem&item=58889743">
<IMG HEIGHT=150 WIDTH=200
SRC="http://www.geocities.com/Hollywood/Boulevard/8785/potp6.jpg"
ALT="Lobby Card #6"></A>
<BR>
```
Good luck and good bidding!

As simple as that, you can add cross-selling strategy to your listings and watch your bidders jump at the easy opportunity to buy more with less effort.

FORTUNE BOOST #47
SOLD TODAY AND AGAIN TOMORROW:
SELLING CONSUMABLES

While unique, rare, and collectible treasures and trinkets always do well at eBay as well as high-priced, high-value specialty and luxury goods, you'll see here that even everyday, run-of-the-mill items are sometimes just as popular with the millions of eBay shoppers. We're a consumer culture so that means, well, we *consume* (and how). Every day, shoppers around the world buy goods to sustain or improve their daily lifestyles, whether those goods are household supplies, clothing, footwear, computer supplies, and even health and beauty goods. Look at your daily and weekly purchasing habits, especially of those goods you buy again and again and again; those are "consumables," and if you can set your sights on selling the sorts of "boring old items" that are purchased by the masses on a recurring basis, you'll be setting yourself up to collecting a fortune on consumables.

Daily Needs

Just as you'd run to your corner market or brave the often-crowded aisles of the local Maul-Mart to grab those routine items you want and need on a regular basis, you can often find the same goods up for bid or Buy-It-Now at eBay. Savvy shoppers, bargain hunters, and those faced with stretching their budgets have found eBay to have become a truly viable alternative for purchasing everyday items. The big retailers have already learned this, those who routinely offer their backlog of brand-name closeouts, excess inventory, and refurbished returns. Consider these numbers: 29,000 lawn and garden items are sold every week as well as 2,000 vacuums. There's nothing terribly exciting about these items, except for the fact that they're selling at a fast rate week in and week out. Therefore, as you're establishing your sources of wholesale goods, don't skip over to the sexier (and far more competitive) electronics goods without stopping to see what's available to sell in the more mundane realm of small home appliances.

Frugal Footwear

And what if the "baby needs a new pair of shoes?" No problem because eBay has likewise become a fast-growing sector in footwear sales, with major retailers turning to the site to liquidate last year's styles, while cost-conscious shoppers are constantly on the prowl for a better price than they can find at the local shoe store. But this isn't a market just to be cornered by the authorized shoe dealers; some entrepreneurs have found staggering success in selling inventory acquired from stores that have gone out of business as well as outlet malls and wholesalers. The folks at eBay indicate the shoe business is booming, indicating that roughly 72 percent of all athletic shoes listed sell within the first 10 days. Beyond the shoes themselves, look to sell the other consumables here like shoelaces, shoe inserts, shoe polish (yes, for leather athletic shoes), and sport socks.

eBay for Babies?

Speaking of baby, expecting mothers are perhaps some of the most-skilled bargain hunters when it comes to providing for their little ones (and if ever you've seen them at garage sales, you'll know this is an irrefutable fact). Many have turned to eBay for their babies' needs and many in-touch sellers have seen this need remain consistent within the auction place. Consider these sorts of baby consumables that are selling at eBay in high numbers every day:

- Baby formula
- Diapers (cloth and disposable)
- Baby bottles
- Baby bedding
- Onesies (can't have enough of these easy-access baby garments)

Here's Looking at You, and You're Looking Good

Perhaps you fancy entering the field of fitness merchandising. If you do, enter eBay today because the site is brimming with all manner of goods to help you look and feel better every day. You'll find everything from vitamins to protein powders to aerobic steps to instructional videos to the latest in top-quality exercise equipment. As the baby boomers continue to age, their interest in staying fit is getting them interested in shopping eBay for their health needs.

And what about body-care products—skin care, hair care, pampering baths, and so on? Here again is another category of everyday goods that are thriving on eBay. Rather than spend premium prices at "body salons," eBay shoppers have found the auction to be the place to purchase their personal care items at fractional prices.

Office Essentials

Don't forget the very instruments of your online endeavor—your personal computer and all its various accessories and supplies. eBay has become a major outlet for buying and selling these sorts of goods, anything from ink cartridges, reams of printer paper, specialty papers, and, of course, plenty of refurbished and remanufactured equipment that you can buy or sell to millions of active shoppers.

If You Consume It, Why Not Sell It?

Consumable goods account for roughly 60 percent of dollars spent by consumers and, in the online realm, this has been translated to billions of dollars spent each year. No matter what the economic climate, goods like soap, diapers, and beauty supplies will always be in demand. Some of the most successful sellers at eBay have learned to look away from some of the glitzy and glamorous goods and have, instead, charted their own regular purchases. These profitable sellers have learned that when customers buy consumable goods, they'll surely be back for more.

FORTUNE BOOST #48
SPRING CLEANING STRATEGIES THAT REALLY PAY OFF

When it's the time of year that both love and pollen are thick in the air, it's also time for that cultural ritual known as "spring cleaning." It's a time in which all manner of odds and ends are wrested from their respective nooks and crannies, items that seemingly secreted themselves away in a last-ditch effort for survival. And although garage sales and flea markets routinely feature the excesses of our lives, so too does the online marketplace. If you're ready to get serious about your spring cleaning in a way that will feed your fortune, here are some points to ponder to better ensure that your efforts pay off in the most profitable ways.

Justify Your Stuff

If you're simply sick of looking at all the junk that has found its way into the corners and crevices of your living space, drag it out—but not to the curb just yet. As you've been frequenting the online marketplace, you now know that folks will bid on just about anything. Log on to eBay first and search for items similar to what you've just unearthed (checking current as well as recently closed auctions) and you'll quickly learn how much demand is out there and what folks are willing to pay for that unassuming item you would just as soon get rid of. And, though you can't be assured of making a fast fortune on each and every one of your soon-to-be-discarded items, you'd be surprised what people are willing to bid to take that clutter off your hands and how quickly it can tally up to a satisfying sum (recall the example from Fortune Boost #2).

Research the Promising Pieces

It *does* sometimes happen—we do come across an item or two that could easily command a significant chunk of change. If you think you've uncovered such a holy grail, do your homework before you offer it up. Besides checking in at eBay, conduct a Web-wide search (using your favorite search portal) to learn more about the piece. Determine the origin, originality, and potential obscurity of the item. Whenever possible, discover what other items might be similar to yours. This will help you associate it to other related treasures, especially if your find is something of a "missing link." The research you do will not only better educate you about the item and its value, but also it will allow you to create a highly informative and well-presented item listing that shows potential bidders and buyers that you *know* what you have.

Some Trash Is Trash

Always keep your feet on the ground. Many of your knickknacks, doo-dads, and gewgaws are truly junk. Many busted, broken, or simply bizarre items are nothing more than trash and, if you can bear to look at them any more, just dispose of them. Of course, even though these odds and ends you may have don't seem to command much attention at your online selling places (eBay or others), you can still make one last effort to pawn them off for a buck or two (or less) at a garage sale or flea market. Key point here: it might not be worth the time and expense to list and ship an item that only pulls down two bits. And, if you still can't find someone to offer you 25 cents for that funky little item, you could still consider donating it to a local charity or thrift outlet. It might amount to a potential deduction on next year's income tax return.

Priced to Sell

While it's very exciting to dream of turning your trash into cash, remember the overall goal of spring cleaning: to get rid of this stuff! Therefore, price your items to sell. If auctioning, offer low starting bids with no reserve. If there's a market for the item and there's potential for decent bids, let the bidders do the work. Price your stuff too high and bidders will look elsewhere. If selling for fixed prices, then price the item to sell (you don't want it languishing and cluttering up your virtual shelves). Either way, it's not necessary to *give* your stuff away (especially if it's something truly collectible or otherwise desirable), but remember that any profit you can glean from your castoffs is better than nothing.

Whistle While You Work

If you're content to just get rid of the junk that clutters you life, enjoy the process of selling it off for whatever you can get (this is an especially beneficial outlook for newer sellers to adopt as they learn new ways to use and harness eBay's fortune potential). Many sellers marvel at the eagerness of bidders and buyers who clamber after your throwaways. It's fun and often amusing to watch others scuffle for the stuff you could give a hang about. You might not necessarily make a mint as you clean out your castoffs, but the little money you might make could fund a more profitable inventory investment or offset the cost of much-needed auction office equipment. In these cases, be happy with what you get and enjoy the fact that others are now paying you to clean out your closet.

FORTUNE BOOST #49
HO, HO, HO FOR HOLIDAY SELLING

Before you've even had a chance to carve up your jack-o'-lantern, it seems the yuletide season has already arrived. Retailers look to the holiday season as their big time to make big sales, and they'll roll out every hook and harbinger to get customers into the spirit of giving (and that means *buying*). Although you may not be ready to pull out your plastic Saint Nicholas and eight "tinny" reindeer, plan ahead as the big day approaches and shift your plan over to some sensible seasonal sales strategies. Here are some things you can do for your listing to entice the most holiday bidders, bring smiles to your customers' faces, and ring up some tidings of great profit for yourself.

Do You See What I See?

A real key to holiday auction success will be offering the items people want most but can't often find. Do your usual market research, trolling the auctions sites to find out if what you'll offer is plentiful or plenty scarce. Remember that quality, condition, and completeness become ever so critical when hooking the holiday hunters. If you see other items like yours, but yours is clearly superior in condition and completeness, it will probably be the one that gift givers will want to give. Be clear in the distinction and even use some colorful ad copy to show that, this season, yours are the best goods in town.

The Price That Entices

If the Hallmark keepsake you're offering is sold out in stores but seemingly plentiful in the auction venues, you'll be in competition with the other sellers to catch the bidders' attention. In these situations, you'll do well to lower your opening bid price and forego the reserve price option. If you've done your research well, you'll know what your item is worth and know the bidders can be trusted to bring you a fair price. Bidders will be looking for a potential bargain, though most hot items with low opening bids often soar past those that have high opening bids or seasonally insensitive high reserve prices. Try to resist plopping a high opening bid or reserve price that could telegraph to bidders that the eventual price of your item might exceed their holiday budget. No buyer likes to think they're going to get gouged during the festive shopping season.

Timings of Great Joy

Never is timing of such importance to auction sellers than during the holiday season—that's because timing is of *critical* importance to bidders this time of year. Bidders are looking for and bidding on items that can be won, paid for, and delivered in plenty of time before the big holiday arrives. Sellers can do well to foresee the shoppers' mire and take steps to make their potential win a smooth and easy task.

Every year folks shop and bid earlier and earlier in an effort to get the "work" of the holiday out of the way. Shoppers have already mobilized in hopes of beating the crowds and finding the items they want most. If you have the goods folks are clamoring for, get them listed now. Shoppers want to finish their buying quickly and, if you wait too long, many of your potential bidders might have already completed their shopping tour of duty, leaving you with a potential decrease in bids.

Then consider the day and time your auction will close. It's a hectic time for most treasure hunters, and many will appreciate the auctions that end at a reasonable hour (around 6:00 p.m. or 7:00 p.m. PST). Weekends are still the best days to end those auctions, but remember that Sundays are going to find more and more potential bidders attending additional church and other seasonal functions.

And while it was mentioned in Fortune Boost #8, it bears reiterating that you should not forget to consider the duration of your auction. Although seven-day auctions are often most popular year-round, three-day and five-day auctions become increasingly enticing to bidders during the holiday season (sometimes even a one-day blitz will work wonders for you and your bidders). A shorter auction spells a quicker transaction and another checkmark of success on a winning bidder's shopping list. This is especially applicable in the last couple of weeks before the holidays arrive.

Oh Come, All Ye Bidders

If you give your item a clear and descriptive title, you'll like find more bidders visiting your auction's doorstep. Bidder-shoppers are often looking for specific items. Give them specific item titles that describe the product by name, color, style, or whatever. Try to use as many keywords that will show up in as many search "hits" as possible. Again, leave out useless tags like "hard to find," "L@@K," "great gift," or other such meaningless additions. If you have what bidders want, they'll already know how hard to find it is or what sort of gift it might make. Give them more definitive information up front and you'll find that more of them will give your auction a closer look. And, if you already have a great description and still have room in your item's title, squeeze in whether yours is a one-day, three-day or five-day auction (if that's the route you choose). This is an immediate enticement to bidders who are running out of shopping days.

Too Much (Eye) Candy Will Spoil Their Appetites

Many sellers like to roll out a barrage of excess yuletide glitter and glee in their listings to the point that it becomes enough to gag an elf. Overdo it and your bidders will grab the next Polar Express out of there. While you've done well to wield your HTML skills sparingly, it's especially important that you fight the temptation to roll out the biggest, brightest, blinking-est holiday listing—it's typically very slow to load and will only succeed in detracting from the great item you're auctioning. If you like, throw in a simple holiday image or a nice holiday font, but leave the intricate animated gifs and blaring muzak out, giving more attention to the picture and great description of your item instead.

Yellow Snow

Tread very carefully here. Although there's a joyous sound in the air, a flat note might be heard if a winning bidder takes the next sleigh ride out without paying up. Though most auction-goers know the routine and frustration of dealing with dead-beat bidders, the holiday season doesn't offer as much time to sort such matters out. If you feel it's necessary, clearly state in your listing description when you expect to receive payment from the winning bidder. Most honest bidders will understand the need to close transactions quickly during the holiday season. If a bidder does stiff you, just move on to the next highest bidder or relist the item, knowing there's a lump of coal coming in that bad bidder's stocking (or feedback profile).

Also, be sure you state your shipping terms clearly in your auction's description so bidders know if they can expect to receive their winnings in time for the holiday. During this time of year, make special shipping methods available to your bidders (Federal Express Overnight, UPS Second Day, or USPS Express Mail). If the bidders are willing to pay the extra charge, accommodate them with the special delivery services your usual carrier provides. Sometimes, offering fast shipping options could determine whether a bidder will bid on your item or shop elsewhere. And, more than any other time of year, be sure you and your buyer agree to the shipping method and delivery expectation *before* the package leaves your hands.

With all those packages being shipped about, damage will strike something, somewhere. Encourage the buyer to pay for insurance and clearly state that you will not be responsible if the buyer waives the extra protection. Then, whether you'll open a virtual returns desk or not, be sure to clearly state your return policy in your item description. During this time of year, many bidders are prone to impulse bidding and buying—some may change their minds after the item is in hand. To protect yourself from those who may bid today and refund tomorrow, make it clear up front what your policy will be if buyers change their minds.

Post-Holiday Sales

Consider this: hasn't there been a holiday in your past when you didn't get *everything* you were wishing for? The same goes for many auction-goers out there today, and there will be hordes of them looking to fill those empty spots on their wish lists. After the holiday passes, sellers can typically find a resurgence of bidders still looking for the stuff they *really* wanted this year, as well as those hungry to feed on post-holiday closeouts and other such bargains. Unless you need a holiday break yourself, keep those listings coming and, if you're looking to unload a bunch of stuff before the new year, list items with low opening bids and positioned as end-of-the-season loss-leaders, then bidders do the rest.

FORTUNE BOOST #50
YIKES! UNWANTED GIFTS: FROM REGIFTING TO DEGIFTING

According to the Seinfeld Primer, *regifting* is that practice of giving a gift you've received from someone else. And while superficially considered bad form, regifting of unwanted items is reportedly practiced by 53 percent of Americans according to those analytical tattletales at the United Mileage Plus Visa Card Shopping Index. The newest twist on the recycling of all manner of gaudy jewelry, garish holiday sweaters, and carbon-dated fruitcakes is the opportunity the Internet provides in summarily *degifting* such goods, offering them outright for sale or bid to the worldwide marketplace. Just be sure your Great Aunt Pat isn't expecting to see her hideous metal sculpture when she visits again this spring (and hope she isn't reading this, too!).

Is It Right to Degift?

Of course, the matter of ethics will be your first hurdle to clear: is it proper to even consider selling off a gift that was recently given to you? Well, as regifting has gained something of a humorous acceptance in our modern society, degifting seems poised for equal acceptance for the frugal, fiscally minded, and Internet-enlightened among us. Besides, there may be someone out there trolling eBay or elsewhere in cyberspace who can truly appreciate the gift that we simply cannot warm up to. Yet, with ethics being the crux of this question of whether it's right to degift, why not take it directly from an ethics expert? According to Judith Martin, a.k.a. "Miss Manners," regifting is fine provided you don't get caught doing it.

"If you're going to recycle a gift, you must cover all traces that it's been given before," Martin warns.

Of course, getting caught *degifting* an item online is much less risky than actually regifting it at next year's gift exchange. Of course, now degifting involves gaining cash in the item's place—an ethical taboo?

Ethics columnist Randy Cohen sees nothing wrong with selling an unwanted gift. "If you accept the idea that [regifting] is okay, then I think a sale is okay unless you believe touching money taints you."

Ultimately, it comes down to your personal value system and how much of a beating your conscience might take if you sell a former gift. Of course, returning the item to where it was originally purchased for cash back doesn't seem to yield a much different result—only the method has changed.

Marketing Your Degifted Goods

Assuming you've decided it's okay to offer your unwanted gifts online, you need to decide where you'll put them up for sale. Naturally, eBay seems the most obvious venue of redistribution. It has become the first site that comes to mind when people think of unloading unwanted goods or seeking out an odd artifact. In fact, analyst Daniel Mackeigan has noted that auction sites like eBay tend to triple their gross sales after the holidays, so you're in good company.

A start at eBay, then, will most likely help you find an appreciative owner for your wayward gifts, given that millions of shoppers continue to scour the online offerings even after the holidays have passed. But the nagging question you might encounter could be, "Should I actually *admit* this is an unwanted gift?" Depending on the item, you might not need to divulge anything—garish holiday ties and Chia Pets seem to shout out their useless yuletide provenance. But, if you want to have a bit of fun, you might explain that you're degifting an item that either didn't fit you or is something you already possess. With a wink and a smile, you will likely add a bit of charm to the item in the bidders' eyes. Why not?

Then again, if the item is more akin to being a collectible, there's really no disclosure required. It's just another item that you're offering up for bid in a marketplace that regularly accommodates such goods. In fact, you may find that these goods you offer, if outside your usual style of inventoried offerings, could lead you to new customers and vice versa. Many sellers have claimed that selling such a "one-off" item ultimately helped them branch into a new commodity.

Then there's the handmade gift that can't be bought in stores (and sometimes for good reason). If you've received a spotted, speckled, sculpted bird that you're likely never to encounter again (if you're lucky) market it as a "one-of-a-kind" piece. Handmade goods are quite popular in the online marketplace and, just because the ceramic gooney won't enhance your current decorating scheme, it might be just the ticket for a customer out there seeking a truly unique item. And how.

And while you may elect to post a degift to your online fixed-price venue (if you have one), you should take heed of the original caveat of regifting: ensure that the original gift-giver will not learn of your activity. Therefore, if your friend Susie likes to frequent your eBay Store or other Web store to see what you're selling, make sure the purple-and-orange ceramic frog she gave to you isn't prominently priced to sell. Oops!

Guilty Conscience?

If you're still struggling with the moral issue of whether or not you should sell a gift that just didn't strike your fancy, avoid the guilt and hang on to the item for 6 to 12 months. If, after that time, you're still no closer to embracing the whatchamacallit, consider again if it's time to set it free in the online wilderness.

FORTUNE BOOST #51
REMARKETING SOMEONE ELSE'S LOW-PROFIT LISTINGS

As was mentioned earlier in this collection of fortune-boosting tips, a good source of profit-bearing goods to sell is available within eBay every day. Often, sellers have found undermarketed items that seem to flounder and flail, never capturing bidders' attention nor garnering their true value in the online marketplace. Of course, to the shrewd seller, these are the "diamonds in the rough" to be eagerly mined and repositioned to benefit the bottom line. In this simple but effective tip, you'll read of an actual example of a poorly marketed listing that bore the seller (that's *me* in this case) not one but two high-profit gains with room to cull even more.

The Smiling Bandit

During a mining session within eBay, I stumbled upon a rather silly little item that plucked a nostalgic string within me: a listing for a collection of Frito Bandito pencil-top erasers, the sort that kids in the late 1960s were able to collect when they purchased snack-sized bags of Frito's corn chips. I saw several listings for these nifty little pieces of advertising yesteryear (albeit sorely politically incorrect today), most for single erasers and most selling for about $10 to $15 each. Searching deeper and using some intentional misspellings ("bandeeto"), I unearthed a listing for nine of these erasers, of various colors, all in excellent, unused condition. Their opening bid was just $19, yet there were no bids. Beyond the misspelling in the item title (the seller's first major misstep), there wasn't an image of the erasers (second big blunder). A quick e-mail later, I learned from the seller that the set consisted of some of the more difficult colors to locate, the sort that impassioned collectors were eagerly trying to uncover. To make a long story short, I won the auction at a final price of just $29 (one other lowballing bidder discovered the hidden gems, too). The seller reluctantly honored my win, noting that I got a "killer deal." So true. From a purchasing standpoint, I *did* find a bargain and the story could have ended there.

Time to Remarket

Of course, the story didn't end there. Upon receiving the erasers and noting them to be in excellent condition, just as promised, I knew that I only really wanted one of them for my personal collection; the rest were intended for resale. A bit more research on my part and I learned which eraser colors were hardest to find and which seemed to be more common (the common colors would still appeal to collectors who hadn't yet rediscovered this fun little novelty from years ago, and the rare colors would attract the hard-core "completist" collectors). My approach: offer a set of three erasers that included two of the more common colors and one of the rare colors. Here's the logic behind that decision:

- At an average market value of around $15 each, the two common colors could garner $30 alone, while the rarer color could double or triple that amount.

- Offering one rare color along with two common colors would ensure that I could sell *all* of the erasers at top dollar without seeing only the rare colors sell and the common colors potentially languish and undersell (had I chosen to list each individually).
- Offering a group of three mixed colors—rare and common—would serve to incite more battling between bidders, casual and convicted collectors alike.

The approach already made sense and stood to gain me a better return than the seller before me, but there was still a bit more opportunity to be seized.

Dressing Up the Bandito

Recall that the previous seller launched a listing with a misspelling and a listing content as bland as an unsalted corn chip. The remedy: apply a bit of simple HTML and imagery to spice up the bandito. A quick search of the Internet provided me with images of the bandito as displayed on collector sites as well as confirmation of the origin and history of the Frito Bandito (it's always a good idea to provide a bit of history, especially when it's of a wistful nostalgic sense, to motivate bidders). Also, I included an image of the three erasers that would be up for bid, as shown in Figure 51-1 (displayed in color, of course, on the eBay site to further incite color-collecting Bandito enthusiasts).

With this, I was ready to launch a mere third of the collection of erasers I had purchased just a week earlier.

Making Out Like a Bandit

Although I considered even $30 would be a great profit on my listing (remember that I purchased *nine* of these for just $29 and here I was offering only a third of that collection), I was pleased to see my remarketing tactics paid off perfectly. When the dust settled and the final bid was in, this remarketed listing collected $89! A great return on an easily repositioned listing for a popular item. I decided to wait a few days and then list *another* collection of three erasers, two common colors and one rare. The result: the second remarketed listing earned $71 (I attribute the price drop-off to the fact that the bidder from the first listing was the most impassioned of the current audience of collectors; the runner-up of that auction won the second listing). Of course, I could have contacted the underbidder directly at the close of the first listing but decided to use this as a way to continue testing my remarketing tactic.

Results Come from Wise Remarketing

As you can see, there's plenty of profit to be found when you discover "lost treasures" amid the tens of millions of listings at eBay. The next time you see a listing for an undervalued item and think to yourself, "Gee, that seller should try a

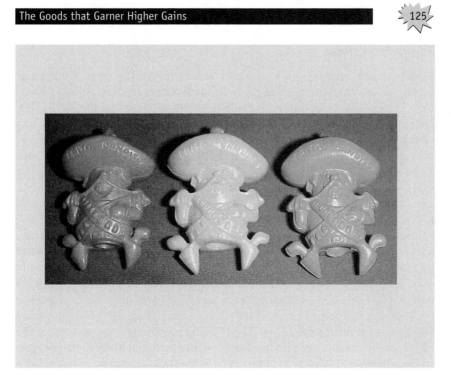

Figure 51-1   This former Frito spokesman sold for mere crumbs when grossly underrepresented. A bit of image management turned him into a fortune-bearing favorite.

different approach to gain what that thing's really worth," consider snatching up the unpolished diamond and practice a bit of remarketing yourself. And of my effort with the Frito Bandito, well I spent $29, I gained $131 ($89 + $71 - $29) in unburdened profit, and I *still* have three more erasers of my own, two common, one rare. *Ayyy-yi-yi-yiiii.*

FORTUNE BOOST #52
BUNDLING FOR BUNDLES OF MONEY

As you just completed reading the example of a remarketing tactic explained in Fortune Boost #51, look again to see the secondary tactic at work in that success story: bundling.

Although, by this point, it might seem unthinkable but, yes, sometimes, a stand-alone item seems to never earn to its potential or, worse yet, fails to find a buyer at all. Despite effective item titles, compelling descriptions, and terrific images, some items seem to struggle—by their own merits—to always attract the bidders' eye. Don't give up hope, though, because with just a bit of bundling, that is offering several items together in the same listing, you can turn a washout into a watershed of profit.

How Bundling Helps

Sometimes, all an item needs to become a successful auction earner is the proper setting. Taken literally, consider items regularly found in table settings: silverware, cutlery, dishes, and such. Considered singly, any one of these items might not have a persuasive draw to bidders. However, collect them together in a way where their interactive purpose is easy to envision and apply, well then you've offered a bundled "solution." When it comes to bundling, think "solution"—what might a buyer need in order to gain an answer to some problem or see immediate value in the items presented in a listing. Back to the table-setting example, consider the offering of napkin rings. By themselves, napkin rings might or might not be so compelling, but pull actual cloth napkins into the rings (maybe festive holiday napkins for appropriately decorated napkin rings) and you've provided a setting, a use, and maybe even the nudge the looker needs to see that those napkin rings are must-haves.

Consider, then, the Frito Bandito example and how a bundling approach not only helped earn a better overall price for the listing (three desirable items offered together) but also helped ensure that the more common-colored erasers wouldn't languish in an inventory. If you have "wallflower" items, the sort that folks simply don't seem to warm up to when you offer them singly, try to bundle them with a complimentary item and turn that stale inventory into more profit.

An Alternative Approach to Bundling

Now recall the discussion of cross-selling in Fortune Boost #46 and how effective it can be to include images and active links within an auction listing, encouraging and enabling shoppers to easily discover other concurrent listings you have running. This was, in actuality, another form of bundling, especially as referenced in the example shown in Figure 46-1. In that example, a group of lobby cards promoting the same film were being offered concurrently. In some cases, this can be a better approach than bundling all in a single listing if you anticipate that you can earn a better per-piece price for the items. The trick is to offer them *all at the same time* to encourage spirited buyers to bid on each of the individual auctions in order to gain a complete set. Use the cross-selling technique previously discussed to ensure that bidders know *and see* the other like-items you have available.

Once you try bundling, you'll surely see how providing grouped offerings can translate into great fortune for you.

FORTUNE BOOST #53
LET'S GO DUTCH

While on the topic of leveraging the power of grouping goods for greater gains, take a quick look again at the historically long-running auction format of the Dutch auction.

Recall that eBay got its start by hosting traditional (ascending-price) and Dutch auctions. Realizing at the outset that some sellers would come to the online auction parlor with quantities of identical goods (cases of crankshafts, boxes of bow-ties, palettes of pot-holders), eBay immediately provided a time- and money-saving vehicle allowing the seller to offer a quantity of identical goods within the same listing. High-volume sellers have found how Dutch auctions can save on listing time and cost while also moving out greater quantities of goods. If you've been selling awhile but have been avoiding the potential of the Dutch auction, here's your chance to get reacquainted with a time-honored money-maker.

Why Go Dutch?

If you regularly deal in large volumes of the same item—perhaps as part of a bulk or wholesale inventory purchase—you may find it easier for you and your bidders if you use the Dutch auction format. Here's why:

- Dutch auctions allow you to list high volumes of the same item up for bid (or sale, in the case of a fixed-price listing where you'll specify that multiple units are available) within a single listing. This saves time and fees over listing the same item, singly, over and over again.
- Dutch auctions allow you to have more of your inventory available at one time (albeit the same item) rather than projecting the perception that you have only one such unit for sale.
- Dutch auctions allow you to sell complete identical sets of items in a way that caters to buyers who often prefer to purchase in multiple quantities (think dinnerware, clothing, picture frames, storage containers, and so on).
- Dutch auctions enable you to sell more and ship less. That is, you can sell multiple units to a single customer yet manage the delivery with just one shipment to one address.
- Dutch auctions allow you to manage tens or hundreds of items all within a single listing, reducing your need to track multiple identical auctions.
- Dutch auctions prevent you from perceptually flooding the market with numerous identical listings that can often become annoying to buyers who are searching for goods.

For these key reasons, if you're selling identical units of an item, consider using the Dutch auction method to push out more inventory with less effort. That alone is a key ingredient to boosting an eBay fortune.

FORTUNE BOOST #54
BECOMING AN EXPERT IN YOUR FIELD

One surefire way to increase your customer base and improve your eBay profits is to become recognized as an expert in offering and representing certain sorts of goods.

A common answer to the question, "What should I sell at eBay" often seems the most obvious: "Sell what you know." By that, new or emerging sellers are encouraged to deal in the sorts of goods they truly understand, personally, technically, and historically. How do you become an expert and turn that expertise into profit at eBay? Good question. Read on.

What Do You Know?

Again, it starts with determining what sorts of items you tend to know the most about. Each of us has plenty of knowledge about certain sorts of goods: crafts, comic books, electronics, Eames-era kitsch, marionettes, or movie memorabilia. The fact is, we have all become specialists in something, either through our work or through our play. Begin with your passions to determine if that's where you can become successful in selling such goods at eBay.

How Do You Learn More?

The best follow-up question to, "Sell what you know," is when the budding seller asks, "So how do I learn even more?" The quest for additional knowledge in a professed area of interest or expertise is what will mark you as a trusted source of information among your customers. The good news is that enhancing your expertise has become easier than ever. Consider these ways to sharpen your acumen:

- Review all the reference books you can find. Scour the online booksellers constantly (and don't forget the used and out-of-print book market represented online by ABEBooks at www.abebooks.com) for materials that deal with your area of specialization. The real experts are always surrounded by a vast and ever-growing reference library.
- Search your local community for local classes (collegiate courses for credit or personal enrichment sessions) and clubs where enthusiasts like you gather to discuss and learn more.
- Search the Internet for information. These days, almost every answer you need can be found online so keep your search engine revving.
- Network with others who share your passion to learn more of what they know and have discovered.

Most often, you'll find there's plenty of information to be gleaned from sources just mentioned; the sort that will give you the background to build an impressive and obvious expertise.

Going to the Source Itself: eBay as a Fount of Expert Information

If it's true that experience is the best teacher, then each of us is a veritable "professor" in our own right thanks to our personal experiences and interactions at the eBay site. As you further enhance your expertise, don't forget the wealth of knowledge all around you at eBay:

What have *you* bid on lately? Review the details of the items you purchase carefully and make note of why you decided to make the purchase. Chances are there was some distinguishing factor about the item, one that other buyers would hope to learn from you when *you're* selling.

What are other sellers saying about the kinds of goods you want to specialize in? In a classic case of "watch and learn," astute sellers continually review other sellers' goods and carefully study images and descriptions, either to validate a present understanding or to discover new aspects about certain goods. As you build your expertise and begin sharing such pearls of wisdom in your listings, it's a fair bet that others will be learning from you, too.

What are the buyers doing at eBay? Look closely at the number of bids and the final high bid values for items like those you'll specialize in. Many buyers, themselves, are experts and many can sniff out an expert's offering over a novice's dabbling. Carefully watch all the completed listings at eBay and study each to see why some sold well while others sputtered and sank.

Most importantly, stay involved in your area of desired expertise. Read constantly, listen carefully, and bid wisely on the sorts of goods you aim to specialize in. Be tireless in your quest for knowledge and you'll soon be an expert yourself. Then, when you list goods for sale, let the appropriate amount of that hard-earned expertise shine to instill confidence in your buyers and gain higher profits along the way.

FORTUNE BOOST #55
LICENSED TO SELL

Depending on how long you've been selling, how much you've been selling, and how much more you intend to sell (hopefully up to the point where you can declare you've made your own fortune), you may or may not have crossed over into the realm of having become a bona-fide business. Many sellers are doing quite well without a license, buying and reselling goods happily and collecting a nice little profit. The only problem is when sellers decide to stay in this business opportunity for good (and why not?) to pursue higher levels of earnings (again, why not?). Are these sellers conducting business lawfully, though? Are they paying their requisite taxes to Uncle Sam? Are they operating within local jurisdiction rules and regulations? If not, and if these sellers are becoming quite fiscally prominent in their auctioning results, the authorities may be paying an unannounced visit—and when that happens, it's usually not a very pleasant experience. Rather than duck and hide in the realm of online selling, here are the ways and means to get officially "licensed to sell."

What Sort of License Do You Need?

First things first: determine which sort of license you'll need to legally operate a "going business concern" within your particular state. Begin by visiting the Web

Figure 55-1 Visit for assistance on how to obtain a license and start up your bona-fide business.

site of your local State Board of Equalization (just perform an online search for "board of equalization" and include your state name in your search string). Once you've found the site, locate a link or perform a search for a "seller's permit." This is so you can properly register your business and set up a schedule to remit *sales and use tax* payments for your in-state sales. Now, if you're planning on operating solely from your residence in a virtual manner, you shouldn't need to register for an actual "business license." Those are required for folks who sell particular sorts of goods (such as food, machinery, and so forth) or perform certain sorts of services (such as beauticians, chiropractors, and others). When your business broaches the realm of providing certain services, especially those that will involve actual dispensing of products or services to customers from your business location, you may need a business license and you will likely need to consult your City Hall to determine if your location is appropriately zoned for such activity (that means you can't start entertaining a flow of customers, deliveries, and so forth out of your home, as it may conflict with the zoning of your neighborhood). And for even more help and guidance, visit the Small Business Administration Web site (www.sba.gov).

Steps to Getting Licensed

Once you understand what sorts of rules and regulations will apply to your business, it becomes a matter of contacting the proper agencies and putting the licensing wheels into motion. Here's what you'll need to do:

1. Contact you local Board of Equalization to obtain an application for the appropriate seller's permit or other such license (these vary by state). You can call, visit in person, or conveniently download and apply online from the BOE web site.
2. You'll need to provide some information about your business as follows:

   a. Business commodity and intent.
   b. Business bank account details (this could be your own account for a Sole Proprietorship arrangement).
   c. Estimated business income.
   d. Copies of your Social Security card and state driver's license.
   e. Applicable processing fees or security deposits (based on the anticipated income of the business).

Depending on the procedures in your state, your application for a seller's permit might also allow you to effectively record the *fictitious business name* for your operation (if not covered in the permit application, you may need to make direct contact with you local county clerk's office). Once you've successfully completed and filed your application, your local Board of Equalization should provide you with all the necessary instructions and forms to begin a schedule of submitting the in-state sales taxes you've collected. Remember, when you're licensed, you're required to collect the appropriate sales and use tax percentage for each sale (eBay allows you to specify this percentage within the item listing form) and then forward the collected taxes to your local government on a regular basis—usually quarterly.

So What's It All Worth?

At this point, many sellers ask what benefit is to be gained by getting licensed. It's a good question; here are "perks:"

- You can legally submit your annual taxes using the *Schedule C, Profit (or Loss) from Business or Profession* form, allowing you to itemize and deduct all incurred business expenses from your taxable income. If you use this form to report your eBay income and deduct expenses yet *aren't* properly licensed, you might be subject to an audit.
- You can qualify for special business accounts at your bank, with a lender, or with a credit card issuer. These often provide benefits only provided to valid business owners.

- You can purchase inventory at wholesale or resale rates, avoiding retail pricing and taxes when you provide your valid business license number.
- Depending on how your business might grow and expand, you can investigate other forms of business structure (e.g. limited liability, S-corporation) and incur protections to your personal assets while also qualifying for employer benefits such as health plans.

Rather than spin the wheel of fate and wonder if the federal and local governments will notice that tidy fortune you've been building for yourself, be sure to look into getting properly licensed and propel yourself forward into the realm of "big business." Oh, and don't forget to check with your local agencies and tax consultants for any and all specific matters that might pertain to you.

FORTUNE BOOST #56
BUYING FOR RESALE

To be a truly successful seller, you'll need to become an especially adept buyer. If you've been selling for awhile, you know that one great buy or an attic full of stuff isn't going to last forever and is not likely to support your auction business for an extended period. In order to ensure your success you can maintain an inventory full of tempting and profit-bearing goods. You'll want to be sure you embody the traits of a savvy reseller and employ the uncompromising tactics of sound reinvestment to keep your business operating comfortably in the black (and on to the land of rolling green).

The Reseller's Resolve

To be a good reseller, it's important to approach that part of your business with only the purist resale objectives in mind. Resolute resellers, therefore, might see great items as great inventory based on the following criteria:

- They appreciate an item for its ability to generate another sale, to broaden their offerings, and to please their customers.
- They are in business to sell. They don't have the luxury of becoming emotionally attached to their resale merchandise.
- They will buy new and different sorts of items if they sense a trend beginning, customers continue to ask for such items, or there's otherwise an opportunity to expand their businesses by appealing to a different customer demographic.

Casting a Critical Eye on Reinvestment

Operating under such an objective mind-set, ask yourself these questions as you consider purchasing an item for resale:

- Can you purchase an item or items at a price that affords a reasonable profit?
- Can you resell the item relatively quickly? You don't want your money tied up in inventory for too long.
- Is there demand for the item that has been proven in the online auction arena?
- If you're dealing in collectibles, do you know which items are rare and which are more common? You'll want to hunt down the elusive items to make larger profits. (Hint: Talk with other sellers and dealers to learn what their customers are most eager to purchase, and then explore the availability of those items yourself.)
- Is there an upcoming event (news development, movie release, and so on) that could reinvigorate demand for a particular item or group of items you have a chance to purchase cheaply?

The Bottom Line

As a final litmus test, you should strive to acquire inventory that will yield a profit in line with your profit margin goals (refer back to the formulas in Fortune Boost #30). Beyond this, seek out a good mix of items that appeal to many customers or a focused set of items that are sought after by serious buyers (if you can achieve both, all the better). And though some of this presented here might seem a bit mercenary in nature, recognize that your resale success will rest with how discerning and objective you can be when you reinvest in your online inventory.

FORTUNE BOOST #57
PROFITABLE PRESELLING TACTICS

When opportunities arise to get a jump on the goods shoppers will be craving (such as those items that are seasonal or coincide with a widely known or regarded event or cultural "happening"), keep a close eye on the manufacturers that are working overtime to release desirable new goods. Fortune-bound sellers have found success in offering *unreleased* items for sale in advance of actual availability. Known as *preselling*, savvy sellers have found this tactic not only advantageous in getting a step ahead of the competition, but have discovered this to be an ideal way to dynamically manage their inventory. It's no simple task, though, and requires special attention to ensure that the item the high bidder wins *will* actually be available to successfully complete the sale.

The Details of Dynamic Inventory

Dynamic goods management (a process where you receive just the inventory you need just as you've sold it) is considered an optimal method of inventory management. By establishing reliable inventory sources (wholesalers, distributors, or manufacturers), it's possible to let the source of supply manage the inventory for you, whether offering you the ability to preorder and presell unreleased items, maintain a source of goods without having to purchase what you haven't yet sold, or even drop-ship sold items directly to your buyers without needing to store the goods yourself.

The key, of course, is to be certain that when selling items you don't physically own, you can still ensure that your suppliers can, and will, deliver the goods quickly and consistently whenever a sale is made. This requires you to keep in constant communication with your suppliers to ensure that *their* inventory will arrive on schedule and will be as described. If not managed and monitored closely, your sources of presell supply might become a supply management nightmare that will frustrate both you and your customers.

To address this potential, eBay has come forward to announce it does allow presale provided the seller assures delivery within 30 days of the auction's close.

Full Disclosure Required

When managing presales, sellers should commit to fully disclosing that an auction item is a presell or otherwise to-be-delivered piece of merchandise. It's in the seller's best interest to be absolutely certain that bidders and buyers understand that the goods they're bidding on are not presently in the seller's possession and there may be a longer-than-usual delivery time due to the fact that the goods are on-order or will be delivered by a third party. To disregard such disclosure (or worse, to misrepresent item ownership) is a sure recipe for all sorts of postauction backlash, including buyer dissatisfaction, demands of refund, negative feedback, and even escalation to eBay or consumer protection agencies.

Satisfaction Guaranteed

Though it's within your right to state that all sales are final, such policy isn't well suited to presell items. Whether an item arrives differently than your supplier (and ultimately, *you*) described or arrives damaged, late, or doesn't arrive at all, you must absorb the fallout to avoid angering and alienating your customers.

Though some sellers have tried to blame problems of item delivery, quality, or content upon their suppliers (sometimes attempting to shift cost, an inconvenience to the buyer), it becomes the seller's ultimate responsibility to guarantee that whatever they sell is "as advertised" in all aspects of the phrase. If not, buyers have the right and responsibility to take protective counteraction.

Manage Presales Well and You'll Do Well

The bottom line, despite the special care and managing you need to provide when preselling goods, is that you can catch a demand wave as it's rising and take full advantage of the hype and excitement of a pending item release that often brings along higher-than-usual selling prices. Work closely with your suppliers, who can provide you full item details and images to help stir up some excitement for the goods you'll soon be delivering. Help allay customer's concerns regarding whether they should take a chance on buying presell goods by posting specific testimony from former satisfied customers who found buying presale goods from you has been a good experience.

FORTUNE BOOST #58
SELLING OTHER PEOPLE'S STUFF

Now consider this situation: you're a seller who's looking for more goods to sell, determined to never run out of goods to auction or offer at fixed prices. You soon meet another person who has tons of great items to sell but just doesn't have the auction inclination, the time, or the motivation to list and sell the goods. The two of you should meet, and soon. The fact is, for every seller who's perpetually on the prowl for more inventory to offer, there are as many would-be (but, for whatever reason, won't-be) sellers who have gobs of stuff but just don't want to get involved in the whole online selling revolution. These folks would *love* to turn their trash into treasure, hearing how so many others have already done so, but they'd prefer if maybe someone else would manage that for them, offering a cut of the earnings for the trouble; enter the opportunity of eBay consignment.

Why Consign?

Ask any current consignor (that is, an eBay seller who actively sells items for other people) why this is a profitable path to fortune and they'll give you plenty of reasons. To cut to the heart of the matter, though:

- You'll rarely (if ever) run out of inventory to sell when other people bring *their* goods to you to sell on their behalf.
- You save time and cost when you don't need to actively source inventory yourself; it practically delivers itself to your door.
- You can test new "markets" or "commodities" by selling other folks' goods that you haven't previously managed yourself. You save cost and the risk of having unprofitable inventory on your hands; you just give it back to the owner.
- You avoid the cost and clutter of managing an inventory of goods; you can elect to simply house those consigned goods that you're offering at the moment.
- You can offer goods with complete impartiality and without emotional ties to any of the items (a problem so many collector-sellers face when they simply can't bear to let go of a treasured possession despite the potential fortune it promises to deliver.)

- You can build an impressive eBay feedback rating and develop a greater expertise in goods when you don't have to bother sourcing the inventory yourself.

These are just some of the many good reasons to consider becoming a consignor of other people's goods when you sell at eBay.

Managing Consignment

When you decide to become a consignor and let other folks bring their goods to you to list at eBay, you need to be ready with an offering of services and stipulations as you engage in a consignor/consignee relationship. Consider offering the following key services:

- Reviewing and appraising items to be offered (helping to weed out the items that either won't sell or perhaps won't earn enough to be worthwhile to you or the owner).
- Photographing and detailing items to be listed.
- Launching auctions or Buy-It-Now listings, depending on the client's wants and the market potential for the items.
- Monitoring the listings and fielding all potential buyer inquiries.
- Collecting payment from buyers and shipping goods (although the shipping task is often negotiated to be managed by the owner of the goods yet must be overseen by the consignor as to safe and timely delivery).
- Delivering agreed-upon profit split to the client.
- Providing ongoing consulting and assessment of future listings.

When you become a consignor, you step into a slightly different dimension of selling at eBay. Not only are you managing a virtual sales enterprise, but also you're managing a source of supply, one that can keep you happily in listings and bring you a profit for your efforts without troubling yourself with inventory acquisition matters.

Determining a Fee for Your Services

As I said, establishing consignment fees is not an exact science and you'll need to decide for yourself how much you should charge for your services and eBay expertise. For this reason, research other consignors out there (visit eBay's Trading Assistant discussion board within the site Community area to see who's doing what) to help you decide on a fair and competitive fee and service schedule. Generally, consignors collect fees in the following manner:

- All eBay and other listing-related fees reimbursed.
- A flat-rate fee charged for each item to cover the services provided (anywhere from $3.00 to $10.00 per item seems to be the norm), assessed even if the item does not sell.

- A portion of the final selling price, usually between 20 and 40 percent, often dependent on the item's final selling price.

Remember, you're now competing with other consignors, so you'll need to try to establish a competitive pricing structure that will attract clients to you while properly compensating you for the services and expertise you provide. Other consignors might be vying for your consignee's goods (though generally, such direct competition only comes into play when you advertise yourself at eBay as a Trading Assistant, that is unless someone in your immediate community is also offering consignment services to the same local folk you're serving). Begin your consignment activities by studying other consignors and developing a fee schedule that you can deliver to potential consignees (either in print or via e-mail). Then start with one or two clients to get a feel for the consignment process and to ensure that you'll be earning a profit on your efforts. Many sellers today, though, are doing excellent consignment business such that they're bringing on additional help. Give consignment a try if you're tired of sourcing out your own inventory and see how well you can boost an eBay fortune by selling someone else's stuff.

FORTUNE BOOST #59
GETTING THE DROP ON DROP-SHIPPING

Drop shipping is enjoying a renewed boom thanks to the proliferation of e-commerce, marrying up manufacturers or wholesalers with retailers ready to sell the products. Not relegated to just online sellers, drop shipping is also being embraced by brick-and-mortar business owners who are likewise eager to expand their product catalogs in serving the wants and needs of their customers. Learn now how drop shipping works, how it can be successfully managed, and how you can reap the rewards of offering vast inventories of goods without spending a dime on product *until you've sold it*. This is no come-on; this is a real opportunity to boost your eBay fortune.

Managing Your Drop-Ship Inventory

Well, this makes no sense at all: manage inventory in a drop-ship relationship? Well, it *does* make sense because the greatest risk you incur in any drop-ship arrangement is when your supplier utters the nightmarish term, "out of stock." As you're responsible to deliver the goods for an auction or fixed-price listing that has just concluded, you need to be sure you can deliver the item in case your drop-shipper can't.

- Keep just a few units on hand yourself. If you have items that are particularly popular or upon which you base the core identity of your business, it's wise to have one, two, or three such items yourself to be used to fill a customer order if the supplier runs out.

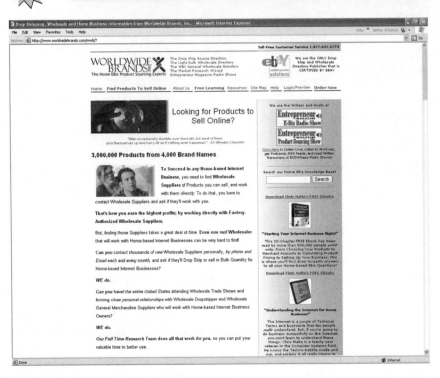

Figure 59-1 Looking for drop-shippers? Visit Worldwide Brands, Inc. (www.mydss.com) for the most reliable list of drop-ship suppliers.

- Identify backup sources that might be able to fulfill orders when your primary source is in a stock-out situation.
- Inquire whether you can reserve quantities of an item, to be warehoused at the drop-shipper's location. This will require you pay for the goods in advance but, again, if the item's a good seller, you may want to maintain a store of goods that can only be used in fulfilling orders to *your* customers and that you could use and monitor as a "safety stock."
- Consider suspending future sales of the item until you're assured inventory is once again plentiful to fulfill customer orders (otherwise, you truly are selling goods you can't deliver).
- Reassess your drop-shipper. Don't be harsh here because often these inventory troubles arise from time to time. If, however, you're hearing more often that your source is unable to maintain a sustained inventory of the goods you're selling, you may want to switch over to another primary source.

Manage Your Drop-Shipper

Beyond inventory matters, establishing and nurturing a good working relationship with a drop-shipper is essential if you're to succeed in selling and managing a virtual inventory. To that end, consider these key points in drop-ship partnering:

- Get it in writing. Be sure to document clearly and agree upon all matters of establishing and maintaining a drop-ship relationship. Be sure you've covered issues of delivery times (remember, the drop-shipper sends goods *directly* to your buyer, not to you), shipping costs, replacement arrangements, and any changes to inventory availability and costs.
- Insist that no additional flyers, promotion slips, or other such literature be included in shipments to your customers other than what you might have requested or supplied yourself. Remember, you want to give the appearance the order came from you or your business, not a third-party.
- Establish and update sales forecasts to your drop-shippers so they can, in turn, adjust their stocking levels to ensure that the product will be available to ship whenever needed. This is that all-important aspect of "partnering" through which you can garner some great returns from a drop-shipper that will equally consider your needs upon seeing how you're considering theirs.
- Define packing and shipping instructions to your drop-shippers. Work closely with them to understand how they'll pack and ship an item (order it yourself first!) to be sure that what they ship (which will bear your business's name) will be representative of the reputation you wish to promote.
- Communicate, communicate, communicate. When dealing with drop-shippers, you'll likely work with a representative that will service your account, working with you to ensure that your orders are shipped as expected. If there are any troubles or potential inventory shortfalls, you'll want to be communicating regularly with your representative to try to identify and head off such situations before they impact you or your customers.

Set Customer Expectations at the Outset

Finally, don't forget the most important players in your business's supply chain: the customers. Not really a part of the chain itself but, rather, the recipient of its function, the customers need to be managed well (without realizing they're being managed) in order for your business to flourish. Although drop-shipping might be new to you, chances are your customers have been the recipient of drop-ship supplied goods for decades (they just didn't know it). Your job, then, is to maintain that level of transparency by ensuring that you're offering reliable goods from reliable drop-shippers, doing your work up front to manage the supply chain so the customer will remain none the wiser. One key aspect of drop-ship supply that you might need to communicate to your customers is that when multiple goods are purchased, some may be shipped in separate boxes (these could be coming from multiple fulfillment points, but *all* should bear your name as the seller). If your customers will be receiving a separate shipment for a drop-shipped items, be sure to let them know, especially if the item will take longer to arrive than others they may have ordered (those that either you yourself shipped or that were managed by other sources of supply, drop-ship or otherwise).

Communication is generally the glue that binds all good retailing relationships, supplier-to-retailer or retailer-to-customer, and it's something you'll want to do well if you wish to avoid fulfillment headaches while simultaneously instilling customer loyalty to the benefit of your bottom line.

FORTUNE BOOST #60
RESISTING BUYING WHEN YOU SHOULD BE SELLING

It's raining outside. There's nothing to do. You've been listing great items faithfully and you have plenty of bids accumulating on your current batch offerings. But, as you take a moment to pause and wonder why you're feeling out of sorts, you realize you haven't bought anything *for yourself* for days—and right now you're bored. If that's what has you feeling a bit unsatisfied, there's always a quick fix: step into the bidders' shoes and hit the auctions. But, as you're gleefully surfing, looking, and bidding, are you sure you're buying things you really want, things you can really afford, and things that won't leave you muttering, "Now why did I buy *that,* especially when I should have been selling instead?" It could have been an impulse moment, but too many long-time sellers who have maintained a steady auction presence, sometimes the temptation to look away from the profit statement and into the allure of all those tens of millions of auction goods is too much to resist. That's OK, but here are a few tips to help ensure that when you are bidding, you do so in a controlled and containable manner.

It's All in the Mind, Y'Know

We've all heard of compulsive shoppers and compulsive gamblers. Online auctions have emerged as an addictive activity, providing a combination of the thrill of buying an item and the excitement of doing so in a sort of high-stakes gaming environment. Some people actually experience a euphoric sensation during the act of buying and definitely in the striving to gain a "win." Psychologists have documented the chemical reactions that take place in the human brain that provide the euphoria: the chemical *dopamine* is released during these activities, which provides the individual a euphoric sensation, albeit short lived. That feeling can actually become addictive and is often cited as the reason some folks shop compulsively or gamble excessively or maybe even bid irresponsibly at online auctions: they want that *high*. This particularly affects first-time eBay bidders but can also sneak up on seasoned sellers.

Do You Think I Have a Problem?

It's hard to say, and you certainly shouldn't feel you're being subjected to some amateur psychology here. However, if ever you're wondering whether you're straying a bit out of control in your online bidding, ask yourself these questions:

- Do the items you win hold little interest to you once they've arrived at your home?
- Do you love the thrill of *winning* auctions, yet hate to pay for the items you've won?
- Has your personal debt increased significantly within a short period of time (especially credit card balances)?
- Do you keep your auction spending a secret from friends and family?
- Do you ever feel guilty about the amount of money you're spending online?
- Most importantly, does it appear your bidding activity is surpassing your selling results?

Though a "yes" answer to any one of these questions isn't necessarily a sign you've developed an auction addiction, it could be the beginning signs that you're caught up in impulsive bidding and buying. That could mean it's time to take preventive action, quickly!

Your Best Defense

It's your financial well-being and online reputation we're talking about here, so take a long hard look at your bidding habits and, if you feel you're losing a bit of self-control, take these steps:

- Take control of your time. Consider all the other activities you need (and want) to complete in a day, especially those that contribute to your bottom-line profits and fortune goals. Allot a more reasonable amount of time to be used for surfing the auction sites, which includes buying as well as selling. Many sellers avoid getting caught up in distracting bidding by setting a schedule where they'll take breaks from the research and listing activities, actually stepping away from the computer entirely to refresh themselves and clearly consider their next "to do" to complete.
- When the day is done, log off. It's too easy to plop into the chair and impulsively surf for stuff when the PC's always warm and running. In your selling activities, set a start and stop time for your work each day and stick

to it. Then, when the veritable quitting whistle blows, log off the computer and tend to other matters, business or pleasure. This way, you'll be out of reach of the computer and should be able to resist a bidding binge.

- Set a dollar limit. Of course, there's nothing wrong with doing some bidding and buying for yourself (you've worked hard and you deserve a bit of reward). Regulate your bidding, though, by establishing a strict spending budget (and sticking to it). You don't have to entirely sign off from online bidding, but by allotting an affordable amount of spending every month, you'll satisfy the desire to bid without jeopardizing your personal fortune goal.

- Make a shopping list. Look for the items that are truly of interest or importance to you and search for those only.

- Don't fall for fads. It's all the rage today, but no one will care tomorrow. Try to avoid hype and trends that often lead to impulsive bidding. Ask yourself if you'll still want it a month from now. And, rather than get caught up on the buying side of such trends, take that impulse and turn it into an effort to secure such goods to offer to other buyers who are seeking the latest craze.

- Do something else for a change. The Internet and online auctions are exciting new forms of interactive shopping, but do you remember what you did before they arrived on the scene? Take time to rediscover an old hobby (or an old friend) and balance your online and offline time.

A Little Help from Your Friends

And, in case you're worried that you've gotten just a bit too caught up in all the bidding and winning and are losing sight of your selling goals, don't keep it a secret—tell someone. Whether it's your spouse, partner, family members, or friends, if you ever doubt your control over your online bidding, let someone know. You may just need to hear another point of view on your activity, you may need to have someone else point out alternative activities to pursue, or you may need someone to help you get a more professional assessment.

Don't panic, but don't take impulsive bidding too lightly. Take control instead.

Arming Yourself for Efficiency

TIME MANAGEMENT YOU CAN TAKE TO THE BANK

At the end of each busy day of selling at eBay, you'll want to know that all of your hard work to get organized is paying off by affording you more time to get more done (not to mention more time to relax). Time management is no longer just a corporate concern. As more and more people have discovered eBay as a bona-fide alternate source of income and an income-generating opportunity that can be exercised from their own homes, good time management reinforces the age-old axiom, "Time *is* money." Your time is so incredibly valuable, and the way you spend it has a direct effect on your fortune-earning potential. Therefore, it's always wise to take time to reflect on time. So, take a break now and consider some of these simple yet effective efforts that will help you reclaim your most precious yet nonrenewable resource: *time*.

Enlisting Tangible Tools to Save Time

First, consider (or reconsider, as the case may be) some "tangible" time-saving tools:

- **Use a bulk lister:** You'll save significant time if you'll upload your eBay listings in volume rather than one at a time. If you're going to be listing a lot of items week after week, let a bulk lister like TurboLister help ease some of the burden, increase your throughput, and save you time.
- **Create and use templates:** Create and reuse HTML listing templates; why recreate the code when all you really might need to do is change some text. Also consider using e-mail templates that will save you time

in your correspondence. No sense in writing the same sentences over and over and over again.

- **Develop a database:** Keep track of your inventory, sales, and customer records by using a software application designed specifically for that purpose. Filing and retrieving information in a database is far more time-efficient than hopeless searches through e-mail or fruitless riffling through a stack of sticky-notes. Use eBay's My eBay to download data to your PC (via the Subscriptions link) for permanent storage and future reference.

- **Check your hardware:** Is your PC out of date? If so, it could be robbing you of precious time as you wait for it to execute tasks that newer PCs simply whiz through. This can be a costly upgrade, but weigh how that cost might be offset by increased productivity and increased sales.

Don't Overlook the Intangibles

Now, consider some of the "intangibles" that can save (or cost) you hours every day of every week of every year. These time savers are more related to your business behavior, and they're often the ones that can bring the greatest returns in the long run.

- **Establish working hours:** At the auctions, you're the boss, so set your own hours. Whether you choose to work hours on end or segmented times of the day, put a schedule in place when work is to be done and do it. So many home business enterprises fail due to lack of discipline in setting regular working hours.

- **Stay in your office:** With so many product and resources now available online, you can save so much more time that was once wasted driving here and there (you know, "running errands"). Today, you can order packing supplies online, you can buy postage online, and you can research your customer market online. What a time-saver.

- **Limit interruptions:** If your friends keep calling to chat, switch over to the answering machine. If "you've got mail" throws you off track, close your e-mail window. If there's a television in your auction office, leave it off or get it out of the room. Granted, working from home was envisioned as doing work with all the comforts of home, but you'll soon realize why traditional employers prefer the standard office space when it comes to productivity.

- **Develop a weekly work schedule:** Monday is e-mail day. Tuesday is listing day. Wednesday is packing day. Whatever schedule works best for you, develop it into a routine so you can anticipate the next day's duties and avoid wasting time pondering, "Hmm. What should I do today?"

- **Focus on the task at hand:** While you're working the auctions, it's all too easy to become distracted and surf off to read, play, or shop. Stick to your task until it's done, *then* play.

Now There's Time for You

OK. Now it's playtime. Yes, time off can be an incredible productivity boost and can save you from wasting time daydreaming or generally feeling sluggish and burnt out. Get away for lunch. Take a midday exercise break. Get up and stretch for 10 minutes. Take regular breaks not only for your physical well-being (get out of that desk chair once in awhile) but also for your mental well-being. It's been proven that regular (but not excessive) breaks serve as a proven mental re-energizer, allowing you to return to work with a refreshed perspective and renewed motivation. So take time management seriously and you'll discover a higher level of productivity that you can take to the bank.

FORTUNE BOOST #62
TOP TIME WASTERS YOU NEED TO AVOID

Since we're fresh on the subject of time management and you've just read about the things you can do to improve your time efficiency, take a look now at those top time wasters (and profit killers) that keep you and your business from reaching full potential. When you're running your own business, be very mindful of those "activities" that may look like work and may sound like work but aren't working to help you increase your income. Here's a list of common time-wasting activities that often *feel* like they're work yet rarely add to (and ultimately subtract from) your business' bottom line.

- **Procrastination:** Sure, I considered writing about this one later, after I had enough time to really feel 100 percent confident about my thoughts. Sound familiar? Some folks feel they need time to let ideas "gel" before they take action, and that often is the excuse given for putting off mundane but necessary tasks that "might benefit if I can just get more time to think them through." You get the idea. If it needs to be done, there's nothing to be gained by letting an important task languish and possibly harm your business (usually encountered when many such tasks pile up to become an overwhelming mountain of I-don't-want-to-do-it chores). Break up larger tasks into smaller, more quickly achievable parts or schedule time specifically to do such things. Plan to reward yourself somehow once the task is completed. Whatever motivation it is you need, be sure to get done the things that your business needs achieved to keep yourself happily in the profit zone.
- **Trips and Travel:** After a time, some folks who work at home in an auction business or other home-based occupation tend to get a bit of cabin

fever. The cure: get out and go somewhere. The ill: always being out and not getting the business's work done. A schedule is needed to allow for both. Schedule the tasks that have to be done in the home office first, then schedule an away-from-the-office task. Spread the travels and errands over a couple of days if you need, but keep in mind that completing multiple away-from-the-office errands in a single trip will be much more time and fuel thrifty.

- **Fast Action, Slow Results:** Have you ever watched those folks who are always rushing around in a flurry of elbows but never seem to get much done at the end of the day? A hurried approach to work is often more counterproductive than you might think. A thoughtful, deliberate approach to your work will usually yield better results.

- **Too Much Chat:** Get an answering machine if a phone call can divert you into an hour-long visit with a friend or relative. If you must get on the phone to talk business with someone, make it quick and get to the point (some folks use an egg timer while others stand and talk to hasten the conversation). If you really want to stay focused on your work, though, consider letting the answering machine or voice mail collect your calls and then schedule time near the end of each day to deal with them directly.

- **Too Much Surf:** Sure, it's already been mentioned in the previous fortune boost yet it bears repeating. The Internet: the great tool, the great time-waster. Yes, you'll need to stay constantly in touch with goings on, especially when you're operating a Web-based business, but continuously checking the headlines, your bid amounts, and whatever else that attracts your attention online can cost you countless hours. Plan surf time or plan to catch up on all your pleasurable surfing on a particular day of the week (hopefully on your "day off") and avoid wasting too many of your work hours.

- **Overly Organized:** And, the need to stay organized can climb to addictive proportions. Ever see someone so obsessed with keeping their desk straight that all the ever seem to do is put things away, stack items neatly, and then methodically move stacks and items around in a seemingly meaningful way? Often, this is a clue that the person isn't sure what to do next, so straightening up a work area seems to be a good alternative to work, yet it won't help the business at the end of the day. Try making a schedule of things to do, whether at the start of the day or, better yet, at the close of the previous workday. A schedule in hand (or captured on your computer) will guide you through the next task and never leave you feeling that you need to organize something in order to *look* productive.

Yes, time *is* money when the time you spend might wind up costing you money lost. Keep ever vigilant over how you're spending your time to be sure every task is one that will feed your fortune.

FORTUNE BOOST #63
MORE AUTOMATING TOOLS—USING AUTO-RESPONDERS

With all you've read and are yet to read in this book regarding the value of meaning-ful customer interaction, it might seem improbable to expect a tip that encourages you to use an automated e-mail response tool, yet…well it's a great way to tame a big part of your auction management activity. Properly worded and frequently revised, an auto-response e-mail message can free you from hours of e-mail duty while still providing your customers with meaningful and engaging postauction communica-tion. Here are some tips on using e-mail "auto-responders"—tools that automatically send messages to your customers and allow you to focus more attention to other aspects of your business without ever neglecting the all-important aspect of timely customer response.

Defining the Auto-Responder

An e-mail auto-responder works very similar to an answering machine or voice mail greeting that you may already have in use. When your customers send an e-mail message to your designated e-mail account, an auto-responder can reply instanta-neously, providing them with key information on how to proceed with a transaction and what to expect next when wrapping up an eBay purchase. If ever you've filled out a form at a Web site or asked a question of an online sales site, you may have received a prompt "thank you" message; that was sent via an auto-responder. When properly and professionally managed, auto-responders can do wonders for a busi-ness in providing important information to customers without appearing overly mechanical or otherwise distant (and *that's* the key to using auto-responders effec-tively). When you properly employ the use of an auto-responder, you'll find you can free yourself of constantly monitoring your incoming e-mail flow while you focus on more pressing profit-bearing matters during your busy day.

Where to Find an Auto-Responder

In case you believed you'd have to have a sprawling Web site up and running to acquire the use of an auto-responder, you'll be pleased to know that's not the case. The fact is you can use an auto-responder e-mail address (or "node") in your eBay account profile. Most third-party e-mail management tools and even ISPs offer auto-responder functionality (as does Bigfoot.com for my designated e-mail node—see Figure 63-1).

Certainly, the key advantage of using auto-responders is that they're imme-diate and provide important first-touch communication to your customers. In addition, auto-responders can be highly effective in the following ways:

- You set them up and they do the rest of the work for you, effectively responding to your incoming mail while also providing you visibility of

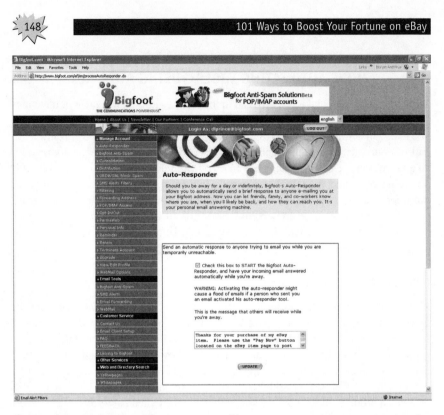

Figure 63-1 Bigfoot.com allows me to provide an auto-response message to my eBay buyers encouraging them to Pay Now for fast shipment.

incoming messages received so you may group and manage that mail at a more convenient time.

- They can help you screen out unwanted mail (spam) through the use of ISP or third-party spam filtering mechanisms so you won't ever need to waste your time with such nonsense.
- They can serve as a means to respond to real customer inquiries and act as a veritable "opt-in" service, sent only to customers who contacted you first.

Best Ways to Use Auto-Responders

By now you're probably already conjuring up ideas for good uses of an auto-responder message. Here are some tips for how the most effective sellers are using auto-responders today:

- Encourage (or remind) customers of your preferred method of payment when they've won or decided to Buy-It-Now from one of your eBay listings.

- Use auto-responder messages to reiterate your sales policies, including information about payment due dates, shipping services, and other terms already stated in your listings (but often well serving to you and your customers if you repeat them in an auto-respond message).

- Create an auto-responder message to provide answers to frequently asked questions to visitors to your commercial Web site, providing detailed information about you, your products, and other services you may provide.

- Provide auto-responder-only discounts, specials, or other incentives to customers who have contacted you, giving instructions on where they can navigate (your eBay listings, your own commercial Web site) to find great items and great deals.

- Provide status messages in case you're vacationing or otherwise unavailable to respond immediately. This is especially important if ever you're away as listings are ending or purchases are being made; never keep your winner/buyer wondering if you'll respond.

- Devise and deliver targeted messages to customers when you seek to specialize in specific goods or services, especially seasonal offerings.

The best news about auto-responders is that most are free for your use. Some third-party providers will limit the number of characters in your auto-respond messages in their free versions of auto-responder tools, yet you can eliminate this boundary by upgrading to a fee-based service (usually of nominal price and of good investment potential to you).

If you haven't investigated an auto-responder yet, do it now. You'll be amazed at the time you'll save, the increased volume of customers you can serve, and the ability to further market your business, hands-free, to boost your eBay fortune.

FORTUNE BOOST #64
POSTAGE AS CLOSE AS YOUR PRINTER

Perhaps one of the best developments in saving time with shipping (next to all the free supplies mentioned in Fortune Boost #29) is the advent of online postage purchase and printing. If you haven't already, you must harness the time-saving value of printing preposted shipping labels from your eBay office, whenever you need. Here's a look at how it's done and how easy it is to say "good-bye" to stamps and long lines at the postal station and "hello" to postage on demand.

Who Offers Online Postage

Both USPS and UPS postage purchase are already integrated with eBay itself, the site having previously recognized the value to sellers who want to squeeze out every bit of inefficiency in their selling activities.

When one of your listings has concluded, you can collect your payment from your buyer and click a link (from within the actual item listing page or from within your My eBay page) and purchase and print the shipping label. To add to the efficiency gain, you'll find that your buyer's name and address are already prefilled into the label, saving you even more time.

You'll be guided to the carrier's Web site, where you'll be prompted to verify the following:

- Shipping method (standard, priority, overnight)
- Package type (envelope, package, oversize package)
- Package weight (in pounds and ounces)
- Insurance option (specify the value of the package contents)

Once that information has been entered, the site will process your input and provide you a cost to deliver the package as you have specified it. At this point, you simply purchase and print the shipping label (you will need to create an account and provide a valid credit card for charging the shipping costs).

Note: If you've received a PayPal payment and complete the postage purchase through the PayPal site, you can elect to have the shipping label costs deducted directly from your PayPal account balance.

Now it's just a matter of printing the label on an attached or network-accessed printer and you're done (see Figure 64-1). Oh, and don't forget to select the "economy printing" mode on your printer properties to save on ink consumption, too.

FORTUNE BOOST #65
TELL THEM BEFORE THEY ASK: AVOIDING
THE COST OF UNANSWERED QUESTIONS

Now let's look at the critical elements of a sales approach that go beyond your well-created auction listings, your clear and precise sales policy, and the overall thoughtful and thorough effort you've already put into your auction offerings. While it's true you need to offer up all telling details of your items in order to establish confidence in your potential customers, there's another dimension of information sharing that is just as telling, possibly more so. Well-seasoned sellers have learned the necessity of answering the other "unasked questions" in order to seal the deal and show they truly have command of virtual merchandising. This Fortune Boost covers the additional details, and approaches to providing them, that you'll need to offer up in advance of a sale to better ensure your online sales success.

People Are Funny

How many times have you ever declined to ask a question of a salesperson at a retail establishment, feeling that they wouldn't answer you clearly, completely, or with much concern for your comfort in a purchase? How many times have those situations caused you to not purchase at all? If you're like millions of others, this

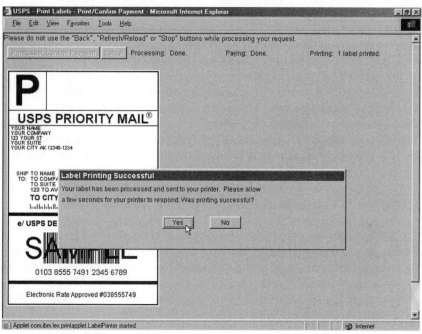

Figure 64-1 Your shipping costs and applied effort just got slashed again thanks to online postage purchase and printing.

probably happens quite frequently. Some shoppers don't like to approach sales-people with questions, either for lack of confidence in the answer they may get, for lack of patience to take the time to ask the question and wait for an answer, or just because the really just wanted to manage their shopping experience on their own terms without having to engage the assistance of others. It sounds funny but it's true and many retailers have learned that this sort of customer—the one who just doesn't feel like asking a question—accounts for significant losses of sales.

Why? Well, according to the testimony of many sellers, online and off, cus-tomers are something of a skeptical lot, and for good reason. Consider how many times, as a customer, you've felt misunderstood, misguided, and even mistreated as you've tried to make a purchase, large or small. After a few such experiences, customers tend to withdraw and mistrust those who proclaim, with their best Cheshire cat grin, "Hello! May I be of service to you?" Yeah, right.

Sweat These Details for Sales Success

If you ever thought a FAQ (Frequently Asked Questions) declaration was just another computerese Web page filler relegated to online geeks who love to speak in TLAs (Three-Letter Acronyms), think again. The fact is that a FAQ has become very much sought-out by online shoppers to quickly find answers to their most pressing concerns, those who prefer the "self-service" approach to their browsing and buying. Therefore, in order to convince your customers that they're truly understood and highly valued, consider providing this sort of additional information:

- **Establish how you differ from other sellers.** Customers have long heard how they'll never find a better deal nor get better service than wherever it is they're shopping at the moment (that is, until they rub elbows with the next plaid-jacketed salesman). If you've crafted your approach well, you've already determined how you are different—and, thereby, how you decided to position your business as you have—among other would-be competitors. Provide information about this differentiation for your customers to read (directly within your online store or as a link from your auction listings). Provide a bit of history of how you've come to be an expert in what you offer and how you determined that you could provide better service and better products—an overall better *experience*—to shoppers.

- **Tell customers how they'll immediately benefit from a shopping experience with you.** This is key: Let customers know what's in it for them. Customers want to feel they've stumbled into an oasis of excellent goods or great prices or supreme service (or all three!) when they visit a sales establishment. If you've culled an excellent collection of goods, show that off immediately. If you've devised a superintuitive checkout process and fast delivery method, let that shine! If you have a "no–questions-asked return guarantee," put that up in glowing lights the moment your customers enter your store. Let them know how they can immediately benefit from shopping with you before they've ever put anything in their virtual cart and, chances are, they'll be much more inclined to make a selection, or two, or more.

- **Provide proof for what you promise.** Testimony can be your best ally, and when you post the positive references from past customers, you're letting your patrons know that you're committed to doing good business.

- **Don't be afraid to accentuate the negative.** Consider again that many of us, as customers, have felt misdirected by sellers or worried that items were intentionally misrepresented. Because of this we've been trained to cast a skeptical eye on most everything. If there are less-than-perfect elements of the goods you're offering, tell 'em all about it. If you've had a dissatisfied customer who has taken exception to your goods or your service level, make the correction to your business approach and then share that with new customers (this shows you're open to constantly improving your business and committed to ensuring a positive shopping experience). Customers love honesty, and if they can determine they've met an honest shopkeeper, they'll be better inclined to make a purchase (and hopefully return for more).

- **Exude extreme respect for your customers.** When you provide all of the above, you show that you care for your customers and, in this day and age when goods have become so much more available to us (thanks to the Internet), it will be service and satisfaction that differentiate sellers from one another. When you go to these extra lengths to satisfy your customers and help them understand, up front, what they can expect from shopping with you, they'll know they've stepped into the right virtual showroom.

FORTUNE BOOST #66
RECORD KEEPING THAT WORKS

Although it's been said a clean desk is a sign of a sick mind, an organized auctioneer is definitely ahead of the pack. While many fortune boost discussions have catered to matters of proper pricing, enticing titles, and effective listing styles, keeping track of your auction sales, bidder information, and everything else that comes with auctioning is paramount if you want to be an auction leader and a fortune finder. Here are some tips that will help you keep your business in order, help you to see the importance of being earnest in good auction record keeping and, ultimately, reduce waste while bolstering your bottom line.

Get a New Plan, Stan

Everyone will have different ideas about the best way to organize records. Because of this, you'll find there is no single way to manage your auction data. However, when devising a record keeping strategy, consider the key elements:

- Is your method easily repeatable and can it be useful for high-volume as well as low-volume auctioning?
- Is your method efficient to the degree that *you* won't be tempted to abandon it in the near future? Record keeping methods can be enhanced, but if you find yourself changing over to a new style every other month, you may have developed something too complex.
- Keep it as simple as possible. You don't have to keep every single bit of data. Decide on the most pertinent information that will serve you for one year's time and go with that.

Of course, there are many tools to help you manage your auction records. From a paper-based system to a PC-based spreadsheet or database application to eBay's own My eBay and other Seller Tools, you'll find there are numerous methods of organization you can adopt and use. Whichever means you settle upon, be sure you're comfortable with it, have the proper storage facilities for such records (physical or electronic), and have some sort of backup or recovery method in case the unforeseen occurs.

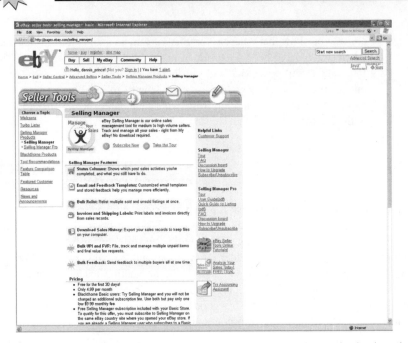

Figure 66-1 Visit eBay's Seller Tools page for time-saving and organization-boosting assistance.

The Need for Speed

Who among us has the time to dig through reams of printed notes, receipts, and so on? Most less-than-organized sellers will typically confess they spend more time looking for something than they care to admit. That time is lost opportunity, plain and simple. Therefore, keep your auction records handy.

Establish a filing plan, be it hard copy or electronic, and stick to it faithfully. Using clearly marked files, you can store and retrieve information in mere seconds. Time becomes important when you're trying to maximize your hours working the online auctions. Moreover, your ability to respond quickly to a buyer who has some question about a current or previous transaction will head off trouble and clearly portray you as a high-quality seller who is in control.

Someone's Been Sleeping in My Bed

Just a quick note about controlling your auction data: be sure you have exclusive access to your auction records. In other words, make sure there isn't someone else in the house who might, unwittingly, reorganize or otherwise disrupt your organization system. And, if you work with a partner, be sure you both agree to the organization methods and communicate excessively whenever a change or enhancement might be useful.

In Times of Trouble

Remember, good auction records can be crucial to sorting out a potential snag in an auction transaction. A buyer could contact you weeks or months after you believe the deal was closed. Though not necessarily a reason to suspect a scam, your ability to quickly present detailed records and accounts of an auction transaction will be your best tool to proving you held up your end of the bargain.

Your Customer Base

As any good businessperson knows, a base of customers can be your best asset to long-term success. Though you wouldn't use their information irresponsibly or inappropriately, keeping track of the folks you've sold to in the past and their contact information will help you recognize a good returning customer, a potential deadbeat, or anyone who has expressed interest in the sorts of items you offer. The Internet was made for helping individuals network with one another. To an online seller, understanding who your best customers are and occasionally notifying them of the availability of the things they desire can leave the two of you standing quite happy and successful.

FORTUNE BOOST #67
RECORD AS YOU GO...*OR ELSE!*

Following close on the heels of Fortune Boost #66, now take a more detailed look into the kinds of records you should be keeping—the tracking of the most pertinent business data—and why that information will be so important to keep you in business, out of trouble, and ever progressing to your individual fortune goals. So while the bids are coming in, the inventory is shipping out, and you feel you're an unmitigated success, are you certain you can put your finger on precisely what costs you've incurred, how much profit you've earned, and what it all means to your bottom line?

To be really sure your eBay business is going in the right direction, you'll need to make sure you're keeping costs under control, records up to date, and tomorrow's goals within reach. Assuming you've heeded the guidance offered in the previous fortune boost, here are the next details to consider as you prepare to keep the records that will serve your business best.

Record Your Expenses

While the appeal of online auctioning is its relatively low cost, many hard-core sellers get a real eye-opener when their per-auction costs begin to tally up. And many others overlook the other expenses associated with buying and selling online. The only way to be sure you can confidently determine if your business is being profitable is to recognize and record each of these expenses:

General Expenses

- **Internet Fees:** Unless you're using one of those "free Internet" services, you're probably paying a monthly fee for Internet access. That's a cost of doing business, so record it.
- **Storage/Insurance Fees:** If you've moved your inventory off-site and are paying insurance to protect its value, it's another expense to consider.

eBay Listing Expenses

- **Listing Fees:** Long-time sellers understand how the generally low-cost-per-item insertion fees at eBay can quickly add up when it comes to hosting a hundred offerings or more. Record these fees because they're your cost of merchandise placement.
- **Special Feature Fees:** If you want special fonts, icons, or price protection, record all the fees that are associated.
- **Final Value Fees:** When your auction ends, eBay's there to levy a commission that is a percentage of the final high bid price. That's more cost to your doing business, and it needs to be captured in your records.

Transaction Fees

- **Shipping and Handling:** The buyer is typically responsible for these, but when you're buying for resale, don't forget to capture these costs.
- **Insurance and Tracking:** A subset of S&H, but one that isn't always recorded on the postal meter.
- **Money Fees:** If you're using an online payment service, an escrow service, or simply purchasing money orders, don't forget the costs of using different payment methods.
- **Travel:** Whether you're off hunting for more inventory or simply driving to the carrier's office to drop off packages, there's a cost involved in whatever method you used to make the trek—be it plane, train, or automobile.
- **Supplies:** Shipping supplies, office supplies, and anything else you need to buy to make your auction business work is an expense that you need to recognize.

You might discover additional expenses that you'll incur as a part of doing business. Whatever those business expenses are, be sure you identify them and document them properly. Generally, here's the information you should make note of for every business expense:

- When the expense occurred
- Where the expense occurred
- The cost of the expense
- The business applicability of the expense

Record Your Sales

Naturally, you'll need to be keeping close track of you actual sales and, to assist you in that task, be sure to capture these details:

- Date of sale
- Sale price
- Customer
- Gain or loss (based on your original purchase price)
- Date payment received
- Payment method
- Payment processing fee (as with credit cards)
- Shipping date
- Shipping expenses

You'll notice that some of the aforementioned information will be necessary for your annual tax records, while other information will be suitable for developing a customer record and an "audit trail" for the completion of the transaction. All of this information is either necessary or highly useful to keep your business under control and help you quickly assess important income information as well as resolve any problems that could occur during the transaction.

Or Else What?

OK. So back to the original thrust of this particular fortune boost—record as you go or else—here's why it's important to identify and record your auction activity as it occurs:

- If you manage high volumes of activity, you'll need to keep records as you go, lest you'll be unable to recall and recount just what you bought, what you sold, and what you earned last week, last month, or last quarter. (Yes, this may sound like an obvious bit of counseling, yet you'd be surprised to learn how many business owners put off this sort of activity.)
- Recording your expenses as you go enables you to clearly and confidently identify those that can be legally deducted from you business' taxable income. If you miss some of your deductible expenses, well that's just like throwing money out the window.
- And, as you're earning profit, you *will* need to report that as taxable income and pay appropriate income taxes on it on a quarterly or annual basis. Avoid the fear of tax time by keeping your records complete and up-to-date at all times.
- Most importantly, keeping track of your records in line with your sales activity will enable you to see just how well your business is doing, how successful you are at progressing to your fortune goals, and whether any

adjustments should be made to keep you profitable. To ignore this would likely undo any efforts or aspirations you ever had for making an online fortune.

It's your business and the way you decide to manage it is strictly up to you. However, if you truly want to compete and succeed among eBay's finest, you'll want to recognize and respond to the need to keep detailed records and monitor your auction activity every step of the way. There's a fortune awaiting you, but you'll need to track it closely to ensure it doesn't otherwise slip through your fingers.

FORTUNE BOOST #68
HELP WANTED! BEING CHOOSEY OVER YOUR ASSISTANTS

Has the sales and marketing potential of managing ongoing auction sales prompted businesses to seek out and appoint skilled "Auction Sales Specialists" to their staffs? If your online business is booming to the point that you're finding you can't keep up with demand or run the risk of missing out on profit-bearing opportunities, it may be time for you to seek some help. But will anyone do—your wife, your mom, your uncle, or your kids? For sellers who are struggling with meeting the flood of customer needs (and that's a good problem to have, by the way), here are some important considerations in selecting the services of someone else who can help you further your sales endeavors.

Who Needs Help?

Whether it's computers, photographic equipment, jewelry, or even movie memorabilia, established businesses have found the online auctions venues to be the emerging new "distribution channels" whereby they can increase sales, extend market visibility, and, ultimately, fortify their customer base. But auctioning is not just a novelty anymore, and astute businesses that recognize the potential of the auction market also recognize the growing need for individuals skilled and savvy in the ways and means of successful business auctioning.

"These days, you need to stay ahead of the curve using the new [sales] tools and technologies that are available," observes Andrew Hortatsos of Shadesaver.com. Though he originally launched his successful business of selling designer sunglasses, watches, and similar products by means of simple Web site marketing, he now proudly asserts that up to 70 percent of his sales are achieved through ongoing auctions.

"We started with a simple direct-sales Web site, but then found eBay and took off from there. At the pace we're going, we might need to hire some additional help and even move the business out of the home just due to the amount of inventory we move and manage."

Chris Aument, who operates BJB International Jewelry, was merely looking for a way to move some languishing goods within his Lancaster, Pennsylvania, showroom. "The online auction process started as an experiment to liquidate some of our long-standing inventory items. Little did we know that it would turn into the viable sales source that it is."

Even entertainment icons like Warner Brothers Studios have recognized online auctioning for the significant yet inexpensive exposure of product and company brands. "Our online auction activity is . . . an extension of our marketing activities," notes Barbara Brogliatti, Corporate Communications for Warner Brothers Studio Auctions (*wbauction* at eBay).

Whether intended to build a business upon, liquidate inventory, or further promote a brand to the millions of regular auction goers, online auctioning is becoming the exciting new channel for businesses to engage. But *who* will be responsible within the company's ranks to make the venture successful?

An Emerging Career Path?

As even casual sellers will attest, selling consistently at online auctions is hardly a mundane or "simple" task. To truly exploit the opportunities for increased sales and exposure the online venues can offer, it's an effort that requires a focused effort by knowledgeable individuals.

"Online auction sales were conceived from the start as both a means of enhancing customer shopping experiences and of selling and marketing a variety of items that wouldn't work well in the standard, static-pricing model," offers Mike Harper, Auction Manager for Ritz Camera auctions (listed exclusively at eBay under seller ID *ritzauctions*). "As *Auction Manager*, I am responsible for ensuring the smooth and continued operation of all the mechanical aspects of our auction program. I [work with] an assistant who has the title of *Auction Specialist*."

As managing auctions is a rather new role that is still being defined, other businesses recognize the role under a variety of names. Whether identified as *e-Commerce Director* at BJB International, *Auction Curator* at Planet Hollywood, or a marketing and sales staff member responsible for auction channel management, it's evident that more businesses are beginning to understand the need for this new role on their organizational charts.

Not a Traditional Role

As Harper notes, it's clear that managing auction sales isn't just a matter of working a Web browser or coding HTML. "We have separate departments for warehousing product, fulfilling auction orders, and supporting customers but . . . I am deeply involved with each of those functions."

Elevating the importance of effectively combining traditional duties to support auction sales, Mike Manoske of TimeShareValues.com explains "we advised people to focus on 'intrapreneurial' types—someone with cross-department skills [including] technical, customer services, marketing, etc. who are used to cutting across company boundaries." But Manoske's vision sees even greater potential for

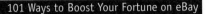

auction specialists: "They should be viewed as trendspotters," suggesting that selling at auction will not only uncover new markets for goods (Manoske refers to this as developing "business intelligence") but will do so in a profitable manner. "Traditional models say business intelligence is a cost. Using the auction model to test [potential markets] is a profit center."

The Right Stuff

Naturally, any business that understands the value of auction sales also understands that the best employees for managing such sales will be highly computer and Internet savvy. "Students coming out of college with some sort of formal training in Web design and creation are desirable," says Andrew Hortatsos. "I've outsourced my Web development needs to a younger fellow since it's a more innate task to him and would take me too long to learn myself to an efficient level of proficiency."

In just the listing process alone, Chris Aument calls out the need for appropriate skills there: "One would need to be very detail oriented and have good communication skills. They [should] know minimal amounts of HTML . . . and good photo editing skills. The items will not sell if they do not appear attractive."

Beyond that, would-be auction specialists should also demonstrate that well-rounded skill set that, as previously mentioned, will break through traditional boundaries and enable a more holistic approach to viewing, analyzing, and addressing sales needs and opportunities.

Yet a common skill that seems to run through all the minds of these businesspeople is that of total customer satisfaction. "Customer service is the number-one requirement to online sales success," advises Hortatsos. It's a sentiment that Mike Manoske also echoes: "I have recommended that people look to their best customer service staff member. You are looking for people who have shown the ability to think 'customer'—to be customer driven as opposed to product driven."

And, understanding that online auctioning grew out of the very goo of the entrepreneurial spirit, Hortatsos finds such spirit as necessary in an effective employee: "I'd be looking for someone that has an entrepreneurial attitude, is an explorer, and definitely a self-starter."

FORTUNE BOOST #69
THE ETHICS OF THE SUCCESSFUL ENTREPRENEUR

Now, if you ever want to stir up an impassioned dialog among eBay sellers, bring up the matter of business ethics. Everyone has an opinion, and everyone generally believes they are operating under the most admirable ethics code around. But what makes the discussion so lively is that ethics are almost spiritual in nature—whether you believe in divine intervention, karma, or the concepts of cause and effect, business ethics will often be at the core of reaping what you sow (and how quickly you can reap and sow your way to a fortune).

To avoid a heated discussion at this time and to partially diffuse any differing attitudes, let's focus on the notion that you need to be clear about your business ethics when you entertain shoppers at eBay and elsewhere online. Determine for yourself how you'll conduct and portray yourself, ethically speaking, online and consider these virtues to get your ethical engine cranking:

- **Honesty.** Well of course you'll be an honest businessperson, but will you go so far as to, say, refund money to a customer who accidentally over-paid you? If you can't deliver the sort of item someone asks about, will you direct them to a competitor who might be offering the very thing the customer is seeking? And, if your customer is less-than-knowledgeable about an item you're selling, will you be sure to fully disclose every detail and correct their possible misunderstandings, even if it costs you a sale?
- **Fairness.** It's an open marketplace, but is it fair to try to lure away another seller's customers (even if eBay wasn't actively hunting for "bid siphons")? Can the potential to make a sale cause your better judgment to become clouded and obscured—even temporarily—in deference to meeting your income goals? Will you avoid bad-mouthing a seller who seems to be consistently doing better than you are? Will you accept the fact that some sellers "have it" and use their success as a motivation to redouble *your* efforts rather than try to undermine theirs?
- **Employ the Golden Rule.** And when you lay your head down to sleep, will you be able to do so with a clean conscience? Will you treat every customer and competitor in the same manner as you'd wish to be treated yourself?

If you ever succumb to operating in unethical ways, you'll be forever looking over your shoulder to see if anyone you've run over is fast creeping back up on you. If, however, you commit to running a clean, honest, and ethical business, your success will surely come in improved sales and an overall truly satisfying experience. How's *that* for a fortune? (see Figure 69-1.)

FORTUNE BOOST #70
THE HOWS AND WHYS OF PROVIDING
EXCEPTIONAL CUSTOMER SERVICE

In today's competitive eBay market, more and more sellers are scrambling to beef up their bottom lines by seeking better ways to acquire and retain customers. At eBay and elsewhere on the Web, you'll find literally millions of sellers who are vying for the attention and patronage of the bidders and buyers who frequent the online marketplaces. There was a time when a good variety of merchandise was the hook needed to attract eager bidders, though now the attitude has shifted in which bidders are just as interested in *how* they will be served as what they will be

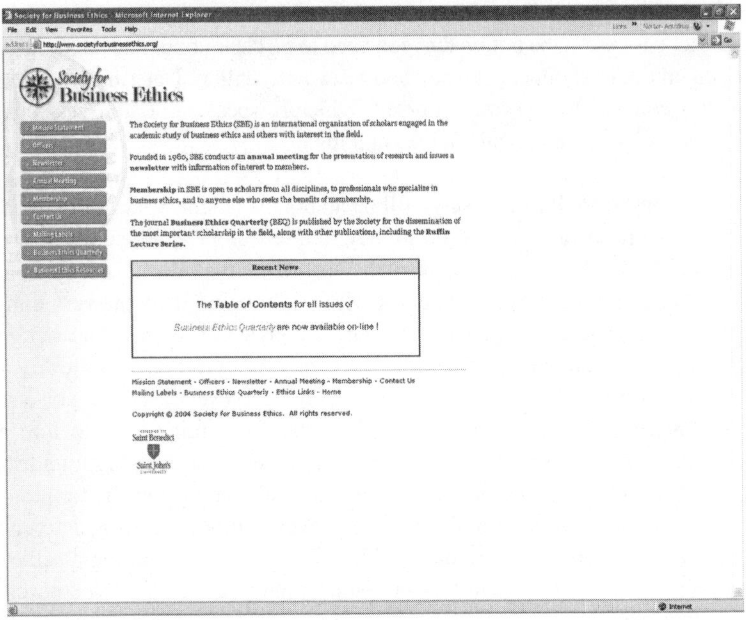

Figure 69-1 Looking for some more ethical food for thought? Visit the Society for Business Ethics online at www.societyforbusinessethics.org.

served. Here's a quick and concentrated overview of the key elements that can make you a stellar seller, helping you understand what bidders are looking for from online sellers and whether your way of doing business will have customers feeling glad they found you.

- **Be interactive and responsive.** Bidders and buyers are usually engaging in business with complete strangers, often across the continent and sometimes across the globe. The attentive seller understands the potential anxiety this can cause and will remain ever ready to respond to any and all bidder inquiries. When a bidder (or especially a potential bidder) contacts you, be sure to respond quickly, completely, and professionally. Answer the bidders' questions directly and then provide extra information that you think could help them better understand your item or your way of doing business. Remember, you're courting potential customers here, so be friendly and forthcoming. Your goal and duty is to help bidders feel at ease when dealing with you.

- **Maintain a visible sales policy.** Bidders and buyers hope it won't be difficult to find or interpret your business terms. Customers want to be clear about how you intend to do business with them. Develop and publish your sales terms and conditions up front so your customers can quickly understand how you will manage an eventual transaction. Then make your policy easy to find by including the terms directly in your auction descriptions or by embedding an active link in your listing (when clicked, the bidders can navigate to another Web page where your policy can be reviewed). The key here it to make your policy readily available and conspicuously visible —customers don't appreciate guessing games or having to hunt down your sales conditions. If you don't think this is a key to customer service, keep in mind that most customers don't feel well-served if they have to hunt *you* down to determine what kind of business you're running.

- **Establish sales terms that are sensible.** It's a subjective matter, yes, though there are many sales terms that are generally accepted among eBay enthusiasts. Bidders and buyers need information regarding what payment methods you'll accept, what sort of shipping charges you'll apply, and how quickly you'll delivery an item purchased. Be reasonable here—don't mandate "money orders only" or "payment by PayPal—no exceptions." The same goes for shipping charges: don't charge a flat rate of $6.00 if what you typically sell only incurs $3.85 in postage costs. Customers don't appreciate being trapped by unfounded terms that make it look as if sellers are more interested with their convenience at the expense of the customers'. That bidder will most likely bolt from your auction and find another seller who's operating in a more customer-friendly manner.

- **Be clear about guarantees or return privileges.** Your customers need to know what protections and recourse they might have if that treasure they've anxiously awaited turns out to be less than what they expected. Clearly, unlimited guarantees can expose a seller to some buyer's misdeeds, such as phony claims of loss or switch-and-return swindles. But if you want to truly bolster bidders' confidence in you and entice them to bid higher and buy it now, offer them the peace of mind that you'll stand behind every item you sell. If you choose the "all sales final" route, that's perfectly acceptable provided you are very clear and honest about the item, its condition, and the fact that no returns will be accepted. Given a choice, though, customers prefer the safety net of a guarantee.

- **Show a little appreciation.** Though some may argue that dealing with customers can be a grueling exercise in patience (which it sometimes can be), the fact is that most bidders and buyers you'll deal with at online auctions are honest folks intent on doing good business. Simple things like including a "thank you" note with their item or suggesting an alternate shipping method that can save them a buck or two can go a long way. If you treat your customers like people, they'll be more inclined to work with you to improve the transaction. Then, upon completing a successful transaction, be fast to post positive feedback for your customers, letting them know how important and appreciated their business has been to you.

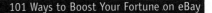
It's been said that to truly excel in customer satisfaction, a seller needs to have a passion to serve customers. "Real customer service comes from the heart," offered a fellow seller. "If you don't truly and deeply value what the customer means to your business's health, you may as well not bother." Your key to ensuring that you remain totally customer focused is to let the customer—not yourself—determine what's satisfactory. Only the customers can tell you if they've been satisfied, and wise sellers keep a pulse on their customers' satisfaction as a means to understanding which direction the business will go.

And by applying these key principles to your business, your approval ratings and profits will have nowhere to go but up.

FORTUNE BOOST #71
REWARD YOUR BUYERS FOR REPEAT BUSINESS

Each of us wants to feel like we're special, like we have a certain "clout" with others. This is especially true of eBay buyers who return to preferred sellers for additional transactions. If you recall the discussion of Fortune Boost #20 (Retaining a Clientele), you'll remember the importance of gaining a customer's trust and the value to your profits if you can encourage a buyer to return for additional purchases. Here now are some simple approaches you can take to further instill customer loyalty and help your repeat buyers feel like they're "preferred" on your list.

- **Relax your sales policies.** If you have customers who prefer to pay with personal checks and you've never gotten one that bounced, waive the bank-clearance delay and show those customers that you trust them since they've been responsible and reliable for you in the past.
- **Offer special services.** Some return customers will have special needs on occasion (perhaps a specific shipping need) and, if you've done good business with those customers in the past and continue to actively receive their patronage, bend a bit to keep those customers active in your sales efforts.
- **Provide discounts.** Long-time sellers know that their customers who spend frequently at their store like the occasional price reduction (who wouldn't). Offer a discount when you can, or offer an additional item at a discount when one is purchased at full price.
- **Give advance notification of the availability of new goods.** This is especially appreciated by buyers who are collectors of rare or hard-to-find items and want to get a jump on competing buyers. When you can, provide advance notice of exciting new items that are coming available, and you might be able to make a direct sale with ease.

Little efforts like these can go a long way in making your regular customers feel special and appreciated. And if you can show a bit of preference to these repeat buyers, chances are they'll continue to consider you among their preferred sellers.

FORTUNE BOOST #72
SELLING OUTSIDE OF eBAY *LEGALLY!*

If you've been selling at eBay for long and have strived to maintain your own con-current sales Web site outside of eBay, you've likely become aware of the site's policies regarding redirecting bidders and buyers away from the auction space; if you're not aware of these policies, you should become familiar with them right away. This Fortune Boost provides key information that will help you better under-stand eBay's policies regarding off-site links and, more importantly, explain how and when you can use such redirection methods to encourage customers to buy from you directly and boost your sales income.

eBay's "Links" Policy

Early on in the eBay experience, savvy buyers found the site to be a fertile ground in which to capture the attention of the millions of registered users and parlay that exposure to pull users away from the site and into a direct-sales Web portal. It makes perfect sense yet eBay wasn't too thrilled that its efforts were being rerouted to help sellers gain greater profits in direct-sales while eBay earned nothing in such transactions. To that end (and whether you agree with it or not), eBay instituted some boundaries to such activity to protect their interests and to protect their users from being lured into unprotected off-site transactions (or so they say).

Item descriptions were the first place that sellers began offering up links to other offerings outside of eBay; it made good sense to do so considering that bidders who were already reading about a desirable item may be interested in other similar goods available directly from the seller. eBay responded by allowing only these sorts of links within an item description (these come directly from eBay's own help pages):

- One link to a page that further describes the item being sold in that listing
- One link to your e-mail address that opens an e-mail client for potential buyers to ask questions about the item in that listing
- Links to photos of the item for sale
- Links to your eBay (including your eBay Store) or Half.com listings
- Links to your About Me page (in addition to the About Me icon already provided by eBay)
- Links to your "Add to My Favorite Sellers and Stores" page
- Links that provide credits to third parties
- One link to your listing terms and conditions (providing that the most relevant information is within the listing itself and that this page does not include any links off of the eBay Web site)

So are these restrictions oppressive or opportunistic? Well, it all depends how you look at it. Actually, there are some excellent opportunities to be gained by working *with* these site polices rather than against them. To wit:

- Links to your own Web site where buyers can find more detailed item descriptions and photos can establish your commitment to providing "disclosure" to aid buyers in being confident in their purchases with you. This helps establish you as a trusted and knowledgeable source of particular goods and information.
- Links to your eBay Store and Half.com listings immediately help bidders find additional goods you have for sale, thus increasing your ability to make multiple sales to a single buyer.
- A link to a more detailed sales terms and policies helps better establish your business practices and (hopefully) will communicate to all buyers exactly how you intend to conduct business to your mutual satisfaction.

OK, but nothing here indicates sales are able to "legally" occur outside of the eBay site. Yes, and no. You need to adhere to eBay's policies or else face the wrath of the site, which could include listing cancellations and suspension from using eBay entirely. So how, then, can you conduct sales off site without getting in the bad graces of eBay? Recall that once an auction has successfully completed, eBay encourages the winning bidder (or buyer) and seller to communicate directly to complete the transaction—and there's your opportunity to market your off-eBay goods. Be prepared to have information about your direct-sales site available in your e-mail communications. Naturally, begin with communicating about the eBay transaction itself to ensure that's completed successfully, then provide additional information as follows:

- A direct-sales Web site name and URL
- A direct-sales Web site logo
- Thumbnail images of other compelling items that might interest your buyer
- Direct contact information, including your direct e-mail address and possibly business phone number.
- A link back to your other active eBay auctions (just to keep visibility of your eBay goods).

Once eBay turns the transaction over to you and your buyers, you're now operating in a free market and you should feel comfortable engaging your buyers in communication regarding other goods (or services) you might have available. Most buyers appreciate this opportunity to buy more items directly from a trusted seller rather than continue to battle with other potential bidders and buyers within eBay. Of course, don't go overboard on the sales pitch or else you'll risk being regarded as bothersome or a possible spammer. Let them know about your business, help them find your direct sales site, keep it all within the boundaries of eBay's policies, and you'll find you can conduct additional business without worrying whether you'll come under fire from eBay. It is the site that's providing you access to millions of potential customers, so treat it with care and respect.

FORTUNE BOOST #73
HANDLING DIFFICULT BUYERS

Though it's been the long-held mantra that "the customer's always right," the fact is that's not always the case. And while committed eBay sellers work hard to be flexible and accommodating to their valued customers, some patrons just seem to be a pain right in the bottom line. To help manage such situations, here are some tactics to help sellers avoid such wayward transactions and what to do when a buyer requires significantly more "hands-on" treatment than originally expected.

Set the Ground Rules

Clear and concise communication is really the best tool for establishing the mood, methods, and motivation for the transaction ahead of you. A good seller gets a jump-start on setting expectations by having clearly stated sales policies within the body of the auction description and following those policies to the "T" when it comes time to engage the high bidder. Though not 100 percent fail-safe, clear sales policies in your auction description will help screen out some bidders you'd rather avoid. Following up with quick end-of-auction communication will make it clear that you're committed to getting the deal done fast and "as-advertised."

Share the Ownership

Remember, it takes two to transact, and a deal can only be successful when *both* parties are committed. As a seller, you state your policies and methods up front—no surprises. If there is concern or disagreement on the buyer's part, you two have the option to negotiate a *mutually agreeable* solution (you can also stick to your original policy if you choose). Whatever is agreed, though, is owned by the two of you. So long as you, the seller, hold up your end of the bargain, there's no room for the buyer to contest the agreement. As seller, you might wish to remain reasonably flexible to a buyer's reasonable needs, though.

Diffuse the Bomb

This goes back to the basic tenets of dealing with customers: kill 'em with kindness. While you should never be a doormat to anyone, you can head off caustic situations by showing understanding and a willingness to make the deal work. If a buyer becomes irritated, quickly ask what the problem is—often, it's simple misunderstanding. If the buyer won't settle down and seems bent on arguing with you, it might be best to respond with, *"Perhaps it would be better if we canceled this deal."* Whether the buyer seemingly doesn't like you or is trying a harsh tactic to weasel out of his commitment, you're likely better off to cut this one loose and move on.

A Word about Feedback

When things get ugly, sellers sometimes throw out the threat: *"I'll post negative feedback against you!"* Anymore, this isn't as effective for coercing cantankerous customers to comply—it's really the last word after a bitter divorce. Post negs if you feel you must, but expect them in return. Though you shouldn't feel unjust in speaking your mind in the public forum, take a moment to ask what the neg might truly achieve. Give it some thought, then do whatever you feel will serve you best, both now and in the future.

Rising Above It All

If you have been through somewhat of a bumpy experience with a buyer but the deal comes off smoothly in the end, recognize that fact and thank the buyer for working with you. Though we often would like to lash out at that incorrigible so-and-so, a professional manner always leaves you standing tall in the face of adversity. Chalk it up as a win for you as you further develop your customer management skills.

(Note: Not *all* difficult customers can be successfully corralled into a good transaction. If you wonder whether you'll need to kow-tow to the truly troublesome, you'll find a bit of relief in Fortune Boost # 76.)

FORTUNE BOOST #74
HOW ONLINE CROOKS CAN HELP YOUR BUSINESS

What? Is this some sort of joke? As absurd as it may seem to suggest that online scammers have benefited the virtual business owner, the fact is that cyber-crooks can and *have* been instrumental in the education and enlightenment of Internet merchants and their customers the world over. Many ill-doers have deftly disappeared into the ether of eBay and the Internet after committing a dastardly deed, but there have been plenty who have been caught and brought to justice. Before you throw up your hands and proclaim that fraud is an ever-waiting killer ready to halt your eBay business in its tracks, take a moment, first, to say "thanks" to this ilk on the online marketplaces—well, sort of.

Flash back to the early days of online buying and selling as Internet newcomers, wide-eyed and worry free, ventured into the virtual marketplace. It was a veritable Eden called *e-commerce*. Yet, the nefarious tricksters slither in, intent on manipulating a sale, duping a buyer, or backing out on purchase commitments wherever and whenever they please. The good people of the Net were left stunned and dismayed—yet ready to take action.

When online fraud emerged as the National Consumer's League #1 complaint in 1998, it prompted an accelerated coming-of-age for the evolving new cottage industry. Just as this online population had demonstrated the original prowess to bring such a virtual marketplace to life in the first place, they proved equally determined in policing their new Internet neighborhoods and storefronts.

Credit Pierre Omidyar, founder and creator of eBay, for launching the Internet's first community feedback system. Buyers and sellers learned the value of conducting themselves in responsible fashion, building an online reputation that would be seen by millions of their peers—the same system that also effectively ferreted out the Net's ne'er-do-wells who believed they could hide within the pixels, never to be brought to justice for their unscrupulous acts. Nice try but no dice.

But has justice been served online? Recall Robert Guest, who in 1999 became the first to be convicted of auction fraud, scamming his unwary customers out of $37,000 for nonexistent computer goods. Then, who could forget Kenneth Walton, convicted in the attempted sale of the phony Richard Diebenkorn painting, nearly racking up $136,000 in the thwarted swindle.

What has helped bring online criminals to the halls of justice is the very alert and sophisticated online community that has become quite adept at sniffing out a rat. Taking a lesson from the online population's vigilance, Vermont Senator Patrick Leahy introduced legislation to provide for $25 million in training state and local law enforcement agencies in cybercrime—how to detect it and how to prosecute it.

So where's the silver lining to this cloud of criminal activity that has partially obscured the skies of the e-commerce landscape? First, it should be expected that anywhere money changes hands—anywhere money's to be made—there will be shady characters lurking about. However, just as shop owners and community members of the offline world have increased their ability to self-police the areas where they work, shop, and live, so too has this concept of civil awareness translated to the online destinations and sales venues. Sellers now astutely establish policies and procedures to protect themselves from risky business; buyers use safe payment systems and virtual report cards to ensure they won't be duped. And consumer advocacy groups and law enforcement agencies have made online crime a top priority.

Yes, some among us have sadly fallen prey to online misconduct, but the end result has been the valuable lessons learned by a virtual population of buyers, sellers, and browsers who now know how to protect themselves, their personal information, and their monetary assets. It's the sort of education you can't get in any school except perhaps the School of Hard Knocks. But, thanks to the interactive nature of the Internet, online businesspeople are actively talking, sharing, and watching—and they're not being ignored.

So, while this particular tip has not been sent *directly* at your bottom line, it's a friendly reminder how the sometimes-unsettling news of online fraudsters can bring about greater awareness and readiness in the thoughts and actions of fortune-bound sellers. Just post the sign in plain sight: "Violators *will be* prosecuted."

FORTUNE BOOST #75
THE KEYS TO BUILDING A STELLAR ONLINE AUCTION REPUTATION

Your good name can be one of your greatest assets at eBay, but if you don't keep it highly polished and squeaky clean, it could become your most limiting liability. In the world of online selling, the bidders and buyers you court don't know you, can't see you, and might not yet even trust you. It's up to you to actively establish an online presence that serves as a beacon to bidders, guiding them to your auctions while easing any doubts they may have. Building a stellar reputation, then, doesn't happen overnight, but there are several steps you can take to gain the customer exposure you need, get the edge on your competition, and ultimately give your customers good cause to trumpet your online activities and spend more money in your virtual store.

Get Noticed

It's tough to be seen among the millions of other sellers online and, as you strive to establish a stellar reputation, you'll first need to take every measure available to be seen as you strive to rise above the crowd. The first step in building an online reputation is by making your presence known. Forget the bold type and fancy icons (those just add to your selling costs, remember). Rather, take advantage of these attention-getting moves:

- **Peak Timing:** Stage your auctions for 5 or 7 days, ending on a weekend, closing between 6:00 and 8:00 p.m. Pacific time for maximum bidder exposure.
- **High Hitting:** Carefully choose keywords that are most likely to be searched by bidders, ensuring that your listings appear in the maximum number of result lists.
- **Category Savvy:** There's a sea of them to choose from, so research which are host to items like yours and where the most active browsing seems to take place.
- **Detail Oriented:** Give ample information about the items you'll sell so bidders won't feel like they're taking a risk.
- **Image Conscious:** Provide clear photos of your items or thumbnail links to a gallery of images in your listings. Don't overdo it or your item pages will take too long to load, causing bidders to lose interest and leave.
- **Cross Listed:** Cross-reference your concurrent auctions in the descriptions of your listings. Use HTML links to make it easier for bidders to jump from item to item.

Being deliberate in how and when you'll list your items will gain you greater exposure to the millions of bidders searching for goods. If you serve up high-quality listings for your high-quality items, you'll be more likely to be remembered by customers who like what you sell.

Get Knowledgeable

To really carve a prolific presence in the auction world today, you'll need to convince bidders that you're an expert who can be trusted and is worth seeking out again and again. If you merely dabble in the goods you sell and have limited knowledge to match, you might be perceived as risky by some.

In order to gain bidders' confidence as well as capture their bids, sellers need to establish themselves as being reliable sources of goods *and* information. If you don't know the facts, find out. Read collector's books, trade journals, historical references, and anything else that will give you the inside information that bidders are looking for. By offering up accurate descriptions, key details, appropriate pricing, and answers to specific questions, sellers provide the proof of their knowledge and become recognized for being trustworthy sources that bidders learn they can count on. With the ever-present specter of fraud lurking online, bidders are taking greater precautions to be choosy about whom they'll buy from.

Get Committed

Your sales are your bread and butter; your customers are feeding your fortune. Strive to *exceed* customer expectations with every sale. Be prompt, professional, and pleasant in all communications—don't make them wait and don't leave them wondering.

Offer clarification about your products and your sales policies whenever asked. Give clear and concise answers to a bidder's questions. Then provide additional information that you think will help potential bidders feel more confident about bidding on your auctions, be it product related or policy related.

And go the extra mile if transactions get a bit muddled and require special handling. Keep those customers satisfied. Show them your commitment to better business by actively working to clear confusion and resolve potential problems. You're not only working for the satisfaction of those customers, but also you're protecting your reputation from the sort of disgruntled retribution that could mar your otherwise blemish-free reputation.

Get Personal

By all means, don't pry into your bidders' private lives, but let them peer in a bit on yours. Given this is the "faceless" Internet you're dealing on, bidders aren't able to make that face-to-face contact as they might at a shop or show—remember, they can't see you and might have trouble trusting you. Remedy the situation by sharing something of yourself with an eBay About Me page or information about how customers can visit your own Web site to learn more about you. Though it might sound superficial and possibly irrelevant on the surface, many bidders are eager to see and know just who it is they might be dealing with; that is far more comforting than an eBay User ID. Consider it an icebreaker as well as another way to gain recognition and rapport with the bidding public.

Get Interactive

One of the most recognized tools for building a reputation at eBay is with a high feedback rating. Work hard on each transaction and your customers will be bubbling over with positive comments to pour into your feedback profile. Sometimes, though, you'll need to lead by example: upon completion of successful transactions, post positive comments for your customers and encourage them to do the same for you (don't be bashful about asking for the props you deserve). Though you can't *force* anyone to post feedback for you, you'll find that most will be more than happy to comply, eager to let other bidders know you're one of the good eggs.

Get it All Together

Gaining a reputation means gaining recognition in the places where you'll conduct business. If you apply these tactics with determination and diligence, you'll become one of those sellers that bidders will be eager to deal with again. And, when those customers begin singing your praises, you'll attract the attention of even more bidders who are looking for a reputable seller worthy of their business, too.

FORTUNE BOOST #76
FLUSHING OUT THE DEADBEATS
THAT COST YOU DOLLARS

While most buyers you'll encounter on eBay will qualify as genuine "good eggs," beware of the occasional stinkers that might come along who'll retract, renege, and refute their responsibilities to complete a transaction. While, as a seller, you can't really hold a gun to flaky buyers' heads and force them to pay up, you likewise don't need to be a doormat to those flighty few who think this online buying is just another form of entertainment. To protect yourself, your business reputation, and your valuable time, here are some approaches to help you prevent the cost of a losing proposition if ever you find yourself dealing with this scourge of the online marketplace: the deadbeat buyer.

The Deadbeat Pool

Ask longtime sellers where they encountered their first deadbeats and, most likely, they'll seethe, "at eBay!" Because the online auctions embody a certain level of gamesmanship in competitive bidding, often emotionally charged, they also incur the sobering *bidder's remorse* not to mention attract those aggravating *gamey bidders* who bid for fun with little intention to follow through.

Of course, while it would be inappropriate to level a wholesale castigation on eBay or slap an egregious generality on the majority of responsible bidders, there is no denying that the online parlor has given rise to the notion that online purchase commitments are only as good as the ether in which they're written. So while it's good news that eBay has done much to verify and virtually indemnify

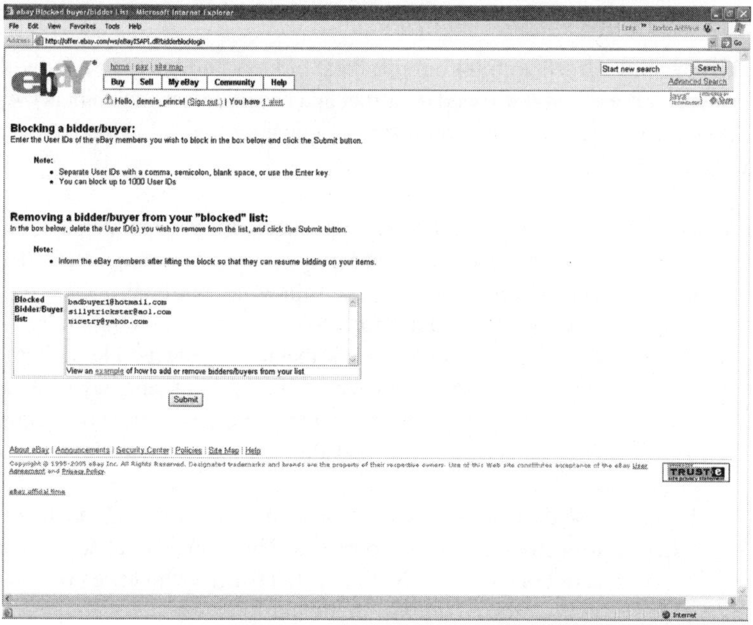

Figure 76-1 If there are deadbeats who have been giving you trouble, get a drop on them by adding their names to you own eBay Blocked Bidders List.

bad buyers, it's still the seller's responsibility to identify ways to stop deadbeats in their tracks, even *before* they can infiltrate your listings.

Head 'Em Off at the Outset

As some undercommitted buyers once merrily cruised the various online auction places and fixed-price sales destinations of old to play their game of yes-I-want-it-no-I-don't, today's sellers have found the need to protect themselves from such capricious shenanigans. Here are some preventive tactics you can use to help thwart deadbeats before they can strike your eBay activities:

- Institute sales policies that clearly state when payment is to be received (either via online payment, phone orders, or snail mail remittance) with the option to negate the sale if payment is not received within a stated time window (usually 10 days).
- Block habitual deadbeat bidders' IDs using eBay's Blocked Bidders List (see Figure 76-1) or by reserving the right to cancel bids of deadbeats you've previously encountered.
- Keep track of less-than-reliable buyers at your fixed-price Web site, too, *a la* a "blacklist." (No, it's not a nice thing to have to do, but you do have to protect your interests.)

Manage the Deadbeats that Slip Through

Despite your best efforts to filter out deadbeat bidders and buyers, some will still slip through (after all, you *do* need to attract and entertain new customers). Again, to help you ascertain a buyer's commitment, consider the following engagement methods:

- Be prompt in your e-mail correspondence with your bidders and buyers and state your expectation to receive an equally prompt reply. If your messages go unanswered, offer a follow-up notification stating your right to negate a sale if your efforts to make contact are ignored.
- Beware "excuse abuse" in which all manner of down-and-out, hard luck stories will come your way as to why the buyer can't send payment just yet if at all. Show an appropriate amount of compassion but don't allow the transaction to become drawn out and ultimately cost you a sales opportunity elsewhere.
- If you've got deadbeats on your hands, cut 'em loose and move along to other customers as quickly as possible. Then quickly relist the item for bid or sale, or contact any other interested parties who have previously or concurrently expressed interest in the item.

Be Positive about Negatives

One conspicuous feature about eBay is its Feedback Forum. While you'll hopefully find yourself in a routine of exchanging glowing tributes with your dependable customers, you might wish to lay a negative comment on the deadbeats you encounter. Take heed in what you do, though, as your negative comment might also earn you one in return (eBay's still pretty slow or nonresponsive to sellers who attempt to have a bad bidder's caustic remarks removed from an otherwise top-notch reputation).

Some sellers will opt to dispense with posting negative feedback while they dispense with the deadbeat at the same time. Other sellers feel the responsibility to post warning of the misdeeds of a deadbeat. Your best advice: allow yourself a day to consider a negative comment and what backlash it might incur. But, if you're confident it's the thing to do, then exercise your right to objectively air your grievance in the public forum.

Collect on Your Loss

Be sure to take advantage of fee reimbursements at eBay when you find you've been stiffed. As you make contact with the site to request your remuneration, be sure to also report the deadbeat's user ID. Even though site suspension is easy for deadbeats to circumvent, you'll still be able to slow them a bit in their evasive efforts and hopefully they'll steer away from you and your well-prepared profit machine.

FORTUNE BOOST #77
STUPID BIDDER TRICKS

OK. So you've read quite a bit now—76 ways to boost your eBay fortune by keeping both your sights and your spirit high. Good for you! But, while the positive outlook is always best to boost your eBay endeavors, I realize that sometimes we bump into folks who really try our patience and test our innate goodness. So, just in case you think I've taken too much of a *Pollyannish* outlook on maintaining an eBay business, recognize that I, too, have my personal limits. So, let's vent a bit, shall we? You may laugh or you may grimace as I shine this chastising light on those annoying little bidders and their asinine little antics that I call *Stupid Bidder Tricks*—but maybe some of this has happened to you, too.

Reading Is Fundamental

Let me start by giving props where props are due: many sellers have worked hard to present a sales policy that's quite thorough (frequently exhaustive) for the obvious intent of setting down their rules, plain and simple. But, along comes a stupid bidder trick and —*poof*—the fruit of a seller's labor is spoiled by bidders who simply refuse to read.

Can these bidders read? *Do* these bidders care? Apparently it's a "no" on both counts.

Whether griping about payment methods, postage costs, or refund policies, it seems some bidders will bid first and ask questions later. What frosts the cookies here is when said bidder becomes irate when the seller won't freely acquiesce to the bidder's wishes. Sellers: stand by your guns. And to those stupid bidders, remind 'em to read the fine print and, if they don't like what they've read, encourage them to bid somewhere else. Don't waste your time with the whining and whimpering about how they're case is special. You have a business to run and, if your temper's at the bursting point, it's OK to let a bidder know it.

Dumb and Dumber

Not only have I encountered the same reading-impaired shoppers as have many of you, but I've also entertained many other curious folk who seem to be playing a few cards short of a full deck. To wit:

- How about the winning bidder who sends you money with no note, no mention of *what* was won, and no shipping address. This makes for an amusing game of "Find the Ninny," and if I'm unsuccessful, I'll donate the funds to UNICEF.
- Then there's the bidder who asks if I accept PayPal. Actually, no—I was intending on selling that large PayPal logo that adorned my listing. The other text and images of an item were merely a smoke screen I use to confuse the less-clever bidders.

- One fellow sent a personal check with this note: "*Please don't wait for my check to clear before shipping—it's good.*" They're so cute when they talk that way.
- And there are also the bidders who contact me when *I'm* bidding, too: "*Hey* [expletive]*! Don't you* [expletive] *have anything better to do than* [expletive] *outbid people at the last second? You* [expletive] [expletive]*!!*" As a matter of fact, I don't have anything better to do and I would never pass up the opportunity to meet such intelligent and interesting people like you.

Hey, everyone's entitled to a goof, a blunder, and even a word out of turn from time to time, but some of the folks I've run up against have me wondering if the gene pool's gone stagnant. And, for sellers, this sort of stuff adds up to more wasted time and biting of the lip.

It's the gold of office chit-chat, though.

This Is Not Funny Anymore

It's one thing to be genuinely silly, ostensibly oafish, or downright dumb in bidding, but some of these stupid bidder tricks aren't so stupid—largely because they're flat out illegal. That's right: I'm talking about all those schemers with an arsenal of user IDs that they regularly summon in their bid-shielding rip-offs and auction-tampering antics. And don't think we didn't see those swap-and-return cretins out there, looking for free upgrades. What makes these bidder tricks so stupid is that most are perpetrated by obvious amateurs who leave an undeniable—and highly incriminating—trail to follow. It's amazing that these folks wouldn't anticipate that today's eBay sellers have seen quite a bit in the past 10-plus years and very few intend to be so easily duped.

And so the moral of the story, I guess, is that these strange, insidious, and unexplainable things will continue to happen wherever people meet to exchange goods. But, remember, just because the virtual venue is relatively new, the tricks are still some of the oldest in the book.

If you need, it's OK to vent once in awhile, but it's usually safest in this manner on a seller-to-seller basis. Whoever said the "customer is always right" failed to note some of these footnotes here. You don't have to blow your customers' hair back at every infraction, but it's best for your business if you take a no-nonsense attitude to those who would attempt to play a stupid bidder trick on you.

Give me a break!

FORTUNE BOOST #78
STUPID SELLER TRICKS

All righty, then. I just talked about all the stupid thing buyers do. Now it's time to turn to sellers. I'm a guy who believes in a live-and-let-live coexistence, but some of the stuff I've seen sellers doing at the auctions is, frankly, aggravating the heck out of me.

Again, here we are, running on 10-plus years of this eBay thing and apparently there's still no shortage of silly sellers who insist on misrepresenting their stuff with cheap come-ons and slack sales pitches. Mind you, I don't hold up some unreachable standards by which all sellers should be measured, but the sloppiness, sly approaches, and, yes, *stupid tricks* being used are really annoying when most of us are seeking out the best and most bountiful ways to boost an online fortune.

Holey moley—sounds serious, doesn't it? Well, you decide 'cause I'm seeing red with the stupid tricks on *this* side of the auction fence, too. Make sure you're not doing any of these deadly sins of selling.

A Rare Bird...Should Be Shot Dead

First aggravation: is *everything* really "rare"? (Short answer: no.) Case in point comes back in 2000 when many newspapers prematurely announced the presidential proclamation "Bush Wins!" (well, eventually, but not immediately.) OK. If you grabbed a copy of the premature publication you'd think it's a real collector's item. Fair enough, but when I saw them being auctioned at eBay and Yahoo as "rare early editions" and "of limited run," a simple search turned up more than 2,000 additional one-of-a-kind *blunder*-ful baubles. Rare? I think not. Show me a "Dewey Defeats Truman" Tribune from '48—that's tougher to come by and your buyers know it. So drop the old "this is really rare and going to be worth plenty, friend" routine. It's a stale act.

And it's not just these newspapers—it's all the other stuff that some sellers peddle as "out of print," "hard to find," and "very limited." Most of the time, I can find such things readily available at retail sites online (as in the case of books, CDs, videos, and so on). And, if the items truly aren't to be bought on the retail circuit, a quick look at eBay, Yahoo, and Amazon often shows ample specimens to choose from. Maybe it's just a matter of semantics, interpretation, or even personal perception. I, however, see the superfluous use of "rare" and the like as nothing more than misrepresentation. Period.

Reserve This!

Next peeve: "No reserve!" Cool. An auction where the bidders get to hammer out the true market value, right? 'Fraid not. I check the starting bid, the one that's well beyond the present going rate and I've stumbled onto another total waste of time. Folks, if you're going the "no reserve" route, the let the bidders set the price; don't set them up for an ambush.

Stingy with a Sentence?

And what else? Well, how 'bout the auction that offers the voluminous 10-word description—which includes the auction title; goes something like this:

Item as shown. Buyer pays shipping. Gee. How helpful. C'mon now sellers. Even if a photo is pointed up, give the bidders a morsel of common courtesy and respect and tell them something useful about the item they might have been interested in owning—of course, your item just fell out of favor in response to your verbal stinginess.

So are these such weighty infractions that I should get myself all tied up in a knot? Maybe not. Perhaps this stuff just gets me a bit cranky, but when I trip over this sort of misguided merchandising, only then to hear sellers sometimes gripe that sell-through rates are down at eBay, it makes me want to blow my top. I see this lazy effort in salesmanship—what I believe forces bidders to play guessing games—and find little sympathy to offer to those who complain that sales are down.

Fair is fair and sometimes sellers are guilty of committing stupid tricks. Enough said.

FORTUNE BOOST #79
WHAT TO DO WHEN eBAY BOUNCES

While the site, thankfully, hasn't experienced a near-devastating outage like the 22-hour derailment of June 1999, eBay has, on occasion, gone dark. Whether the fault of incomplete disaster prevention measures or the result of another maddening Web-spread virus, eBay remains vulnerable to those times when the virtual plug gets kicked out of the socket. Although it's infrequent, it's still a potential impact to you and your business. Therefore, here are some things to consider as you, too, prepare for a time when eBay might bounce.

Understand eBay's Site Outage Policy

First, be very clear on how eBay responds when its site gets sluggish. The site currently defines two types of outages:

- **Title Search Outage:** If ever you've accessed eBay and attempted to search for items, only to be greeted by a screen that indicates the Search function is temporarily unavailable, you've seen a Title Search outage. When this occurs for more than an hour, eBay indicates it will automatically credit back-listing fees for any listings scheduled to close during the outage period.
- **Hard Outage:** When the entire site is inaccessible (you try to navigate to www.ebay.com only to find that your browser is unable to resolve the host argument), the site is undergoing a complete outage—a *hard outage*. If the outage lasts between one and two hours, eBay will offer the same automatic listing fee credits as during a Title Search outage. If the hard outage extends beyond two hours, though, eBay will provide the same credits, plus eBay will automatically extend the ending time of a listing by 24 hours.

Naturally, you'll want to fully review and understand the site's outage policy, so be sure to visit http://pages.ebay.com/help/everyone-outage.html.

Have Your Own Plan

After you've understood how eBay will react in the event of an outage, you'll also need to determine if their actions reflect your needs and desires in case the site slips. Here's what you can do to protect your efforts—and your bottom line—from outages.

First and foremost, make sure your sales policy includes provisions in the event of a site outage. Longtime sellers have learned it pays to indicate what is to be expected if an outage occurs during an auction's run. To that end, some sellers will indicate that they reserve the right to nullify any final bid amounts in the event of an outage, that they reserve the right to cancel all bidding activity and relist an item, or that they can proceed with a sale if they so desire. Take time to fully evaluate how an outage could affect your listings—in terms of when a search can't be completed, a bid can't be placed, or a user's question (via eBay's "Ask the Seller a Question" link) can't be answered. Hopefully it isn't a policy that you'll need to utilize often, but if the unexpected situation arises, you'll want to be prepared.

If an outage occurs and you believe it has disrupted your ability to achieve sales or satisfy your customers, be ready to leap into action, recover any site fees due to you, and intervene directly with your customers to sort out the matter and regain your footing as quickly as possible.

FORTUNE BOOST #80
TAKING A BREAK WITHOUT BREAKING YOUR BOTTOM LINE

While it's true that fortunes are made when sellers run at the speed of business, it's just as valid that even the most well-oiled machine needs a rest once in awhile. Whether you intend to take one extended vacation a year or several minibreaks along the way, it's important you stop and rest to maintain your stamina and stability in the online marketplace. But can you really take a vacation from you eBay activity and not lose your place in customers' minds? Sure you can. Here's how.

First off, eBay already has a provision for their storeowners who need to signal that they'll be vacationing for a time. If you've kept a store well stocked with tantalizing goods yet are going to be away for a period of time, do the following:

1. Go to the My eBay area of the site and select the "Manage Your Store" link in the My Subscriptions box.
2. Once inside the Store management area, select the "Change vacation settings" link.
3. On the settings page, enable the vacation alert, "Turn vacation settings On."
4. Click on "Save settings" and you're done.

So what happens to your eBay Store while you're on vacation? Well, all of your Store inventory items will be hidden from site searches while the vacation setting is enabled. This prevents buyers from finding and purchasing your goods while you're away. Otherwise, they'd await response from you or arrival of the item they purchased, unaware that you're away from your store and unable to tend to their purchases or inquiries (which would make for a pretty unpleasant shopping experience).

But what about your auction items? Well, setting a vacation flag on your eBay Store won't affect any auction-format listings you might have active, so you'll need to tend to these separately. Consider timing auctions to end around one week prior to your vacation so you can ship all goods before you depart. Some sellers elect to keep listings running during their vacation and add a special note that they're away and cannot respond directly to any questions during that time (you'll need to decide if you think that will work for you and your customers).

One more thing to enable, after you've set your eBay Store vacation setting, stopped the mail, and told the milkman to suspend deliveries: enable an extended absence auto-respond message in your e-mail (this is especially effective if you have a mail node dedicated solely to your sales business). Leave an auto-respond note enabled indicating you're unable to respond to messages for a particular period of time and that you'll reply upon your return. In this way, you'll prevent customers from wondering why you're so unresponsive to their e-mail messages. And, while that's working for you, you can be taking a well-deserved break from your online work.

FORTUNE BOOST #81
WHAT A DAY FOR A DAYDREAM...TO DOLLARS!

"A little nonsense now and then, cherished by the wisest men."

—*Roald Dahl, Willy Wonka and
the Chocolate Factory*

While this quote may seem pure whimsy and designed to merely entertain children with its rhythmic meter, the fact is that author Roald Dahl had pierced to the core of what makes good thinkers into great thinkers. If you've been working your fingers to the bone and taxing your mind endlessly in your online endeavors, it might be time for you to take a break lest you lose sight of the fortune that is easily in reach. When it comes to taking a mental break—short or extended—it's important you realize the value of stopping once in awhile to catch your breath and regain your perspective on your activities and your goals.

Burnout is a reality of the 9-to-5 workforce, those who trudge off to an office or some other place of employment, punching a time card and watching the hours and days of their lives click by. When overwhelmed with the "routine" of task-mastering, many folks lose their ability to invoke vision into their efforts. That is, some folks, when they get so wrapped up in their day-to-day duties, often fail to see greater efficiencies and profit potential in front of their noses. Therefore, at this point in your online selling, be sure you're avoiding the mechanics of your work such that they'd fog your ability to see new options and new opportunities. In a word, dare to *daydream.*

Step One: Avoid Burnout

Although many high-volume sellers believed they'd find true freedom from the daily grind if they could only break the shackles of their "regular job" and migrate to an occupation of fun and fulfillment in online auctioning and selling, some of those same dreamers have once again found they're becoming overwhelmed by their work. No doubt about it, online selling takes work, effort, and a commitment to succeed. Many such self-employed individuals have found they work more hours in their online endeavors than they did in their former time-card existence "working for the man." If you're in this boat (or if you'd prefer to avoid ever getting into it), here are the signs to watch out for that could indicate you're burning out:

1. An increasing feeling of fatigue.
2. Increasing loss of interest in your online activity.
3. Lack of motivation.
4. Anger.
5. Decreased job satisfaction.
6. Depression.
7. Increased substance use or abuse.

Yes, this sounds serious because it is. It can be avoided, however, by planning time to push away from it all and gain perspective on your purpose. Therefore, if you sense the onset of burnout or prefer to never get so overwhelmed in the first place, consider these tactics:

Plan a start and stop time for your work, each day, and then plan on which days you'll work and on which you'll rest.

Set tomorrow's work goals tonight. Plan what you'll need to do and what you reasonably *can* do for the next day at the close of every preceding day (this helps avoid starting the day in the confusion of, "where should I start?").

Plan breaks throughout every day to do the relaxing things you enjoy. Whether sitting outside, sipping a cup of tea, or listening to music, plan 10- to 15-minute breaks at least once every two hours to keep yourself fresh and focused.

Allow for minor interruptions to your work, but *never* allow for interruptions to your breaks. Too often, breaks and lunchtime are whiled away by phone calls or other unplanned activities, preventing you from getting a true respite from your work and leaving you ultimately unrefreshed.

What to Do with Your Break

Here's where the real discipline comes in and where too many great opportunities are lost for lack of recognition. When you take your breaks, relax and let your mind run free. Look to the sky, stare at the wall, go exercise, or just close your eyes and let your mind unravel. This is when you'll be doing your best problem solving and fortune finding—when you're not *actively* trying to. It's for this same reason that many of us bolt up in bed with a great idea, one that could only be discovered when all the day-to-day business has been put to sleep to allow the creative influences to overtake our thought processes. So, when you break, give your mind a break, too, and you'll find more answers and better ideas when you least expect them. Before you know it, you'll be daydreaming your way to dollars like you never before thought possible.

Boosting Your Business
at eBay and Beyond

As we get ready to leap ahead into matters that will take your business beyond eBay, take a moment to revisit the tenets of customer service and maintaining satisfaction in each and every one of your business transactions. Perhaps the sharpest dual-edged sword you'll face in your business regards your claim of "100 Percent Satisfaction Guaranteed." It's truly the best policy for encouraging new customers to do business with you but at the same time many sellers fear it will open the door to unscrupulous buyers who will attempt to make a doormat of you. The good news is you can do both: provide a policy that treats the customer like royalty without leaving you feeling like a fool.

To establish a successful guarantee program, be sure to do the following:

- Post your guarantee plainly and clearly on your business site and/or within your auction listings.
- Explain exactly what you guarantee, but don't get caught up in a lot of small print and conditional text. The best policy is "100 percent guaranteed, full refund if not fully satisfied."
- Be friendly in all dealings, especially in times of expressed customer dissatisfaction.
- Be genuinely concerned if a customer raises a complaint or feels the need to exercise your guarantee policy. This could tell you something about how you're positioning your products or perhaps how you're potentially misleading customers.

- Always work to make the sale right. Ask if the customer wants a replacement, credit, or a refund. Give them options so they can choose what's best for them. The best sellers are those who can leave a customer feeling confident about having dealt with you and eager to come back even if a deal fell apart or a product failed to satisfy.

That all sounds fine from the customer's standpoint, but how can you be sure you won't be target for false claims, switch-and-return scams, and generally having your good business nature taken for granted? Well, it's a very fine line, but you can satisfy customers while still protecting yourself in the process.

- Anticipate your customers' needs and goals to determine if they appear as good prospects or potential sources of discontent.
- Try to pick up on your customers' attitudes as you begin to arrange a sale with them–are they pleasant and agreeable to your products and policies or are they immediately taking exception to some of your business stipulations?
- Establish policies in which you can explain how *both* of you will be protected; never accuse a customer of being suspicious but explain your need, as a businessperson, to protect your interests.
- Beware of customers that seem overly interested in your return policies–they may not intend to stick with the deal.
- Don't be afraid to turn a customer away if you feel doubtful about the final outcome–explain that you don't feel you can meet the customer's needs and that the transaction should be avoided.

In the end, though, expect that a 100 Percent Satisfaction Guaranteed policy will cost your business from time to time. Whether it's claims of broken merchandise, lost packages, or a change of heart, sometimes your best efforts will go unrewarded. Typically, this is considered a cost of doing business and will most often be the smallest minority of your dealings. However, the fact that you are willing to offer such a guarantee can often bring in even more business than ever because it shows your commitment to fair, honest, and customer-driven business tactics.

FORTUNE BOOST #83
CLASSIFIED INFORMATION

It's funny how business and technology can be so cyclical. Recall that eBay got its first big boost into dot-com awareness thanks to classified "for sale" ads listed within the Usenet. Back in the mid-1990s, sellers who used the rec.collecting Newsgroup (among others) listed ads for items available for bid at a site called AuctionWeb (eBay's former moniker). In short order, Usenet traffic streamed into the AuctionWeb site and, well, the result is eBay.

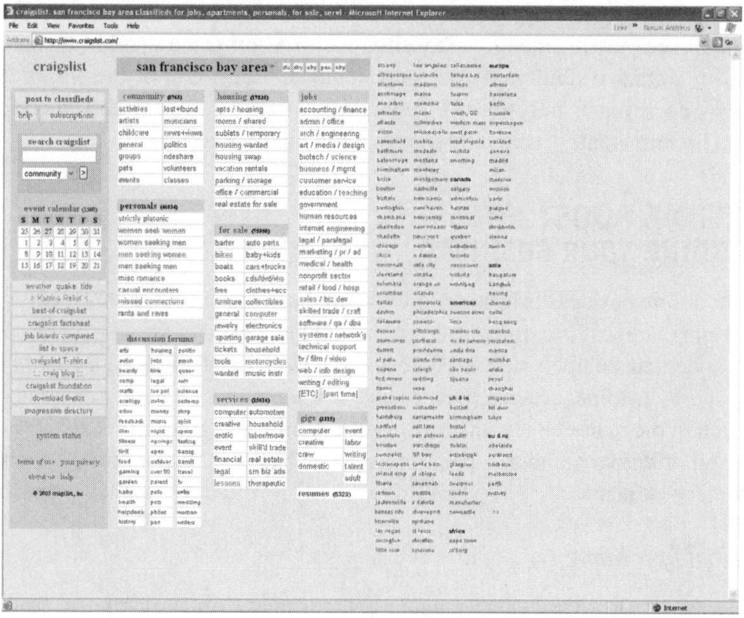

Figure 83-1 Not just a piece of high-tech nostalgia, Craigslist has become a worldwide classified ad phenomenon. Be sure you advertise there, too.

Today, though, there's been a return to the simplicity of the classifieds model with the unbridled success of Craigslist (www.craigslist.com). Originally founded in 1995 by Craig Newmark for use in the San Francisco Bay Area, Craigslist never competed, just coexisted, alongside eBay and others. After incorporating in 1999, Craigslist began to expand beyond the boundaries of the City and, as of October 2005, it has become established in more than 150 cities throughout the United States, Canada, the United Kingdom, Ireland, Europe, Australia, and beyond. Though simple in design yet complex in scope, Craigslist is a bona-fide success. (See Figure 83-1.)

Those sellers who have seen the value of extending the visibility of their goods and their Web presences have used Craigslist to maintain a presence there, bringing customers back to the eBay Stores and self-run Web stores.

And how can Craigslist help you extend your online offerings? Take heed that the site is a preferred hunting ground for folks who are in need of some sort of help or assistance with their daily needs. If you have a knack for Web design, you're a crack tutor for an academic discipline, or you just have a big truck that can be immediately put to use in helping someone move a big sleeper-sofa across town, be sure to actively market your "services" because that's what many folks are actively seeking.

Craigslist currently serves over three billion page views per month, is in seventh place overall among most visited Internet companies, and is the place you should maintain visibility of your goods and services. Use of the site is free (it receives its revenue only through charging for paid job ads) and, therefore, it should be immediately added to your overall online presence.

FORTUNE BOOST #84
BRANDING YOUR BUSINESS

If your online business is brimming with terrific products but seems to struggle in developing a repeat customer base, you might be in need of brand–a name, a look, and a style that shoppers will remember and will associate with high quality goods and superb customer service. Don't leave it up to chance whether customers will find you in the marketplace. Instead, consider employing these methods for developing an effective brand and positioning your business' name in the forefront of customers' minds.

Developing a Name that Sells

Choosing an effective business name is no simple task (just ask the firms who spend millions of dollars on such efforts). It's not necessary, though, to seek out an advertising firm to develop a winning name. According to some of the greatest marketing minds, an effective business (or product) name should have the following characteristics:

- It defines the benefit of your product or service.
- It's easy to remember.
- It's not too similar to any other established business name or brand.
- It differentiates your business from your competitors.
- It's multinational.

Of course, the online realm requires that a few extra considerations be taken into account when developing a cyber-moniker. First, keep the name as short as possible yet try to ensure that it is mentally and verbally "pronounceable." Try to eliminate use of special characters (such as hyphens, ampersands, and the like) as well as numbers; these are the sorts of characters customers tend to forget easily.

Above all, select a name that's appropriate to your business or product. If you're in the business of selling books, choose a fitting name like "BookWorld" or "RareBooks." More colorful names work well (consider "ReflectionsPast" for an antique mirror business) though you'll need to be careful the name isn't so esoteric that it's difficult to associate with your products. Expect that securing a desired online name could take some work–many of the most desirable domain names have been duly snatched up in over the years. At the very least, acquire an e-mail address with your business name (e.g., RareBooks@mysite.com).

Adding Visual Recognition

Once you have a great business name, consider creating a uniquely recognizable business logo (after all, where would eBay be without that highly-recognizable upsy-downsy emblem of theirs?). Be it an evocative artistic representation of the name, an identifiable color scheme, or a some sort of clever character, logos can be as big as the name in perpetuating a business' brand. If you develop a logo design, be sure to make it plainly visible (but not obnoxiously so) whenever and wherever you have items for sale.

Delivering on Your Business Name

It's one thing to have a name that easily rolls off customers' tongues or a logo that's quickly recognized at first glance, but it's another thing to ensure that a brand unequivocally delivers the sorts of goods it implies. While you shouldn't relegate yourself to only selling one specific product (antique stoves, mirrors, carnival glass, or what have you), you should ensure that you're well stocked on what the name promises. Once you assure that you can deliver what you advertise, it's easy to include additional items of interest that might likewise tempt your visitors shopping and collecting tastes.

Developing Mindshare

What it all leads to is firmly establishing a spot in your customers' minds. But to make sure that your brand can be working for you at all times, use it in all of your customer correspondence. If possible, overlay your business name in the corner of every item image you post (many photo editors allow the addition of the semi-transparent "watermark"). Include invoices or "thank-you" notes that bear your brand in all of your shipments.

Beyond this, recognize that your *style* of business will also make or break your brand. Keep your online destination tidy, well organized, and informative. Be sure you've developed considerable "expert knowledge" about the featured commodity such that you can easily and reliably assist customers in their quests for information as well as merchandise. Establish operating policies that meet your customers' needs, taking into account the unique needs they might have as related to your product offerings. And keep your inventory fresh and enticing by actively rotating the goods for sale. Having done all this, your business name will likely mean more to your customers and they'll be eager to return time and time again. And every time they specifically seek out your business (whether online or elsewhere), your business's name will become further ingrained into your customers' consciousness. *That's* a successful brand.

FORTUNE BOOST #85
WHEN YOU FIND A NICHE, SCRATCH IT

To many would-be sellers, the notion of competing with the big firms seems overwhelming and under-rewarding. It's true that it makes little sense to posit your small book business against the likes of Amazon or Borders; nor does it seem reasonable that you'd succeed in your own small fashion outlet while standing in the shadow of Macy's or Nordstrom's. Don't throw in the towel just yet, though, because here comes your mantrum to a fortune:

> *"Don't compete—be unique!"*

Indeed, if there's one thing the Internet and online merchandising has enabled is the potential for establishing a flourishing niche business. Millions of other folks have already done it…and so should you.

Niche marketing is the simple prospect of identifying a product or service that seems to be in reasonable demand yet has been significantly underserved by larger businesses. For large retail outlets and manufacturers who avoid specializing in some commodities or smaller markets for fear of not reaping high-end profits, these become the niche opportunities for small businesses. Most niche market opportunities are encountered when customers find difficulty in acquiring goods or services they need, and they are frustrated that few–if any–sources exist. In a previous issue of *Entrepreneur* magazine, Ira Krenzin, proprietor of The Button Shoppe in Carmichael, California, told of her frustration when she couldn't find suitable buttons for her hand-tailored suits and blouses. Knowing that other seamstresses had this same problem, Krenzin set about to establish her own sources of quality buttons and, after some diligence, found the goods she needed and also found that others like her were eager to purchase from her inventory. A niche was born.

Tips for Finding Your Niche

Niche marketing is another term for "differentiation"–establishing how your product or service is better, faster, more attuned, and generally more desirable to a customer than those offerings from be-all-have-all businesses. With "shopping experience" and "total customer satisfaction" being key drivers in today's marketplace, here are four ways you can best establish your niche and ensure that you're differentiating your approach in a way that will matter most to your customers:

1. Define a target (niche) market and focus squarely on it. If you're eager to compete in the kitchenwares segment, differentiate yourself by, say, catering to bachelors or single parents, offering the items and even recipes that will help them make the most of their unique kitchen and cooking needs.

2. Identify your customers and talk to them constantly. As you encounter the sorts of folks who might serve as the members of your target market, engage them in conversation, asking what their needs are and, more to the point, which needs of theirs seem to continually go unmet. This is the secret sauce of your recipe for success.

3. Research your market before you launch into your business. When you have the information you think has positioned you with a terrific niche opportunity, research its potential by visiting retail stores, scouring the Internet, and reviewing topic-relevant magazines and other publications. Verify your understandings, determine who might be competing in your space, and make adjustments to greet your niche customers in a refreshing new way.

4. Determine the other demographic details of your market and potential customers. Determine if you should be offering high-quality, high-end products or if your customers truly need median-quality, lower-priced items. Investigate whether your market prefers to purchase in a brick-and-mortar setting or if they're better served by an online option where goods can be shipped directly to their doorsteps. And determine what other useful information, beyond products, your clientele desires and be sure to offer that up alongside your inventory to create a completely satisfying customer experience.

Niche marketing isn't typically an overnight success and often takes months or years of tweaking to find the perfect approach. Once you've found it, however, it might be the bearer of fortune that you envisioned. and it could be your shining stage of booming business.

FORTUNE BOOST #86
INTELLECTUAL PROFITING: SELLING WHAT YOU KNOW

If the best proof of a theory is experience, then each one of us is brimming with the sorts of knowledge that others would gladly accept ... and even pay for. Indeed, the very premise of the late 1990s buzzword that made a spike in nearly every corporate expense sheet–*consulting*–was born of the notion that there is immense value in securing the knowledge and experience of those that who have succeeded before us. Rather than travel the sometimes thorny path of learning, many folks are looking for a shortcut to treasure and will seek out the skills and expertise of those more indoctrinated in whatever fits the bill.

When it comes to online selling–especially auctioning and mastering eBay–some of the original community members (including yours truly) found the opportunity to help others by saving them the time and effort of learning what we had already experienced. Able to point out pitfalls as well as profit pools, experienced eBayers reduced the learning curve for others and helped them become successful in a fraction of the time. Now, as you look at your experiences–good and bad–look to see if you have the sort of knowledge that others around you seek out. Don't limit yourself to just matters of eBay and online selling. If you have expertise in just about anything, from marketing to mathematics or anything else, chances are you could offer what you know to others. This is especially true if you found a way to acquire expertise by simplifying your approach to learning as an alternative to more traditional educational methods. (People today are often impatient about reading voluminous texts, no matter how rich in content they may be, in order to get to the desired end-state; hence, the quick and easy-to-use book). If you devised a method to "crack the nut" that few others have employed, you may have an opportunity to share what you've learned in order to teach others how they, too, can be successful. And, when others discover they could find success faster and with less risk than they previously thought, they're usually willing to spend a bit of money to save the expense of potentially costly mistakes.

When you decide to market your "intellectual property," you need to be sure you can present it in a clear, concise, and easy-to-apply manner. For some, this comes naturally, while for others, it can be beyond reach. If you're a natural teacher, then tell what you know in the form of a newsletter, a Web page, or even an e-book. Research if others are serving the same market and determine if their approach has already satisfied the need. If not, or if you believe your approach is different (even *revolutionary*), then gather your information together in a way that it can be easily distributed and digested by your eager students. Determine what sort of price your market will bear and help your customers to rationalize the cost by offering details on how they can recoup on their investment.

When it comes to what sort of information to offer up, just ask yourself, "What have people been asking me?" Chances are you've been sought out on more than one occasion for help with some matter, whether it's been performing simple electrical repairs or installing a swimming pool. If you're adept at landscaping and have found hassle-free, cost-saving methods to beautify a backyard, you might consider writing that down and even offering specialized consultation to your clients. I found my way into sharing my eBay expertise after the people in my office continued to pepper me with questions once they discovered I'd been bidding and selling since the site's inception. As it was something of a technical challenge for some to understand (dealing with computers and other high-tech "scary stuff"), I employed my years of technical documentation skills, tempered to be digestible to the veritable "everyman," and there came my success.

Often, you'll be unaware that you have information to share–and sell–until you find your customers clamoring for more of what you know. As you operate your Web business and develop your expertise, remain continually attuned to the way in which your customers inquire of you and how you might be able to help them with their specialized needs (I know one fellow who began selling curio cabinet instructions after building one for his own collection; those he sold collectibles to saw an image of it and asked where they could get one; you see how it goes). Never shortchange the value of your personal knowledge and experience because you may be sitting on a gold mine of your own; an intellectual fount that never runs dry.

FORTUNE BOOST #87
GO TO THE HEAD OF THE CLASS:
TEACH AND YE SHALL RECEIVE

Here's another idea that's akin to Fortune Finder #86. This concept runs as something of a spoke off the hub of selling information in that you should look for opportunities to actually develop and deliver information in a classroom environment. Again, this is an opportunity I discovered as I sought new ways to help folks get online and involved with buying and selling at eBay. Check with your local community college or personal enrichment organizations to determine if they need programs and instructors to lead a class through the details of a particular area of expertise. Chances are you may be on a community-based mailing list for catalogs that offer details of upcoming classes. Check these catalogs closely to determine if they actively encourage potential instructors to submit a proposal for a new class. Determine the need and content and work with the program administrators to develop a class of your own. Then you can determine what sorts of materials students will need and if it's the sort of thing you can provide (for a materials fee) to ensure that your students can get the most from their time with you.

Again, determine what sort of knowledge you have to offer and decide if it's suitable for a classroom setting. And, while you're teaching, don't forget to provide plenty of information about your other endeavors; your students might just become your ongoing customers.

FORTUNE BOOST #88
BLOG, BLOG, BLOG

While it may seem like a fad whose day has come and gone, there's still plenty of life and opportunity left for the notion of blogging for your business. For those who are new to blogging or simply don't understand its origins despite having been beat over the head with the term of late (especially during the raucous 2004 presidential election in the United States), here's some quick background. First, "blogging" is a nifty abbreviation of "Weblogging," a practice where folks have turned to the Internet to create their daily diaries, only they've made it visible for all to read. Big-time news services jumped on the blog bandwagon during the 2004 political season in order to compete (and sometimes combat) independent bloggers whose sites became heavily trafficked via simple word of mouth; that's right, *word of mouth*. If you recall how quickly the term "blogging" became a part of our kitchen conversation across the nation and around the world, then you probably already realize the potential for using that same "tell another friend" exposure for purposes of increasing the reach of your online business.

Successful blogs are those that contain random thoughts, observations, and sometimes even rants that center around a topic of interest. For your business, a blog can include details about the items you're selling, trends you're noticing, special events (local or global), and so on. The key to making the blog compelling, though, is to write it in a very relaxed "folksy" fashion, as if you're capturing water-cooler conversation in an online forum. When you blog, sharing your thoughts, ideas, and experiences, you also invite responses and reactions from your readers (blog software allows for reader response). You can also post pictures along with your blog entries, adding visual appeal to your thoughts, especially when you talk about a latest great find or the subject of your upcoming sales promotion. When you open the communication in this manner, you stand to learn more about your customers' wants and needs, to learn more about your own area of expertise (readers love to affirm or add to another's shared details), and ultimately gain more customers. Your best bet for fashioning your blog is to read the blogs of others and determine which seem to compel you to read on.

How to Start a Blog

Simply enough, go to a website that helps you start a blog. One of the easiest out there is Blogger (you'll find it at www.blogger.com; see Figure 88-1).

Blogger was started back in 1999 by a few friends who struggled to keep the site afloat until Google offered to purchase them. The site is now quite prolific and offers a free blog-hosting service. You simply create a free account, determine the URL for your blog space, and then link that to and from your online sales site. In addition to this, you should also register your blog URL with a blog directory to help you gain better exposure. Visit sites like www.BlogStreet.com, www.BlogDex.com, or www.DayPop.com to get your blog into a directory and gain more visits.

Blogging is definitely not a fad and for many online business owners, it has proven to be a low-key alternative to a monthly newsletter. It's not just an exercise in vanity, though, because online shoppers are always looking for new information *every day*. Through the use of a blog, you can quickly and easily offer new content to your customers such that they'll become compelled to visit your online sales venue more frequently. What can you share on a blog that can translate into an improved boost to your bottom line? How about these enticing tid-bits:

- New product releases
- Recent finds and acquisitions (especially pertinent to antiques, collectibles, and the like)
- Alerts of upcoming sales or promotions
- Casual commentary on developments in your commodity area or industry
- Helpful "how-to" information such as care and storage for particular goods or collectibles

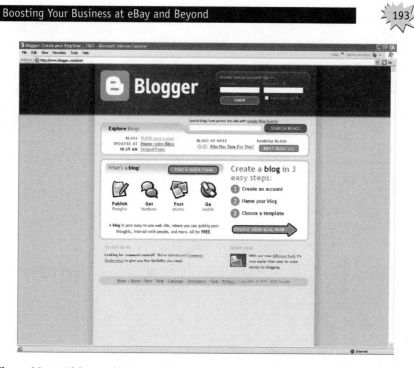

Figure 88-1 Visit www.blogger.com for your quick and easy entrance into the wonderful world of blogging.

Truly, the list of what to include in a blog is virtually endless as you ponder more ways to engage and entertain your customers.

Give blogging a try and keep reading other blogs. Pretty soon, you'll find it to be an excellent tool to further the reach and recognition of your online business.

FORTUNE BOOST #89
HOW BECOMING AN AFFILIATE CAN PAY OFF

Affiliate programs were created years ago in the online realm to essentially recruit others to help spread the word of a Web site, its products, or its services. For instance, Amazon.com was an early user of an affiliate program whereby it would pay Internet publishers, Web masters, or other online authors to provide links to Amazon pages and product areas. If a site's visitors clicked the Amazon link and purchased something, Amazon would pay the affiliate a commission. Essentially, it's a pay-for-referral program and it's actively in use all over the Internet.

For the Web sites who offer such affiliate partnerships, it works out to be an inexpensive form of mass marketing, leveraging off the reach of individual Web masters to help drive traffic to a site. eBay, in fact, has also devised an affiliate program for the same purpose and will pay affiliates every time a link is used to

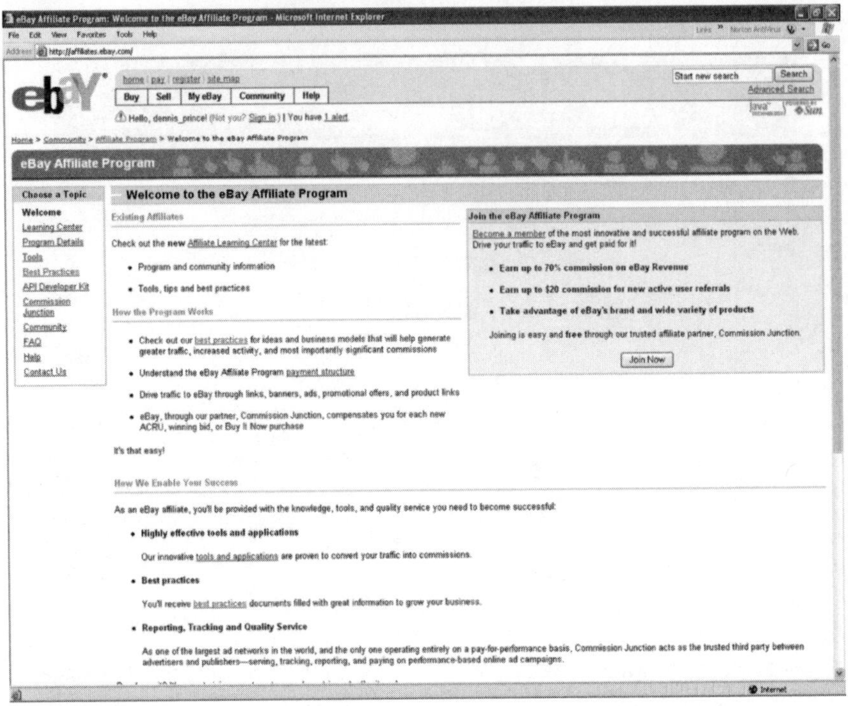

Figure 89-1   Visit the eBay Affiliate Program pages to learn how you can earn profit when others do the shopping.

navigate directly to eBay and results in either an item bid on and won or the registration of a new user.

Affiliates are instructed and encouraged in the ways to promote the eBay site through the use of banners or text links to help drive visitors to the auction site. In return, the affiliates receive commissions for driving new users as well as bids and "Buy-It-Now" purchases. Currently, eBay pays its affiliates from $5.00 to $13.00 for each new active user and from $0.05 to $0.09 for each bid or "Buy-It-Now" transaction. As an incentive, eBay also proclaims that its top 25 affiliates in the program are averaging above $100,000 in monthly commissions (your results may vary).

To become an affiliate at eBay, all you need do is sign up for the free program at http://affiliates.ebay.com (see Figure 89-1).

As an affiliate, you place targeted advertisements on your own Web site, within e-mails, or newsletters for specific products, categories or stores at eBay. Every time one of your site visitors navigates to eBay through an affiliate link, you can earn commissions if that customer registers or buys/wins an item.

Optimizing Your Affiliate Links

No doubt, when you become an affiliate to eBay (or to Amazon or any other Web site), you're clearly recruited into helping *them* succeed. However, this doesn't mean you're an underpaid stooge or corporate pawn. Remember, if you can drive more traffic to a site, you can earn more commissions for doing so. The trick is to learn how to appropriately balance your affiliate links with the other content of your own business interest. Of course, your site visitors will be quickly put off if they're greeted by a barrage of affiliate links, banners, and annoying animations that portray your site as being nothing more than an affiliate hub. If you want to ensure your site remains relevant and will incite visitors to return, you'll need to strategically place affiliate links in and around your otherwise rich content pages. Keep the content rich and worthwhile as if your site would stand alone without affiliate links (which it always should be able to). If an area on your page is discussing a particular item or commodity, it might make sense to include an easy-to-use affiliate link to eBay that would automatically launch a search for similar items. If your visitors are inclined to learn more about such a product, they'll turn to your site for information; if they're then eager to buy such a product for themselves (and one that you don't directly offer), then provide them with the appropriate eBay link where, hopefully, they'll find the item, win or buy it, and you'll receive a commission.

Experiment with the eBay Affiliate Program and take care how you integrate such links within your own Web site. When you strike a perfect balance, you'll see you can maintain a steady traffic on your own site while also helping your visitors find what they're looking for at eBay (or elsewhere) in a way the still earns you profit.

FORTUNE BOOST #90
LAUNCHING A MARKETING CAMPAIGN

As defined by Webster's, a campaign is "a series of activities designed to bring about a particular result." If you seek to further enrich your sell-through rates and sales prices, online and off, there are several things you can do to propel your results upward and increase your business's visibility to as many potential customers as possible. If you're ready to hit the campaign trail, here are several paths you should consider traveling.

Mining the Marketplace

Before beginning any marketing campaign, it's imperative to fully understand the market itself. Therefore, the pre-work of thoroughly reviewing online and off-line venues is a must. Visit local trade shows, consignment stores, and antique and crafter's malls to find out what's up for sale, how it's priced, and how well it's selling. Then, turn your attention online and scour the Internet for Web sites and auction venues to gather the same sort of data. (For past sales auction info at eBay and Yahoo, be sure to review "completed" auctions). As you begin to analyze the data you've collected, you'll likely find many items like those you wish to offer and, more importantly, glean the knowledge of where and how these items seem to sell the best.

Crossing Over

While it's of terrific benefit to rotate your inventory within your virtual store, ensuring that customers will find an ever-changing selection of items upon each visit, keep in mind that you should also seek to rotate your products *across* multiple venues, too. Long-time sellers have learned that some items just seem to sell better in certain settings. High-end antiques might be better suited to shoppers who frequent the upscale antique mall and who regularly visit similar specialty Web destinations. Collectibles, of course, seem to be the draw at eBay and the bidding wars that go on there can typically land final sales prices that would likely be scoffed at in a fixed-price venue. Consider also that some items are simply "tactile" in nature, seeming to sell better in off-line venues where customers can touch, feel, and even smell merchandise. Your task, then, is to rotate your items through the various venues until you find that perfect match where your goods will be noticed by the largest audience of buyers and can be sold at the best possible prices. And, as nothing is static anymore, you might find that some items will do well in a sales setting for a while but might soon require replacement to reenergize demand.

The Venues Well Traveled

So, besides your Web site and auction listings, what other venues might help you increase visibility and, ultimately, your sales? Consider these:

- **The Usenet:** Remember those newsgroups like rec.collecting and others? They're still quite active and they're a viable venue to sell through.
- **Related Sites:** Don't be afraid to make contact with the webmasters of other sites that sell or discuss items like yours, inquiring if they'd agree to posting a banner or link to your destinations. You'd be surprised at how many are more than eager to online space to bring more cross advertising to the online sales marketplaces.
- **Trade Journals:** No, the Internet hasn't completely rendered those print journals as completely obsolete (believe it or not, there is a large population of shoppers who *still* haven't gotten online).
- **Flea Markets and Garage Sales:** And, for those items that just won't seem to sell online or might be too cumbersome to ship across country, these time-tested venues still work well. Plus, you might get a snicker when someone slyly whispers, "I'll bet I can sell this on eBay."

Cross-Promoting

The big retailers are never bashful about telling you of their satellite stores, factory outlets, or subsidiaries, so why should you be? If you're seriously marketing your sales business, you've likely established a presence in multiple venues, online and off. Be sure to liberally promote your other sales destinations in all of your advertisements and customer correspondence. When you're selling at a local show, be sure to have fliers on hand that tell of your other sales outlets and always provide Web addresses. At your fixed-price Web spaces, promote *all* the different online destinations where your products can be found. And, when auctioning goods, make reference to the other items you concurrently have up for bid. Oh, and even if certain auction venues try to discourage you, reference your fixed-price destinations in every auction listing you post.

Good Timing, Better Results

Don't forget that timing can play a big part in your marketing campaign. Besides finding the right venues to sell in, you'll also need to consider when would be the best time to sell in a certain venue. Again, turn to your market research and keep records of *when* items sell best, then rotate, rotate, rotate.

FORTUNE BOOST #91
TRYING ON A TRADEMARK

When you spend a significant amount of effort and money devising a business name, a product brand, or a stylized logo, you ought to complete your work by protecting it, too. Oftentimes, small business owners consider trademarks as the stuff of big companies or large-scale manufacturers but the fact of the matter is that any great emblem or idea, no matter whether it came from a large or small concern, could be worth a fortune.

Trademarks are important to businesses because they offer protection to a recognizable name or design that customers will associate with a company. Consider the Nike swoosh, the Coca-Cola bottle, or the eBay logo–all are trademarked because all connote an idea of product and value in a consumer's mind. Knockoff competitors or copycats would unabashedly leverage a design or name or phrase to confuse consumers to believing an alternate product is the real thing (remember Coca-Cola's slogan of the late 1960s?), whereas it's actually a cheap imitation and one that could dilute consumers' perception of the bona-fide company. Trademark registration provides legal recourse should such an infraction be attempted, imposing severe penalties on anyone who would attempt to infringe.

Properly defined, a trademark is either a word, phrase, symbol or design, or a combination of words, phrases, and symbols that identify and distinguish the source of products or services. A "trademark" is used to identify products whereas a "servicemark" can be used to identify services (such as Enterprise Rent-a-Car or

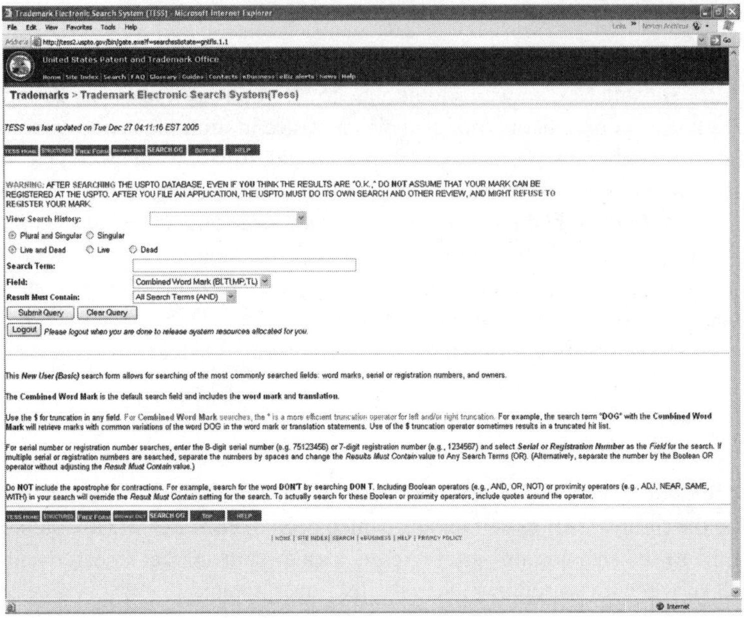

Figure 91-1   Visit www.uspto.gov to begin a trademark search.

Jiffy Lube). Trademark rights are implied to be enacted the moment a mark is used in actual commerce in conjunction with a product or when an *intent of use* proclamation is filed with the United States Patent and Trademark Office. Common law is understood to protect the initiator of a trademark's use but formal registration of a mark is required to secure full federal protection. Trademarks, once filed and fully registered, can be kept alive indefinitely or can be allowed to age and expire (upon which time someone else may file for exclusive use of an expired mark).

Before you file for a trademark, it's wise to perform a search to see if any other same or similar marks have already been registered or are in process of being registered. Do this by visiting the United States Patent and Trademark Office online at www.uspto.gov (see Figure 91-1).

From the USPTO home page, click on the "Search" link under the Trademark section. In the simple search window, enter the name of your mark or phrase and search to see if others like it already exist. You'll be able to examine any similar marks already registered or in the process of registration as well as those that have been allowed to expire by their previous owners. If your mark is unique and available, you should proceed to submit a trademark application.

To submit an application and get your trademark registration process underway, return to the USPTO home page and click the "File" link under the Trademark section. The site will guide you to the Trademark Electronic Application System

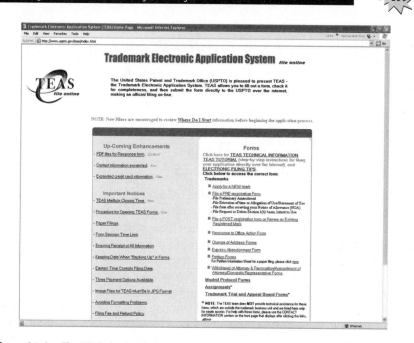

Figure 91-2   The TEAS site is where you can begin your trademark filing process.

(TEAS) and will step you through the filing process including explaining how to determine the "classes" for your application as well as the required attachments and fees (see Figure 91-2).

Trademarks are registered by class of product or service—for example, Toys and Sporting Goods is deemed as Class 028, while Clothing is deemed as Class 025. You'll be required to file for each class of product or service that you intend to bear your mark and thereby protect you from infringement. During the filing process, you'll also need to provide a digital image of your mark for review by the USPTO examining attorney (the assigned attorney that will review your application and also search existing marks to ensure that your application doesn't infringe another mark already in use). As for the fees, the USPTO currently requires a filing and registration fee of $325 for each class in which a mark is to be registered.

Once you've submitted your application, be patient—the process can take more than a year, maybe two. Your mark will be closely examined against existing marks, your application will be closely scrutinized for completeness and clarity, and your application will be posted publicly for opposition (allowing for other trademark owners to oppose your mark if they believe it materially infringes on theirs). However, once your application is in process, you should begin using the superscripted "TM" whenever your mark appears (e.g. Monster Scenes™). Use of this denotation indicates that you are actively pursuing a trademark registration for the mark. When your mark is officially registered with the USPTO, then you may switch to use of the circle-R notation (e.g. Monster Scenes®).

Don't gloss over the value of a trademark and the special protections it provides you in your business. If you've invested significantly into your brand or product mark, be sure to protect it properly.

FORTUNE BOOST #92
REPOSITIONING YOUR COMPETITORS
TO PROFIT FROM THEIR WEAKNESSES

See if you've experienced this in your online endeavors: You've decided on a product or commodity and you know you have an excellent offering. However, there doesn't seem to be anything particularly "new" about what you want to sell. Even though your analysis shows you can strike a profit, it seems virtually impossible to distinguish your offerings from those of others (like pool toys, barbeque accessories, or warm and fuzzy footwear). Your products are good but the competition's seems to be good, too. How will you rise above the fray? Well, without resorting to underhanded tactics, you do have the opportunity to elevate the desirability of your goods by essentially redefining the desirability of those goods available from others.

If it appears that your competitor has a stranglehold on a particular market segment and customers believe it, too, then you need to effectively deposition that competitor. Consider eBay itself, the leading online portal that comes to the public mind-set whenever someone utters "online auction." Although Amazon.com and Yahoo and others tried to topple the 300-pound gorilla, they all did it by attacking eBay directly with their alternative bid-and-sell solutions rather than going after the public mind-set. *Repositioning* is all about gaining favor for your offering by first displacing a current market leader. Consider the recent Hertz Car Rental promotion where they promise to work harder for you. While Avis and Enterprise and other companies have been flourishing in the car rental space, effectively having painted Hertz as old and stodgy, the former leading company *repositioned* their competition–all of it–by referring to newcomers' inferior service and substandard customer care. Hertz has regained market share after first displacing its competitors from their perches. That's how repositioning works. (Just be sure not to be directly disparaging to a competitor; consumers don't typically take too kindly to such a confrontational attack.)

So, how can you know how to reposition your competition? Well, in order to cut into other sellers' business as you manage your enterprise, you'll need to remain continuously aware of how they might be trying to cut into yours. If other sellers seem to be countering your repositioning tactics, study their moves and motives closely and watch how their sales activity changes. Have they employed a different pricing strategy than you? Have they made adjustments to their sales policies? Have they made more compelling allowances during certain seasons (free shipping upgrades, bonus items, and so on)? The trick about working among competitors is not to disregard them as inferior to you. Rather, be savvy enough to shop among your competitors' virtual aisles, taking note of what features, facts, or selections they offer that make you feel that even you would like to make a purchase. With that information, return to your offerings to see what you can do to engender the same compelling desire for your goods.

FORTUNE BOOST #93
IS YOUR ONLINE STORE STICKY?

No, this isn't an examination of your good housekeeping skills nor is it another "Helpful Hint from Heloise" for eliminating grubby fingerprints from display cases. Stickiness here refers to how well your showcase attracts customers, whether it entices them to thoroughly explore your virtual shop, and if it will compel them to return again, soon. If your online store (eBay or otherwise) seems a bit dusty–that is, not getting the sort of traffic you'd like nor keeping visitors around longer than a few seconds–then here are some ways to improve its drawing power and encourage visitors to shop longer and return more often.

Keep them Browsing

It's disheartening to learn that visitors to your online store have dropped by, taken a cursory look around, and then headed out as quickly as they came. Why did they leave? Well, like any of us, your customers are likely looking not only for quality merchandise but also a quality shopping experience that caters to their needs and interests. Though you'll naturally begin with desirable merchandise that is (hopefully) enticingly priced, don't overlook these other "products" that will attract more customers, extend their time of stay, and establish your showcase as a favorite and frequent destination:

- Provide useful and interesting articles that further discuss the sorts of things you sell. Written by yourself or gleaned from other sources (with permission, of course), added information that helps educate your visitors about your wares and related items–be it historical data, industry trends, or even trivia–gives your showcase increased value in your customer's eyes.
- Customers love a forum where they can offer their opinion or ask a question. You can satisfy this urge by providing even the simplest of customer surveys, reader polls, or suggestion boxes. The information they share benefits you, too, as it helps you learn more about what your visitors want, like, and seek in an online dealer.
- Serve up plenty of useful links that can further benefit visitors. You can cooperatively exchange links with others online–you promote their site and they yours–while your customers benefit from the "hublike" quality your showcase now provides.

- And don't overlook the oldest form of promotion: a contest. Be creative and challenge the astuteness of your visitors. Reward the winner with a discount or some sort of freebie.

Keep Your Storefront Fresh

This is the most enticing aspect of a well-maintained destination yet the most difficult to sustain. Once you've succeeded in keeping your visitors browsing your showcase and purchasing your goods, you'll need to ensure there's something new for them upon each return visit.

Online studies have concluded that if you can offer new content (either information or merchandise) on a daily basis, visitors will return every few days. If you only update weekly, visitors will likely return once every few weeks. And, if you're limited to updating just once a month, visitors will probably only visit once every few months. As these findings bear, the more often you can update your online store, the more frequently your customers will return. And, the more they visit your showcase, the more likely you remain in the forefront of their mind when it comes to shopping for the sorts of goods (and information) you regularly offer.

Keep Your Online Store Simple

Once you get into a rhythm of updating your storefront you might find it tempting to go all out and deliver so much content (especially images and cute decor) that you risk bogging down the display. Aside from large images that can take long to display, over-decorating your storefront can become counterproductive, often hiding your great offerings amid excessive visual hoopla. Avoid clutter by keeping your store neat, well organized, and fast loading. If possible, adopt a design that customers can become familiar with, navigate easily, and feel at home in upon future visits. This, again, makes your online store a pleasure to visit, helping visitors easily find what they're looking for while quickly determining what's new for today.

Keep 'Em Coming Back for More

If you'll take to heart the suggestions made here and keep yourself attuned to what *you* like and dislike about the online destinations you frequent, you'll be likely to develop an online store that will attract a reliable base of repeat customers. Remember: Put yourself in their shoes at all times. Think like a customer, and you'll excel at meeting and exceeding their expectations upon every visit.

FORTUNE BOOST #94
THE POWER BEHIND META DATA

Don't let the terminology intimidate you–meta data *is* your online business's best friend. Simply defined, *meta data* is "data about data," and *meta tags* are those special lines of HTML code that contain the keywords (meta data) that represent the style, topic matter, or actual items you're offering to online shoppers. It's these meta tags, then, that tell the Internet's search engines what sorts of items can be found at your Web site. Because search engines actively seek out meta tags, the data within them becomes key to helping more online shoppers find your items, your site, *your business*. Meta tags are easy to use and, with some insight on how to maximize their usefulness, they can help guide millions of online shoppers to your virtual front door.

Understanding Meta Tags

Meta tags are embedded into the *source* of a Web document (the source being the complete code that would generate and display your Web site, for example). But, the meta tags aren't displayed when your page appears on a computer screen. Instead, they work behind the scenes, facilitating the categorization, classification, and retrieval of your page by Internet search engines.

If you're designing your own standalone page on the Web, the design tool you use might prompt for entry of meta data (though some folks actually write this information directly within the HTML code itself).

But what does a meta tag look like? Well, here's a snippet of the tags you might expect to find in the source code of an antique and collectibles Web store:

```
<meta NAME="keywords" CONTENT="antique, antiques, collectibles, glass,
china, fifties, decorative art, Noritake, Art Deco, mid-century, 20th cen-
tury, shabby chic . . .></meta>

<meta NAME="description" CONTENT="I specialize in decorative articles
from the 1925-1939 period. I try to always have in stock Harlequin china,
Noritake Art Deco . . . ></meta>
```

If ever you'd like to view the meta tags of your page or any other page on the Web, simply use your browser's "View" menu and then choose "Source"–you'll be shown the actual source code of the page you're viewing.

Keys to Keywords

While constructing meta tags is easy, don't underestimate the power of the keywords you'll specify within. Besides wanting to ensure that the keywords properly reflect what you'll offer at your site (unrelated, irrelevant, and excessively repeated words could be considered "spam," you know), you'll also want to note these "key" factors:

- Use the keywords your customers use most! Know the most common terms your buyers are likely to use and be sure to include those in your meta tags.

- Include words that *generally* define your site, showcase, and items. For example, consider additional terms like "decor," "collectibles," "keepsakes," "crafts" or "handmade goods."
- Incorporate words that reflect the *style* or *period* of items you offer, such as "vintage," "contemporary," "elegant," "retro," and so on.
- Specify your geographic location to further define the source of your goods.
- Include common misspellings your customers might use in their searches. You'll want to cover every angle for greatest success.

Where Will You Rank?

Your final task in establishing your meta data is to construct and position it in such a way that search engines will rank your site highly within search results lists. As studies have shown, the most popular sites online are those that rank within the top 30 "hits" of an online search result. Here's how you can improve your site's chances of being among the top matches:

- Include keyword combinations ("Harlequin china," "Hallmark keepsakes") in your meta tags that will more narrowly define your site, boosting you higher in specific search hit-lists.
- Use keywords in your site title ("Movie Mania–Original Theatrical Posters, Stills, and Memorabilia") that reflect the meta tag keywords you've listed. Search engines assume a Web page is more relevant to a search if the search terms used are found in the page title.
- Include a descriptive sentence or two at the top of your Web page design that contains your most relevant meta tag keywords ("Welcome to the home of handmade country crafts, direct from America's Heartland"). Many search engines assume that if a specific word is mentioned in the top several lines of a site, it's likely the page is highly relevant to the search term.

So, whether you misunderstood meta tags before or simply considered them as being of little consequence, now is the time to give them another look. By establishing thoughtfully constructed meta tags, you'll not only succeed in helping more customers find your site, but also you'll excel at ensuring that the *right* customers find your online store–customers looking to purchase exactly the items you're offering.

FORTUNE BOOST #95
MAKING COUNTERS COUNT FOR YOUR BUSINESS

One of the best ways to determine how well your online marketing efforts are paying off is by monitoring the amount of traffic your Web site and auction items are attracting. A simple tool that's been available for some time is the online counter.

Here's some insight into counter use and how to distill the information you might gather.

Why Count?

I once read the following sentiment about online marketing: "Fifty-percent of my advertising doesn't work. I just don't know which 50 percent." Though relatively clever in content, there's truth to this statement as online sellers struggle to determine when and where their online offerings and enticements are most effective. The best way to gauge the appeal of your products and sales strategies is to quantify the public response–that's where counters come into play.

Counters can tally how many people have visited your main Web page, a particular featured item, or those goods you may be offering for bid at eBay. Every time a particular item is viewed, the tally is incremented. In this way, you'll see how much relative activity an item is generating, helping you to determine which items seem to be the most popular (by way of comparing the counter "hits"). Immediately, you'll be able to identify those items that draw more attention from visitors and those that seem to languish undisturbed on the virtual shelf. This might provide valuable insight to which venues are attracting the most traffic for your items, which item key words seem to get the most search hits, which pricing strategies seem to lure more potential buyers, and, overall, which combined marketing approaches seem to be working best for you. Armed with these statistics, you're in a much better position to make well-reasoned adjustments as the numbers dictate.

Do the Numbers Ever Lie?

But understand that a high number of counter hits doesn't necessarily ensure a successful sale or higher auction bids. In fact, an item that receives a high number of hits but still doesn't sell might indicate your price needs revising, your description needs revamping, or perhaps your images need sprucing up. Be especially watchful of an item whose images take an extraordinarily long time to display–visitors may have decided not to wait around even though their attempt to view the item was tallied.

More to the point of counter accuracy, simple counters you might use for free from various destinations online are often limited to capturing either item *hits* or item *visits*. A simple hit counter will typically tally up the number of page elements (text content and each individual image) that are displayed; an item with text and two images could tally three "hits." More common is the *page view* counter–it tallies how many times a particular online page (such as an eBay item listing) is viewed irrespective of the number of text and graphic elements. For the online seller, page view counters are more revealing than hit counters.

Many of the online counter providers (such as Honesty.com, Vendio.com, and RubyLane.com) provide counter overviews that, in a single view, allow you to assess your use of their counters over several venues, all visible to you from the counter host's page.

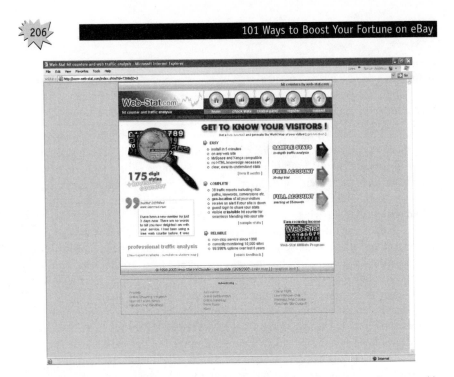

Figure 95-1   Visit www.web-stats.com for a complete suite of counter tools, reasonably priced and ready to provide you the stats for success.

But the most granular and most telling statistic would be that of *unique visitor hits*, that is how many *different* visitors have viewed your item (as opposed to the same visitor viewing your item page several times or more). Generally, to gain this sort of specific information, though, you'll need to purchase specially developed online tracking software (see Figure 95-1).

Better Seen or Unseen?

Here's where the discussion often picks up–the argument whether it's better or worse to include visible counters on your item pages. One side states that a visible counter can help motivate buyers and bidders, citing that a high number of registered page hits will telegraph the item to be potentially high in demand; a subsequent buyer might be prompted to take the item quickly before someone else snatches it away.

From the other side comes the argument that visible counters might dissuade a buyer or bidder for a couple of reasons. First, an item with a high counter value might indicate belief that something's wrong with the item; if not, why wouldn't someone have already purchased it? In a bidding scenario, a high count might foretell a bidding war that will likely ensue, a competitive showdown that many buyers choose to avoid. And if the count is low; well, that could also indicate a perceived problem with the item yet might also act as enticement to bargain hunters.

Either way, there are pros and cons to using visible counters. It's wise to use invisible counters at the outset as you learn which items and sales approaches seem to be most popular, without tipping off or otherwise influencing your visitors. Then experiment with making those counters visible and determine if they have a positive or negative effect.

Whatever your approach, using counters makes good sense and will help you learn more about online marketing as well as your online customer base. And while some statistical data can be a bit misleading, any sort of numerical results can typically aid you in honing your approach to improve your business' bottom line.

FORTUNE BOOST #96
PACING YOUR FLOW FOR PROFITS

With so much in place and so much going well in your business, it's tempting to work your gold mine around the clock, grinning all the way as practically each new hour shows rewarding new returns. It's terrific that you're so motivated and you've found success, but be sure you've consulted your business plan and your natural abilities as well as you begin to push harder for more profits.

Finding a pace in an online business is important to the stability and consistency of your livelihood. Not only do you need to balance your time between listing items, collecting payment, shipping goods, and keeping records; you also need to balance your sales activity to ensure that your inventory doesn't drop dangerously low and put you in a dreaded "stocked out" period. You'll find times when everything seems to be selling and it's natural and necessary to capitalize on those moments. However there's a dangerous tendency that some sellers fall into, that being the temptation to begin cutting corners and taking shortcuts to keep up with the flow. Be careful that your customers don't feel they're getting the bum's rush and decide you're strictly profit motivated at the expense of the customer experience. If your customers perceive you're willing to sacrifice the long-term character (that is, reputation) of your business in deference to a fast buck, they'll likely tend to drift away.

Pacing yourself–using a well-thought-out business plan that's adjusted through business analysis–will not only allow you to keep up with all aspects of your business but will also allow your customers to keep up, too. If you specialize in a certain type of item, you'll probably develop a base of return customers. They'll hope to get first peek at your new goods coming up for sale or bid, eager to make yet another purchase. If, however, you surge your offerings–buffeting the marketplace with a sudden onslaught of goods for sale–your loyal shoppers may find that you've posted too many choice items and they can't possibly afford them. When this happens, you're customer base is unable to secure the goods they most desire and will usually stray off to seek out other sellers who may offer what they just had to pass by. Soon enough, they've found another seller to suit their needs and you may have difficulty luring them back. If you can spread the flow of such goods smoothly over an offering period, you may be able to help your shoppers buy more as they'll be able to plan ahead for your next great round of goods.

FORTUNE BOOST #97
MONITORING YOUR BUSINESS PERFORMANCE

When your business is running along at a nice pace, it's easy to take your eye off the original goal–profit. That's right. Even though you'll be seeing a steady inflow of cash and a steady outflow of goods to keep the bottom line growing, it's important you ensure the growth is as expected and always on the upward trend. It's hard to tell if you're running in the black or in the red if you don't have numbers to back up your beliefs that your business is happy and healthy. The only way to be sure is to perform an occasional but regular checkup on the health of your enterprise.

At least twice a year (better yet, aim to establish a quarterly timetable), schedule time to look over your records. Although you might be eager to do this every month–and there's nothing wrong with that–it's not until three or six months have passed that you can analyze the bigger picture. Your goal is to see if your business is remaining profitable over longer spans of time, to see if you're developing the necessary consistency in your business results, and to determine if any trends are developing. What trends? How about casting an analytical eye on the following?

- Are your expenses in control or are they running higher than you originally planned?
- Are you making the most of the money you're investing into you business or is there a bit of additional fat that you could trim to bolster your bottom line?
- Are there any business costs that, after reviewing their return on investment over a period of months, you think should be cut out entirely?
- Are you able to re-invest a level of profits that enables you to make targeted (planned) acquisitions or improvements to boost your business?

Beyond these points, as you close out a yearly cycle you'll be able to see and track signs of ebb and flow of business income and business expenses that should be compared to your annual business plans and goals. You'll be able to identify cyclical patterns–some good, some not–such that you can steer your business activity into more advantageous directions. More pointedly, consider close analysis of these trend areas:

- **Expenses:** Look at your cost of doing business and determine if you're running a lean ship (any waste is profit thrown away). Are your office supply expenses on the rise due to purchase of non-reusable goods? Is your fuel bill skyrocketing due to too many trips in and around town? Do you have business-related subscriptions or memberships that don't really seem to fit your needs yet are still tallying a cost month by month? Look at all elements that find their way on your expense sheet and determine if they're carrying their weight to improve your profits. If not, reign them in or cut them out completely.

- **Inventory:** Besides operating expenses, you should regularly review the performance of your inventory. This is key to staying profitable and increasing your bottom line: sell the stuff that sells well. While that may sound all too obvious, many sellers become too attached, entranced, or otherwise devoted to their chosen goods, regardless of whether the sell-through rates support such adherence to a commodity. You needn't abandon your choice goods, those that drove you to enter the business in the first place yet you should try to capitalize on the goods the sell most frequently, in the highest volumes, and which bear the highest profits. Again, it sounds obvious yet this is a key contributor to why many small businesses fail. Let the numbers lead you.
- **Industry and Consumer Trends:** Don't ever forget nor underestimate the fickleness of the marketplace. Online auctions and commercial Web sites typically represent what I call *pop-commerce*, that is whatever is the hot ticket tonight could be a stale offering tomorrow. It's a fine balance to strike and you'll need to anticipate the rise and fall of trends, yet you should still strive to serve the masses what they most crave in a way that, once satiated, they don't abandon your hot selling goods and leave you with a warehouse full of inventory that's no longer desirable.

Keeping a pulse on your business is tantamount to your success yet it can often become burdensome (some even lament that it's boring). Whenever you feel that reviewing your records is a drag, just remember that these numbers rarely lie and they're screaming for your attention in a way that can help you steer to pools of profit. Embrace your business results because they'll always tell you, without equivocation, just how well your business is doing.

FORTUNE BOOST #98
VENTURING OUTSIDE THE HOME OFFICE

Don't be surprised if one day, while you're confidently working your business–listing items, updating an online inventory, collecting payment and making shipments–you suddenly experience a feeling of limitation. Whether you feel the need to spread out or the desire to balance your business between cyberspace and the real world, you might find yourself considering breaking free of the confines of your home office.

To be sure you're truly ready and able to broaden your physical horizons, take each of the following into consideration:

- Assess your true motivation for leaving your home office: be sure it's due to a solid business need and not a personal or emotional whim.
- Be certain your business is safely and consistently operating in a positive balance.

- Determine if and how your present business will be interrupted as you set up a new headquarters and how that will financially impact you.
- Understand the actual costs of relocating (moving expenses, setup expenses, rent, utilities, and so on) and if your present and future income will cover the costs while still providing an acceptable profit.
- Determine if there is truly a better venue that will help your business grow (if it merely stays the same, it's probably not worth the relocation costs).
- Determine if moving your business will negatively affect your ability to operate as you presently are (provided you're presently doing well) as you encounter a change in routine adapting to a new location.
- Be ready and willing to delegate some of your current business activities if growth entails bringing helpers on board.
- Be sensitive to your customers and their acceptance of a relocation: Can they still contact you as easily? Will customers benefit from being able to visit you in a physical location?

But if you're business truly needs to spread out, then take a first step to consider establishing an outside-the-home business office. In this effort, you determine if it's administrative space that you need. Sometimes, your business productivity can suffer due to common "home interruptions": a television set, friends calling, neighbors popping by, kids and pets running about. For some, a separate place is all they need to focus more intently on managing their business, and they can often perform far more if away from the domestic distractions.

When considering an office space, keep these points in mind:

- Find an office space that is relatively nearby, reducing time lost in commute.
- Find an office in a quiet part of town where other more active businesses or traffic activity won't distract you.
- Find an office *upstairs*–many private office-dwellers proclaim that an upstairs office is less likely to invite misguided visitors or delivery personnel looking for so-and-so's suite.
- Find an office that, preferably, has all the amenities you'll need: multiple phone lines, electrical facilities, adequate lighting. Remember that you'll need to pay for office amendments to fit your business' needs.
- Find a reasonably priced office. It probably won't be the fanciest (hence the reasonable price), but administrative tasks don't require waterfalls and metal sculptures.

Venturing out to establish a separate business location might seem daunting yet it might be the step you need to take to raise your income to the next level. You'll need to manage the additional cost of affording the designated space and the next Fortune Boost will help you manage that aspect of growing your business, too.

FORTUNE BOOST #99
LEANING TOWARDS A SMALL BUSINESS LOAN

Assuming that you'll be making a go of it out of your own pocket (and hopefully through the reinvestment of your business income), you'll almost certainly find that your ability to successfully expand your business could be directly related to the amount of money you have to invest. Unless your home-based, 'Net-based endeavors have provided you with a financial windfall, figure that getting out into the physical business world will require a bit of financial assistance.

So what kinds of financial help can you expect to find? That's the good news: there is a variety of loan programs that are aimed at helping small business owners make a bigger splash in their market.

- **Personal Loans:** You can fund your business expansion (or start up) on your good name. Savings and loan institutions as well as commercial banks regularly grant personal loans for business ventures, though it's usually not important to them *what* you intend to use the money for–just as long as you can pay it back. Expect to provide full disclosure of your credit history as well as your employment history and current status. And, expect that personal loans often carry a higher interest rate than commercial loans, so pay it off quickly.
- **Lines of Credit:** Many banks and credit unions offer access to money that you can use much the same as you do your credit card (but typically at much lower interest rates). Check with your financial institution to determine if they offer such services (most do) and determine if the limit imposed will be enough to help your business surge ahead.
- **Commercial Bank Loans:** Most business owners pursue the good old commercial loan. Commercial banks are getting much more liberal these days about granting such loans, dependent, of course on your business plan. However, commercial banks are more inclined these days to offer varying sizes of loans–you don't need to be borrowing $75K in order to have your loan application looked at anymore. Be on the lookout for loan offers from some of the larger commercial lending institutions such as Citibank, Wells Fargo, and American Express.
- **SBA Loans:** Naturally, the Small Business Administration is the entrepreneur's advocate in building strong businesses. Visit their Web site (http://www.sba.gov/financing/) or call their offices directly to learn about a wide variety of business loan programs they sponsor such as SBA Express Loans, Capital Term Loans, and Micro-loans. (See Figure 99-1.)

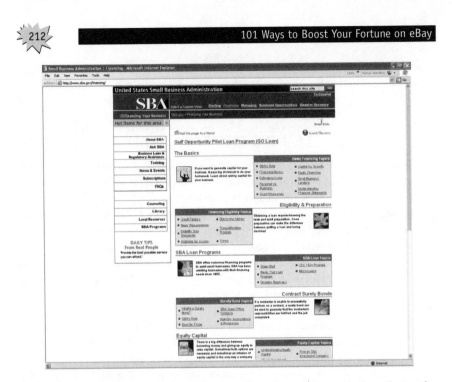

Figure 99-1 If you're in need of small business financing or just need to investigate other solutions to funding your enterprise, visit the United States Small Business Administration site for assistance and advice.

Naturally, people are not too excited about laying out their needs and baring their souls to lenders. But if you thought getting the capital you need for your business expansion means groveling on your knees in some banker's plush office, put it out of your mind–these days, lenders are looking for entrepreneurs who show good business sense and have achievable goals in mind.

Now, to increase your chances of success and ensure a smooth time of securing the loan you desire, do the following pre-work to help instill confidence in the people with the money you want:

- **Have a well-prepared business plan in hand.** Lenders are eager to make interest on the loans they grant, but they're more interested in loaning money to individuals and businesses that have logic and facts to back up their loan requirements. Know exactly how much you'll need to borrow, show which expenses the loan will be covering, and why you'll need to incur those expenses (an obvious notion that many loan applicants seem to overlook more often than you'd think).
- **Have a business cash flow projection.** You'll probably need a business advisor and/or accountant to help you with this one. Provide the lender a projection of income and expenses you would expect of your business.

Lenders want to see that the money they're ponying up won't be squandered on nonconsequential expenditures and that won't garner income for your business. After all, they want to see a healthy income for your business so they'll know you'll be able to repay your loan.

- **Provide a reasonable loan payoff plan.** And from that previous point, again confer with an accountant to develop a reasonable pay-off plan. This shows a lender that you have thought farther ahead than just the acquisition of initial capital and are as eager as they are to see the loan paid back.
- **Have the professional advisors you need.** If you invest in proper consultation, such as accountants, business advisors, and lawyers, you'll gain a better understanding of what taking out a business loan really means to you and your business. Professional advisors can help you understand the language and terms of different business loans and can help you choose the best financial options that will serve you and your business best.
- **Collateral. That's right.** Lenders want some tangible assets that they can claim should you default your loan. Lenders often need stocks, bonds, equipment, or structures that they can hold claim against to "secure the loan." Often, you can remain the physical holder of the collateral and the claim will be lifted once you've paid off the loan amount.
- **Anything else? Yes.** Also be prepared to offer up your personal profile that includes your credit history, your expertise in the field of business, and your sincerity that you're a good risk for this loan.

No doubt, securing a business loan does involve risk—that on the part of the lender as well as that of your expectation that you can put the money to good use fast and begin to turn a higher business profit. Don't fear seeking out a loan, though, because it may be just the extra nudge you need to get over the hump and begin coasting toward a new world of big fortune.

FORTUNE BOOST #100
WHY LOOK BACK?

With 99 Fortune Boosts behind us now, it makes sense to pause a moment and reflect upon where we've been and how far along we've come. The eBay experience has been one that has changed the way we think about many things in our culture today, from the ways and means to enter business to the longevity and value of what previously would have been rightly regarded as trash. Those who have participated in the eBay revolution since its beginning often wax nostalgic about the journey. Some, however, have proclaimed that the eBay experience is dead. Wistfully, they look back to those vintage times when the fledgling site was a refreshing oasis of unique goods and amicable atmosphere, lamenting that the aura of excitement and community goodwill is no more. They say eBay's gone mainstream.

True, but why is that so surprising?

Though I, too, have fond recollection of the site's infancy in late 1995, I seem to recall just as poignantly how the community members were eager to grow the site, attract more users to it, and to make it a brimming, bustling online marketplace. Well, we got what we hoped for, and now we're sorry?

Sure, it's been a bumpy ride at times–some say heartbreaking–as the once lively and electric atmosphere we once enjoyed was replaced by a more stoic, sterile and shareholder-conscious corporate mind-set. While there's no denying the transformation, I would counter that it was bound to happen–it *had* to happen–if this new marketplace was going to achieve any sort of legitimacy or longevity. eBay's no longer a lark–it's legendary.

Think about it: In 1995, who would have believed you if you had announced you were going into business for yourself, enjoying decent profits with very little overhead burden–not to mention achieving your task in a few short months and in the comfort and privacy of your own home? Be honest here because, whether or not you like what eBay has become, it has been successful in making online trading a reality–a viable alternative for buying and selling goods where virtually any private citizen can step in and hitch a ride on the path to profitability.

From where I'm sitting, I'd say the eBay experience has been exactly that: an *experience* that has given us invaluable instruction in operating a business on our own terms. I've yet to find a conventional occupation where I'm free to work as little or as much as I like, whenever I like, and with the residual benefit of gaining real-world exposure to the dynamics of marketing, economics, and global commerce.

But back to the melancholy sentiment about eBay's departure from its more innocent times, I have to weigh the fun and folly of those golden days against the power and possibility we've gained throughout the journey and to the point where we stand today. I mean, looking back is fine–good for perspective and even a bit of healthy daydreaming–but as I look at how this fun little jaunt has evolved into a plethora of possibilities, I don't see how I would be as well off if still bopping about in the "novelty" of an online auctioning white elephant sale. No, I have skills and insight, thank you, and thanks to the fact that eBay has been the flagship and proving ground of the individual's empowerment in the e-commerce marketplace.

Look back at those early days and tell me whether you were ever so poised to make such a bold yet achievable step. Today, you are. So why look back?

FORTUNE BOOST #101
LAST LOOK: STRIKING A
BALANCE TO BOOST YOUR FORTUNE

To wrap up this journey of 101 ways to boost your eBay fortune, let's perform a review of sorts to ensure that all boxes are checked, all to-do's have been addressed, and all factions of your online endeavor are in balance. It all boils down to ensuring your budget, your inventory, and your efforts are aligned such that each contributes to your sales goals without colliding or otherwise undermining your aspirations. So, in this last look at ways to boost your bottom line, here are a few final points about what to keep in balance and how to ensure that you're continually moving your business in the right direction.

Balancing Your Budget

Though members of local and national government's struggle with this at every go-around, balancing your budget is not such a harrowing act as you might think. However, there's no lying that it does require effort and a diligent approach.

As you approach and continually revisit budgeting, consider that you'll be looking to keep an eye on and control over the following:

- **Your Cash Flow:** how much money are you spending and how much money are you earning month to month?
- **Your Cash Cycle:** when do you regularly need to invest money in your business and when can you count on receiving income as a return on that investment?
- **The Realistic Nature of Your Financial Success:** Are you bringing in enough income to cover your expenditures?
- **The Flexibility of Your Budget:** does it respond to spikes and dips in your business, possibly in line with seasonal factors that might affect your business?
- **The Bottom Line:** How much money are you really making, how much can you safely consider "wages," that is, the profit from your business that pays you for your efforts?

And, as maintaining a budget can be a dreaded prospect, remember that the numbers rarely lie and taking an analytical view of your cash flow will help you determine how you should establish your business, how well you might expect to do, and what you think it will cost to reach your goal. In your planning, be sure to think about the following:

- Will this be a part-time or a full-time venture? (The answer can change over time and will definitely dictate how aggressive your financial goals need to be.)
- Will what you intend to sell be more cost-laden than some other sort of commodity? (Consider initial cost of inventory, special storage needs, shipping costs, and so on.)
- As you budget for inventory, consider how much time you'll have each month to turn your goods around and help ensure that inventory doesn't accumulate too much faster than you can sell it.

So, in a nutshell, make sure your budget accounts for the following:

- Your ongoing balance of cash and assets.
- Your anticipated costs during the month (or other accounting period you decide to adopt).
- A buffer or "safety net" of funds for unexpected costs.
- Your desired profit (positive incoming cash flow) after all costs have been deducted.

As previously noted, keep a close eye on your business activity and monitor your actual results as compared to your planned goals. Tweak your figures and revisit your bottom line to be sure your business is staying on a growing and profitable track.

Balance Your Inventory

Recall the financial ramifications of the style of inventory you keep and how that can affect your operating budget. As a point of review, be sure to consider the following key points that can have significant impact on how your business runs and your cash flows.

- Will your inventory consist of high-end goods that, even at wholesale costs, are a significant expense?
- Will your inventory require additional insurance and other protections that you'll need to add to you list of regular expenditures?
- Can your inventory be easily replaced if damaged, lost, or stolen? (Don't think it can't happen to you.)
- Can you relatively assure that you can make regular sales throughout the year (or whatever your targeted selling season will be)?
- If selling extremely low-end goods, can you sell enough items to bring in significant levels of income?
- Can you modify your inventory easily throughout the year to ensure that certain merchandise can pick up the slack when sales of other merchandise trails off?

Inventory balance is important to ensure that you can always have sales coming in and you can always replenish with something you know will contribute to your bottom line. The good news is you can tailor your inventory to suit your goals whether you want to sell high-end goods, low-end bargains, seasonal offerings, or year-round favorites.

Watch Your Assets

You probably have a nice office with all sorts of great tools to help you in your work. Part of keeping control of your auction expenses will also include keeping an eye on how your tools are holding up. Do they require maintenance? Will they be due for replacement? Whether your printer needs a new ink cartridge or your PC monitor fizzles out, be sure to keep track of the often-overlooked costs of keeping your office machinery and other equipment up and running.

Prepare for Hard Times

Then there's the reality check that goes something like this: What if your auction business takes a nosedive? How will you survive lean times? Well, there's not really a checklist to this discussion. The simple matter is you need to be prepared for tight times because the online auction market can change as quickly and unpredictably as the wind.

Any business counselor will advise that all entrepreneurs maintain a safety of at least six-months worth of living expenses. This will be especially true if your sales might be considered seasonal. For that matter, many auction goers have seen a seasonal slump in auction activity that usually occurs during the summer months when many folks are vacationing.

Though you may be thoroughly excited about some great initial sales of items, keep yourself grounded and recognize that not all auctions are high-flying successes and make sure you have a little nest egg to fall back on when the excitement dies down a bit.

Summing It All Up

Understand that any business venture needs to be firmly supported by a financial plan and recognition of the costs of doing business. Develop a clear goal for your auction business and determine what sorts of resources will be required to meet that goal. Develop a budget to help you predict and control your start-up as well as ongoing business costs.

Review your budget regularly to ensure that you're keeping your business above water. Be rigorous in recording all or your business: from inventory to expenses to sales, keep all pertinent data that will help you better report, analyze, and monitor your business activity. And finally, don't fall into the trap of thinking your business will be roses at every turn; there are bumps in the road and you'll need to be properly prepared to endure some less-than-stellar times. But, with careful planning and attention to the numerous details at your fingertips here, your business promises to be a booming endeavor.

Enjoy your fortune!

Index

Note: Boldface numbers indicate illustrations.

About the Author

 **Dennis L. Prince** is a prominent eBay powerseller and the #1 authority on the subject of eBay. His articles on Internet auctions have appeared in *Goldmine, Bottom Line,* and *Entrepreneur* magazines. He was named one of the Top Ten Auction Movers and Shakers by Vendio.com.